Visual Guide to

ETFs

Since 1996, Bloomberg Press has published books for finance professionals on investing, economics, and policy affecting investors. Titles are written by leading practitioners and authorities, and have been translated into more than 20 languages.

The Bloomberg Financial Series provides both core reference knowledge and actionable information for finance professionals. The books are written by experts familiar with the work flows, challenges, and demands of investment professionals who trade the markets, manage money, and analyze investments in their capacity of growing and protecting wealth, hedging risk, and generating revenue.

Books in the series include:

Visual Guide to Candlestick Charting by Michael Thomsett
Visual Guide to Municipal Bonds by Robert Doty
Visual Guide to Financial Markets by David Wilson
Visual Guide to Chart Patterns by Thomas N. Bulkowski
Visual Guide to ETFs by David J. Abner
Visual Guide to Options by Jared Levy

For more information, please visit our Web site at www.wiley.com/go/bloombergpress.

Visual Guide to
ETFs

David J. Abner

BLOOMBERG PRESS
An Imprint of
WILEY

Published by John Wiley & Sons, Inc., Hoboken, New Jersey.
Published simultaneously in Canada.

For general information on our other products and services or for technical support, please contact our Customer Care Department within the United States at (800) 762-2974, outside the United States at (317) 572-3993 or fax (317) 572-4002.

Wiley publishes in a variety of print and electronic formats and by print-on-demand. Some material included with standard print versions of this book may not be included in e-books or in print-on-demand. If this book refers to media such as a CD or DVD that is not included in the version you purchased, you may download this material at http://booksupport.wiley.com. For more information about Wiley products, visit www.wiley.com.

Library of Congress Cataloging-in-Publication Data:

Abner, David J., 1969
    Visual guide to ETFs / David J. Abner.
        p. cm. — (Bloomberg press series)
    Includes index.
    ISBN 978-1-118-20465-8 (pbk.); ISBN 978-1-118-22838-8 (ebk); ISBN 978-1-118-23158-6 (ebk);
    ISBN 978-1-118-26561-1 (ebk); ISBN 978-1-118-52394-0 (ebk); ISBN 978-1-118-52387-2 (ebk);
    ISBN 978-1-118-52397-1 (ebk)
    1. Exchange traded funds.   I. Title.
    HG6043.A263 2013
    332.63'27—dc23   2012030737

Printed in the United States of America

10 9 8 7 6 5 4 3 2

For Denise

Contents

List of Exhibits

How to Use This Book

The Bloomberg Visual Guide to . . . series is designed to be a comprehensive and easy-to-follow guide on today's most relevant finance and investing topics. All charts are in full color and presented in a large format to make them easy to read and use. We've also included the following elements to reinforce key information and processes:

- **Definitions:** Terminology and technical concepts that arise in the discussion.

- **Key Points:** Critical ideas and takeaways from the full text.

- **Step-by-Steps:** Tutorials designed to break down the steps in a multiphase process.

- **Bloomberg Functionality Cheat Sheet:** For Bloomberg terminal users, a back-of-the-book summary of relevant functions for the topics and tools discussed.

Go Beyond Print

Every Bloomberg Visual Guide is also available as an e-book, which includes the following features:

- Quizzes to reinforce your newfound knowledge and skills.

- Pop-ups with definitions for key terms.

Preface

ETFs are the democratizing structure of investment management. They enable investors with portfolios of all sizes to play on the same ball field with the same information at the same low prices. Investors can now use the ETF market to build fully diversified portfolios to rival the returns of the best money managers. Investors can have access to short exposure without a stock loan account. They can have access to precious metals without the need to pay for a far-off storage bin. They can trade whole indexes with a single keystroke. And they can do it all at a fraction of what it once cost. These are indeed glory days of investment products providing real value and indisputable benefits to investors and their investment managers.

Two decisions lie at the basis of every investment: What is the desired exposure, and what is the correct product structure to efficiently achieve that exposure? The ETF market explosion of recent years has provided a resounding answer to the second question. This growth has created a tremendous need for education about utilizing this modern structure. That is the direct reason for the existence of the *Visual Guide to ETFs*.

The trusted financial advisors and portfolio managers that investors turn to for help in all matters financial have now become the navigators of the ETF marketplace. This is no easy task. The ETF market is a close cousin to the mutual fund market, but the products possess some unique intricacies that must be fully understood. This book presents the keys to a vast world of modern financial products. The material is presented in logical order and in small, easily digestible pieces. It can be used as a reference guide to the ETF universe and its tools for investment management. If you are managing any type of portfolio that includes ETFs, the information presented in this book can save you vast amounts of money.

The *Visual Guide to ETFs* begins with a clear and concise description of ETFs and their differences from mutual funds and closed-end funds. In Chapter 1, you will gain a deeper understanding of the basics of the structure: transparency, exchange listing, tax efficiency, and lower costs. You will also see some interesting statistics about the growth of the products and what the future may bring. Then in Chapter 2, you will find a detailed explanation of how the underlying portfolios of the funds work. The details of asset growth and the creation and redemption process enable readers to more fully understand what is happening as assets move in and out of the funds. This is followed by a deep analysis of the short interest of ETFs in Chapter 3.

In Chapter 4, we start to look at the trading of the products in the secondary markets. We examine trading strategies for positioning the funds in your portfolio and delineate the various market participants and their roles. The *Visual Guide to ETFs* provides the most in-depth available analysis of the liquidity of ETFs. There is a full explanation of ETF implied liquidity, the implied daily tradable shares, and the completely new and unique ETF basket implied liquidity scale (EBILS). In Chapter 5, there is a detailed accounting of what

occurred within the ETF market during the flash crash of 2010. In Chapters 6 and 7, you'll see detailed explanations for executing order flow in ETFs and strategies for trading the products. In Chapter 8, we look in depth at the various structures of exchange-traded products and how they can provide very different return results than those from seemingly similar investment exposures. And in Chapter 9, we look at some additional sources of information that are available. Finally, in the Appendix, there is a guide to the numerous Bloomberg functions for analyzing ETFs. The book is packed with more than 200 Bloomberg screens and callouts highlighting key points and important terminology for investors.

The thorough information in the *Visual Guide to ETFs* enables readers to deftly navigate the ETF marketplace. You will understand the product structures along with their benefits and pitfalls. You will understand different ways to determine the potential liquidity of ETFs. And you will learn strategies to trade ETFs like a professional trader. Readers are able to use this information to confidently and competently build ETF portfolios.

Acknowledgments

My goal with *The Visual Guide to ETFs* was to distill the necessary information for readers to use as a guide for their own investment situation, whether a small personal account or the largest institutional portfolio. In gathering my thoughts, organizing my data, stress-testing my conclusions, and formulating my words, I've had much assistance. Two people who have been involved in every step of both my books are Lynne Cohen and Anita Rausch. It's incredible luck to have a mother-in-law who is a good sounding board and also a brilliant editor. Thanks, Lynne! Anita has read and rephrased many sentences in my books, applying her mastery of the product set to my thoughts or, sometimes, toning down my emotions. It's incredible that she found the time while busy as a new mother, and for that I'm forever thankful.

The entire WisdomTree team has always been supportive of my work.[1] I cannot thank them enough. It's truly an honor to work with such driven and dedicated people. Zach Hascoe, my reality sounding board,

is one of the most rational and clear-thinking people I've ever met. I also want to specifically thank Luciano Siracusano for helping me clarify my thinking on many points and Evelyn Hu for putting together a significant portion of the chapter on structure.

I am lucky to have great friends who are also incredibly knowledgeable industry participants: Robert Bastone, Eric Biegeleisen, Tim Coyne, Rob Dailey, Greg Gliner, Dana Martin, Andy McOrmond, David Morton, Adam Phillips, Damon Walvoord, and Robert Wedeking. Their different views of the industry enabled me to see from various angles and be certain that what I have presented passes all the tests. Sumit Periwal was a great help with some of the data found throughout the book. Gabe Pincus is a veritable wealth of information regarding underlying industry processes. He is almost solely responsible for Chapter 9 and would have written the whole book if I had let him! Eric Balchunas deserves special mention as a friend and supporter. His industry insight is responsible for bringing the implied liquidity function to Bloomberg terminals and enabling the client base to finally have a quantified measure of ETF liquidity.

This book would also not have been possible without the thousands of meaningful conversations I have had with the community of ETF users and traders around the world. I also thank the team at Wiley for making this book a reality. Pamela Van Giessen and I hit it off from our first breakfast together. And Evan Burton and Meg Freeborn have been instrumental in bringing this book from concept to reality.

Lastly, I owe a tremendous debt to my family. I am grateful for the continuing support of my uncle, Howard Abner, throughout my career.

My kids still think writing a book is pretty cool but wish Dad would finish already and ride bikes with them. The fact that my wife doesn't hate me after this project is a testament to her vast stores of patience and understanding. And Mom, for the thousandth time, the book is coming along fine!

Note

1. Please note the views in this book are my own and do not necessarily represent those of WisdomTree or anyone else.

2. This book was written entirely on an 11-inch Macbook Air.

CHAPTER 1

Characteristics of Modern Investment Products

The world has changed drastically since the turn of the century. Some of the recent changes we have experienced in our lives today are as significant as last century's introduction of the television or the automobile. The technology revolution is changing and shrinking the world. It's getting harder to track and enumerate the rapid transformations in many of our daily life activities. If you've taken a plane or train recently, you have noticed that most people seem to be interacting and paying attention to a screen. From a train seat, you can read a newspaper, pay your bills, play a game, and even trade and invest on these portable screens. There's even a good chance you're reading this book on some form of electronic device.

The Internet and the miniaturization of electronic devices have been disruptive and game changing to many businesses and industries. Where have the stores that sell albums and CDs gone? Where is the Blockbuster video store that used to be on your corner? Banking is another industry that is undergoing its own transformation because of modern technology. Every aspect from commercial banking, I haven't written a check in years, to investment banking and trading has been affected by technology. Just the way the news is always at our fingertips now, so is our ability to trade and invest.

This is a book about change. The use of exchange-traded funds (ETFs) is a revolutionary change for investors and for those in the investing business. Never before have investors been able to get the transparency, the liquidity, or the access now available in the form of ETFs. ETFs have packaged indices and other forms of asset classes and benchmarks neatly into the palm of your hand. A recent report claims that "ETFs have democratized access to an array of asset classes and strategies."[1] The report further details change in the financial advisory business with ETFs giving advisors the ability to monetize their investment advice by giving them access to almost every asset class in the simplicity of a brokerage account. ETFs give you the power of choice for your asset allocation and modern technology gives you the easy access to implement it.

In this chapter, we'll take a look at the growth of the ETF market and what the product array looks like. We'll delve into the characteristics that stand out as unique to ETFs. In addition, we'll look at the two other major products in the investment landscape that vie for the attention of investors: mutual funds and closed-end funds. It will be valuable to look at the advantages of ETFs, in comparison to other products, to determine how to fit them properly into your own portfolios.

Four Types of Investment Products

According to the Investment Company Institute (ICI), there are four types of products that fit into the definition of investment companies: exchange-traded funds,[2] mutual funds (also known as open-end funds), closed-end funds, and unit investment trusts.

Exchange-traded funds are the newest and fastest-growing category, and are the second largest category by assets. ETFs are open-ended investment funds that have a process of issuing or redeeming their shares in blocks, typically 50,000 shares or more based on customer demand. ETFs also have an exchange listing feature that gives investors access to the funds throughout the trading day on public stock exchanges.

Mutual funds are the biggest category of investment products, both by assets and number of available products. They can be either actively managed or designed to passively track an index. They are open-ended funds, meaning that they stand ready to issue new shares or buy back existing shares on a daily basis, typically at their current net asset value (NAV).

Closed-end funds (CEFs) are another type of investment product, but, as the name suggests, they are not open-ended. They issue a limited number of shares once during their initial offering process, and that share amount remains mostly constant throughout the life of the fund. The fund shares trade on an exchange, like an ETF; however, they tend to move to prolonged discounts and premiums, primarily due to the limitations on new share issuance coupled with changes in investor sentiment and demand.

Unit investment trusts (UITs) are a combination of several of these product types. They issue specific amounts of shares that are called units. They trade on exchanges but typically only to facilitate redemption of shares by investors. And the portfolio is typically fixed until a predetermined termination date.

The growth of assets in each product set over the last 15 years tells an interesting story. You can see in Exhibit 1.1 that two types of the products, ETFs and mutual funds, have grown at a very rapid pace.

	ETFs[1]	Mutual Funds[2]	CEFs	UITs	Total[3]
1995	$ 1	$ 2,811	$143	$73	$ 3,028
1996	$ 2	$ 3,526	$147	$72	$ 3,747
1997	$ 7	$ 4,468	$152	$85	$ 4,712
1998	$ 16	$ 5,525	$156	$94	$ 5,791
1999	$ 34	$ 6,846	$147	$92	$ 7,119
2000	$ 66	$ 6,965	$143	$74	$ 7,248
2001	$ 83	$ 6,975	$141	$49	$ 7,248
2002	$ 102	$ 6,383	$159	$36	$ 6,680
2003	$ 151	$ 7,402	$214	$36	$ 7,803
2004	$ 228	$ 8,095	$254	$37	$ 8,614
2005	$ 301	$ 8,891	$277	$41	$ 9,510
2006	$ 423	$ 10,398	$298	$50	$ 11,169
2007	$ 608	$ 12,002	$312	$53	$ 12,975
2008	$ 531	$ 9,604	$183	$29	$ 10,347
2009	$ 777	$ 11,120	$220	$38	$ 12,155
2010	$ 992	$ 11,821	$234	$51	$ 13,098
2011	$ 1,048	$ 11,622	$239	$60	$ 12,969

Exhibit 1.1 Investment Company Total Net Assets (in $billions) by Type

1. ETF data prior to 2001 were provided by Strategic Insight Simfund. ETF data include investment companies not registered under the Investment Company Act of 1940 and exclude ETFs that invest primarily in other ETFs.
2. Mutual fund data include only mutual funds that report statistical information to the Investment Company Institute. The data do not include mutual funds that invest primarily in other mutual funds.
3. Total investment company assets include mutual fund holdings of closed-end funds and ETFs.
Source: Investment Company Institute and Strategic Insight Simfund.

Closed-end funds have grown slowly, and UITs actually represent a smaller amount of assets than they did 15 years ago. The recent rampant pace of growth in the ETF industry is astounding. Overall, the products are still somewhat small in total assets, representing only about 8 percent of the mutual fund industry. However, the rate of asset growth and customer adoption is definitely bringing more and more attention to the newcomer among investment companies.

The growth rates tell the story about an investing public that is becoming savvier about its use of investment products and more demanding about the characteristics of those products. The CEF and UIT are examples of products that tend to exhibit less desirable traits, such as higher fees, lower liquidity, and a focus on a small, select group of investors. You can see that assets are subsequently lagging in those categories

As a result of the technology revolution, products are evolving as systems, and regulatory structures develop. The ETF structure, from its creation about 20 years ago, is an example of taking a mutual fund structure and combining it with some of the benefits of the closed-end fund structure to develop a product that provides new and unique benefits to investors. When coupled with the development of stock market infrastructure that facilitates increased electronic access and advanced trading speeds, we have created a fertile climate for an investment product revolution not seen since the early days of mutual funds themselves.

Coincidentally, studies have shown that asset allocation is responsible for a significant portion of portfolio returns. There really is no better tool than the ETF for easy and quick access to a wide swath of asset classes. Let us take a look at some of the main features of ETFs and what I like to call their "cousin" products, the mutual fund and the closed-end fund. This analysis will help explain the rapid growth of this newer investment company product versus its more traditional counterparts.

Exchange-Traded Funds

The growth of assets in exchange-traded products and the development of the ecosystem of businesses around that growth have been stunning in recent years. Numerous factors have contributed to this growth, from the Wall Street marketing engines, to the regulatory changes that provide for significant structural advantages, to the growth of electronic trading. What is rarely mentioned, however, is that investors have simply been demanding a way to invest with reasonably low fees and through a straight-forward structure. The main tranche of the ETF market provides this, along with a level of transparency and other benefits that were unavailable in previous products.

Let's take a look at the characteristics of this product structure and why it is taking the investment world by storm. In Exhibit 1.1, you were able to see the dramatic asset growth. There are some defining characteristics that are attracting investors to these products, either for new portions of their portfolios or for transitions of their entire investment strategies. The main ones are:

- Transparency
- Exchange listing
- Tax efficiency
- Lower fees

In the following sections, I'll go through these main characteristics and explain their differences from alternative products.

Transparency

When transparency is mentioned as a defining characteristic, it sometimes takes a minute of personal product inventory for an investor to realize that there is really no other fund product available that provides a daily accounting of exactly what the fund holds. Before ETFs, portfolio holdings were typically only released on a quarterly or semiannual basis. ETFs make their portfolio publicly available daily. This has a host of ramifications, from eliminating style drift to creating the basis for an arbitrage that keeps the trading price close to fund value. One would have thought transparency should have been the gold standard in investment products from their very beginning, but it does not seem as if investors learned anything from watching the *Wizard of Oz*!

Regarding the transparency of ETFs, it is important to understand that the majority of assets are in index tracking products. Daily transparency works well for passive index tracking. Conversely, a majority of mutual fund assets are in what are called actively managed funds. These are funds that have a portfolio manager whose intention is to manage the holdings of the fund to perform better than some specified benchmark. A prevalent argument for not disclosing a daily portfolio of an actively managed ETF is a fear that investors would purchase the portfolio themselves instead of putting assets into the fund and paying the manager for their trading ideas for outperformance. That may be true if it was more economical for investors to do that and gain efficiency. It is also feared the disclosure would drive costs to the fund higher because of the front running. In reality, it would probably drive the management fees for those funds lower in order for them to compete. We are already starting to see that happen, and it is slowly squeezing industry margins.

In addition, portfolio managers of actively managed funds may be concerned about investors backing into their supposedly magical proprietary strategies. I don't think these concerns outweigh the benefits to clients of knowing what is in a fund portfolio on a daily basis. Currently, there are active ETFs available that are providing baskets daily without announcing changes before they occur. That is working very well as a model, and the assets in those funds are growing rapidly. In essence, I agree with the Blackrock goal of "daily disclosure of holdings and exposures"[3] as defined in their recent recommendations on the ETF product set.

DEFINITION: Arbitrage

Arbitrage is a term used in finance to describe taking advantage of price differences between two similar assets. In this case, the ETF and its underlying basket represent the same thing and can be converted from one into the other. For example, if the price of the ETF gets too high, traders would be able to sell the ETF and buy the underlying basket, capturing the price difference between them.

DEFINITION: Front Running

Front running is the practice of purchasing stocks, or other assets, in anticipation that a portfolio manager is imminently coming in to purchase those same assets. The practice describes investors buying stocks in anticipation that a large fund manager will be making similar investments for the fund portfolio. This can theoretically drive costs higher for the fund.

Exchange Listing

There is sometimes confusion that exchange listing is all about liquidity, but that is just one of several benefits. The three major positives of exchange listing are:

1. Standardization
2. Intraday trading
3. Liquidity

Standardization is proving to be a tremendous benefit to holding multiasset portfolios all within the same account structure. ETFs neatly package all asset classes into an equity structure that can reside in the simplest of brokerage accounts. This was impossible just a few years ago. Now you are able to keep your bond position wrapped in an ETF structure within your investment account, instead of having your portfolio separated in different account types with attendant complications. You can even include your commodities ETF piece and your alternatives ETF selections in your investment account. Trading in the products also becomes standardized. If you understand how ETFs trade, you'll be able to trade all the asset classes in your portfolio easily from the same account, probably using the same tools.

Intraday trading of exchange-traded funds has been the characteristic that presents itself as both a blessing and a curse. The mutual fund industry has the benefit of never having to explain to a client the concept of how to achieve best execution. They rarely even have to explain poor trading practices within the performance of a portfolio. While intraday trading adds to the transparency and liquidity of the ETF product class, it puts the responsibility of understanding how to achieve best execution on the investor. The execution portion of the equation is a very important part of the investment process. Every new client has to climb the learning curve of how to achieve a good execution in the products. The ETF industry has given investors the ability to manage their own executions. But with this responsibility there is a learning curve that is proving to be somewhat steeper than the industry may have expected. I've been involved in the trading of ETFs for almost 15 years, and I am still answering basic questions about liquidity and trading. Part of that problem is the slowness of systems and processes to adapt to this new necessity. It is critical to become an advocate for yourself and your clients when trading ETFs. Advances in execution when managing a portfolio of ETFs can save millions of dollars annually.

For many investors, the intraday trading aspect of ETFs is not that important, nor should it be. This is why I have broken it out from liquidity as a separate factor. If you are using an investment process that instructs you to buy a fund today, hold it for some extended period based upon various parameters, and then sell it, then trading intraday, except on those execution days, is like a good insurance policy. It is there if you ever need it, but most of the time you won't. In addition, if you're trading in ETFs with foreign underlying assets, the intraday trading of a fund in the United States adds an additional dimension and time zone for trading the foreign assets. There are some

ETFs that can even be traded 24 hours a day through your broker dealer, which adds a never before seen flexibility to the management of portfolios.

As the trading industry evolves to a more process-driven business based around customer service and continues to attract different kinds of liquidity providers, the customer experience in ETFs will continue to improve. Several of the large customer execution providers are offering commission-free ETF trading on many of their platforms. Essentially, we are seeing a full-scale change in the way equities orders are executed because they now include ETFs. ETFs trade differently than stocks, although they share similar characteristics, so the major execution platforms servicing advisors are retooling to understand and achieve better liquidity in the ETFs. In this book, you will read more about this evolution of providing better execution services to all ETF investors, from the growth of liquidity aggregators to agency executions of baskets with an exchange for ETF shares.

Listing a product on an exchange and creating a standardized format provides access to a wider variety of market participants and can increase liquidity and participation to a level that could not have been previously achieved. This has also helped to decrease trading spreads for many products. You can see in the grid in Exhibit 1.2 where the ETF price is actually trading between the bid and ask spread of the underlying basket. Listing on the exchange has brought multiple sources of liquidity into one location creating a tangible benefit for investors.

This extreme liquidity injection does not happen in every product but at the very least exchange listing adds to the liquidity base. The trading that takes place in some of the highest-volume ETFs has had the effect of causing the ETF itself to trade at a tighter spread than its underlying basket and in much greater size than would be expected. In Exhibit 1.2, you can see the market price and the indicative value (IV) of the SPDR S&P 500 ETF Trust (SPY). There are many more details about indicative value in Chapter 2.

If you look at the spread column, you can see that the basket is showing an implied ETF spread of 4 cents wide. However, the fund is showing a trading spread of only 1 cent wide. The fund is trading at a tighter spread than would be available if you traded the basket. This anomaly becomes much more pronounced in some

DEFINITION:

Indicative Value (IV)

Indicative value is the calculated value of the underlying assets in an ETF. This is typically calculated by using the last price of each underlying component and presents a close to real-time value of the fund for investors.

KEY POINT:

One difference in trading between an ETF and a stock is that an ETF trade is typically between a customer and a liquidity provider. Very rarely are two end customers trading against each other without an intermediary in between. The liquidity providers, or other professional traders, are usually providing liquidity from the basket to the ETF shares for the client, utilizing the arbitrage function that keeps the trading price right around the value of the basket.

	Bid	Ask	Spread	Last Price
SPY Price	$119.25	$119.26	$0.01	$119.25
SPY IV Basket Value	$119.22	$119.27	$0.04	$119.24

Exhibit 1.2 SPY Price Spread Example
Reprinted with permission from Bloomberg. Copyright 2012 Bloomberg L.P. All rights reserved.

products that trade high volumes or have underlying assets that are not readily accessible. The exchange provides a secondary gathering place for a wide variety of market participants that might not have found each other otherwise. The advantages of this become even more evident as products emerge providing access to formerly hard-to-access asset classes. In many cases, the ETF is becoming a vehicle to aid liquidity growth in the underlying basket itself. Bringing together multiple different investor types into one standardized vehicle is centralizing product liquidity as is the purpose of an exchange listed market. As you can see in Exhibit 1.3, the wide array of ETF users all come together in the products on an equal playing field. There are no multiple shares classes or alternative structures for institutions versus smaller investors.

The tighter spreads are also possible because of the arbitrage available when you have two products, the

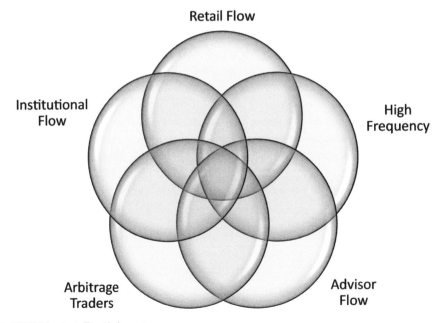

Exhibit 1.3 ETF Market Participants

basket and the ETF, that can easily be converted into one another. This is known as being fungible. There is a lot of competition in the trading industry to capture any spread between the ETF price and the basket price. This is advantageous for investors because, as those trading firms compete, they drive spreads ever tighter and keep the ETF trading near its fair value. There are also alternative trading vehicles like futures and options that trade in conjunction with some ETFs and this only further enhances the liquidity pool. For investors, the centralizing of users into the ETFs is very beneficial because the presentation of tighter spreads and more liquidity than had previously existed translates into cheaper execution costs for the end investor.

Tax Efficiency

I present the basics of why ETFs are different than other investment products in terms of their tax consequences, but I am not a tax attorney or an accountant. Each individual situation is different, and you should consult your own advisors regarding your personal tax situation. I am also discussing the funds in a normal taxable environment. Things can change when the funds are held in tax-deferred accounts and other structures.

The concept of the tax efficiency of the ETF structure is another major feature that is helping to drive growth. In trying to simplify the discussion down to its most important aspects, I have isolated three subcategories:

- Tax efficiencies within the portfolio management process
- Tax efficiencies within the distribution process
- Structural differences that affect tax efficiency

The major tax advantage of the ETF structure within the portfolio management process derives from the concept of in-kind creation and redemption. I will cover the details of how creation and redemption works in Chapter 2 but for now will explain the differences between ETFs and their mutual and closed-end fund cousins.

When investors add assets to mutual funds, the portfolio managers are taking in cash from the investors and then purchasing the underlying basket of assets. The reverse happens when an investor wants to redeem shares of the mutual fund. At that point, the mutual fund manager has to raise cash to deliver back to the investor. In general, they need to sell assets that the fund holds. This selling of assets typically generates a taxable event for the mutual fund. Funds do hold certain cash reserves to accommodate some redemption, but this can lead to performance lag and so needs to be done sparingly. There are also other minor techniques to manage the portfolio, but at its essence, when investors come into and out of mutual funds, the portfolio managers are buying and selling the underlying assets. This is creating taxable events within the funds that will need to be distributed among the remaining shareholders. Then at some point in the future, depending on the distribution schedule,

KEY POINT:

The ETF industry makes use of two parts of the capital markets: the primary market and the secondary market. The primary market is where issuance takes place. All creations and redemptions are considered to be taking place in the primary market. The secondary market is where previously issued securities trade. When you are trading a stock or ETF on an exchange, you are trading in the secondary market. Do not confuse this with the primary exchange listing of an ETF, which delineates the exchange on which a product was first listed to begin trading and that affects the official opening and closing auction and prices.

KEY POINT:

ETFs do not do IPOs to raise assets. Every ETF launches with some amount of seed capital so that the shares can be brought to the secondary market. Typically, this is a process whereby an *authorized participant* goes into the markets and purchases the required basket for the new ETF and then processes an initial creation. Once an ETF has shares outstanding, they can be traded on an exchange, and the ETF begins to take on a life of its own.

the mutual fund will make distributions of short- and long-term capital gains that will be taxable events for shareholders.

The way a typical equity ETF takes in and disburses assets is quite different. It surprises me how many users of ETFs have not gotten a firm grasp on how the ETFs take in assets, unwind assets, and even make money on those assets. The first stage is taking in assets. An ETF transacts on two levels in the markets, the primary market and the secondary market.

When an ETF is trading, the process of taking in new assets actually begins away from the ETF portfolio itself in the secondary market. When an influx of investors want to buy the ETF, the liquidity-providing community sells the shares of the ETF to those buyers. They then typically buy the shares in the underlying basket to hedge their trading books. As this continues throughout the trading day, the liquidity providers are accumulating larger short positions in the ETF, and at the same time they are continually growing their long exposure to the underlying basket. At the end of the trading day, the liquidity-providing community assesses their own trading portfolios and takes actions to clean up their balance sheets. This is where the magic happens in the ETF structure. If the liquidity providers have done everything correctly, they have two positions on their trading books, short the ETF and long a basket of stocks that represents perfect creation units of the ETF portfolio. They can then effect a creation. In this process, the liquidity provider delivers the basket of underlying assets to the

ETF issuer's portfolio management agent, and new shares of the ETF are issued. This is a primary market transaction that is not considered a trade by the ETF portfolio, and is separate from the secondary trading activity that was taking place throughout the day. But the distinction that needs to be made here is that the AP is the one gathering and selling the assets of the ETF when creating and redeeming and not the ETF portfolio managers as would be the case in a mutual fund structure.

The activity in the secondary market can have varying effects on the primary markets, which I discuss further in Chapter 4. At this point, the ETF has grown the assets it is managing, and that growth has been represented to the public via an increase in the shares outstanding number. Now let's look at what is going to happen in the reverse situation. In our hypothetical example, there are sellers in the market. Investors want to do nothing but sell the ETF shares. All day long, they are selling the ETF to liquidity providers, who are, in turn, selling shares across the underlying basket of the ETF. This is the key transference between liquidity in the ETF and activity in the underlying baskets. In this reverse example, at the end of the day the liquidity provider may have a large position of long the ETF and short the underlying basket in perfect unit sizes. Remember, if done correctly, this is a perfectly hedged position, so there is no market exposure, but there are financing fees on the various long and short positions. To manage the balance sheet costs and exposures, the liquidity provider decides to affect redemption of the

ETF shares. In this case, the liquidity provider will be delivering the shares of the ETF back to the ETF issuer, and the issuer will be delivering units of the underlying basket to the liquidity provider. The ETF shares outstanding will decrease because those ETF shares are no longer in existence and tradable in the market place. The assets in the fund have also decreased because the underlying shares that represented those assets have been delivered out.

This primary market transaction is not considered to be a trade and is therefore not creating a taxable event for the ETF. The in-kind creation and redemption process enables the delivery and receipt of shares into and out of the portfolio but are not considered to be trades for tax purposes which can cut down on capital gains distributions. This is all very tax efficient for the ETF and is a critical concept that I refer to as a piece of the structural alpha of the products.

The taxable events of trading the underlying equities and the actual ETF shares have been moved back to where they should be, at each particular end investor involved in the transaction. This removes from the equation the risk of large investors creating taxable events that affect all the other investors of the fund. It also highlights the importance of investors being their own advocates on the trading side, because it is now more likely to have a direct effect on their particular portfolio, while in other fund structures, many of those costs are allocated across all holders.

These efficiencies of moving baskets into and out of the ETF without doing trades enable the portfolio managers to maintain a highly efficient tax strategy within the portfolio. There are portfolio rebalances and corporate actions that take place that do require some trading to be done, but for the most part, large asset moves are done efficiently. If you look at the history of ETF distribution numbers, you can see that they have a small fraction of the tax distributions as compared to other investment products. In addition, since you can see the portfolio movements within the ETF, diligent investors are able to closely monitor what any distribution might actually be if there was to be one. This whole process enables investors to manage their own tax situations at the fund ownership level without being vulnerable to tax consequences created by other investors moving in and out of the ETF.

Structural Ramifications and Taxation

It is important to understand that different types of ETFs structures can affect their tax efficiency. As the ETF structure has evolved and the funds have begun providing exposure to more esoteric underlying assets, they have evolved into utilizing a cash creation and redemption feature. This cash creation/redemption feature is usually only used when the underlying is regulated and/or difficult to trade. In the standard in-kind creation and redemption process, the transactions by the fund are not considered to be trades. In a cash creation and redemption, the fund is acting more like a mutual fund in taking in cash and going out and purchasing assets. Since these asset purchases and sales are actually taking place within the fund portfolio, they are actual trades that can generate realized gains or losses in the portfolio. They are also treated like all trades for tax purposes. There are also hybrid structures that will use cash for some underlyings and in-kind for others. The tax liability will be different for each piece. In Exhibit 1.4, you can see the third page of a Bloomberg description screen showing creation and redemption details. Bloomberg provides you with information on the creation redemption mechanism for each ETF. In this case, the ETF has an in-kind creation and redemption process, indicating shares are delivered in and out of the fund.

ETF Product Proliferation

One question I encounter repeatedly in client meetings and at conferences is whether we have reached a saturation point of product in the ETF market. To address this question, begin by looking at what has been happening in product proliferation both in the United States and globally. The number of ETF products in the United States has been growing at a fast pace, far outpacing other investment products. The graph in Exhibit 1.5 is probably the most widespread graph in the ETF industry. It is in nearly every research publication about the products. The bars represent the main trends of assets under management (AUM) growth, both globally and in the United States. The lines, which I've highlighted, represent the number of outstanding products.[4] Notice the rates of change in the product lines.

The number of ETFs globally is growing at an even faster pace than in the United States. The demand that I see from clients clamoring for ETF product would seem to be saying that we are nowhere near a saturation point. Clients are looking for the ability to build portfolios of multiple asset classes in the ETF wrapper, which is driving a lot of new product innovation.

The next piece of the puzzle would be to look at assets raised in new funds. Are new funds still picking up assets? The logic would say that if new funds are not picking up assets, then we possibly have reached a saturation point. In this case, I have run a search using the Bloomberg search function and come up with 122 funds that were newly listed in the United States in 2012 through June 27.

Exhibit 1.6 shows the top 17 new funds of 2012 sorted by assets through October 29. It shows that those 17 new products have raised more than $4 billion in assets already, in the first nine months of the year. What you see in these new products are unique concepts that have not before been available in the ETF structure, or where investors have not been able to attain exposures, or different aspects of investment themes that have been in existence. In particular, a significant amount of the assets were raised in an actively managed ETF that is designed to be the ETF version of a very popular mutual fund. Many industry participants and potential investors have been watching this launch closely. It could have groundbreaking ramifications for the future of the product set and is proof that ETFs as a product category are still evolving. However,

```
GRAB                                                        EquityDES
 At 11:06   Vol 24,380  Op 50.71 P  Hi 50.71 P  Lo 50.51 D  ValTrd 1234458
DTN US Equity        99) Feedback                  Page 3/5   Description: Holdings
   1) Profile      2) Performance     3) Holdings     4) Allocations   5) Organizational
Benchmark       WTDXFTR Index
6) Top 10 Fund Hlds (MHD)   Net Fund   Net Index  Top 10 Index Hlds (MEMB)   Net Index  Net Fund
 CenturyLink Inc             2.536%      N.A.
 Reynolds American Inc       2.269%      N.A.
 FirstEnergy Corp            2.234%      N.A.
 Lorillard Inc               2.146%      N.A.
 Altria Group Inc            2.100%      N.A.
 NiSource Inc                2.044%      N.A.                No Holdings Reported
 Progress Energy Inc         2.023%      N.A.
 Verizon Communications Inc  1.930%      N.A.
 Duke Energy Corp            1.895%      N.A.
 Eli Lilly & Co              1.852%      N.A.
Creation/Redemption Basket                        Holdings Statistics
Total Cash                      USD 20.6k  Rebalancing Frequency              Yearly
Estimated Cash                  USD 20.5k  Replication Strategy            Optimized
Creation Unit Size                 50,000  Fund Holdings As Of Date         12/09/11
Creation/Redemption Fee         USD 500.00 Fund Number Of Holdings                87
Create/Redeem Process             In-Kind  Index Number Of Holdings            N.A.
Creation Cutoff Time            16:00 EST
Settlement Cycle                      T+3
NAV Pricing Methodology   Primary Market Close
Australia 61 2 9777 8600 Brazil 5511 3048 4500 Europe 44 20 7330 7500 Germany 49 69 9204 1210 Hong Kong 852 2977 6000
Japan 81 3 3201 8900     Singapore 65 6212 1000     U.S. 1 212 318 2000     Copyright 2011 Bloomberg Finance L.P.
                                              SN 192825 G638-450-0 12-Dec-11 11:10:27 EST  GMT-5:00
```

Exhibit 1.4 ETF Description (DES), Holdings

Reprinted with permission from Bloomberg. Copyright 2012 Bloomberg L.P. All rights reserved.

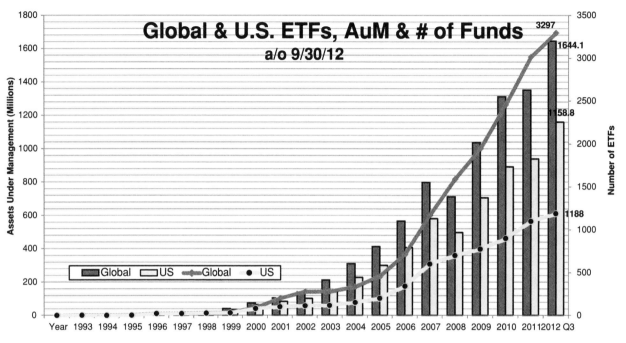

Exhibit 1.5 Number of ETFs and Assets Both in the United States and Globally
Source: BlackRock ETP Landscape Industry Highlights.

there are many variables that cause newly launched ETFs to gather assets quickly or slowly and most have to do with the market timing and investor sentiment in the theme.

The number of products listed over the last several years has definitely accelerated, as compared to recent history. In Exhibit 1.7 you can see product issuance by year and the amount of assets. The graph shows the

number of funds launched each year and the assets those funds have attracted from inception until June 2012. It highlights the dramatic increase in issuance and also the clear decline in assets that were raised in newer products. This shows the difficulties in raising assets when launching new products. However, also take into consideration the market environment and the trend of other investment products in raising new

GRAB
<Menu> to return

Ticker	Name	Inception Date	Tot Asset (M)	Avg Volume 30 Day	Tot Ret 1Y	Parent Comp. Name
1) BOND US	PIMCO TOTAL RETURN ETF	2/29/2012	2,895.38	499,213.00	N.A.	PIMCO Funds ETFs/USA
2) SJNK US	SPDR SHORT-TERM HIGH YIELD	3/15/2012	409.31	252,484.00	N.A.	State Street ETF/USA
3) QLTA US	ISHARES AAA-A RATED CORPORAT	2/14/2012	302.29	188,592.00	N.A.	iShares/USA
4) GOVT US	ISHARES TREASURY BOND FUND	2/14/2012	231.72	455,339.00	N.A.	iShares/USA
5) PICK US	ISHARES MSCI GLBL MTLS & MNR	1/31/2012	219.04	19,028.00	N.A.	iShares/USA
6) FBG US	FI ENHANCED BIG CAP GR ETN	6/8/2012	113.03	46,280.00	N.A.	UBS ETNs/USA
7) EMHY US	ISHARES EM HY BOND	4/3/2012	92.01	109,196.00	N.A.	iShares/USA
8) ILB US	PIMCO GLOBAL ADVANTAGE INFLA	4/30/2012	88.52	55,526.00	N.A.	PIMCO Funds ETFs/USA
9) EMLP US	FIRST TRUST NORTH AMERICAN E	6/21/2012	88.43	95,808.00	N.A.	First Trust/ETFs
10) IEMG US	ISHARES CORE MSCI EMERGING	10/22/2012	81.48	N.A.	N.A.	iShares/USA
11) YMLP US	YORKVILLE HIGH INCOME MLP	3/13/2012	75.84	60,001.00	N.A.	Exchange-Traded Concept
12) IYLD US	ISHARES MORNINGSTAR MULT-ETF	4/3/2012	73.93	47,730.00	N.A.	iShares/USA
13) EMCB US	WISDOMTREE EM CORP BOND	3/8/2012	70.73	10,220.00	N.A.	WisdomTree ETFs/USA
14) MOAT US	MARKET VECTORS MORNINGSTAR	4/25/2012	66.78	39,667.00	N.A.	Van Eck ETF/USA
15) PFXF US	MARKET VECTORS PREF EX-FINAN	7/16/2012	66.37	84,465.00	N.A.	Van Eck ETF/USA
16) IEFA US	ISHARES CORE MSCI EAFE ETF	10/22/2012	66.32	N.A.	N.A.	iShares/USA
17) IXUS US	ISHARES CORE INTL STOCK ETF	10/22/2012	62.30	N.A.	N.A.	iShares/USA

Exhibit 1.6 Fund Search Screen
Reprinted with permission from Bloomberg. Copyright 2012 Bloomberg L.P. All rights reserved.

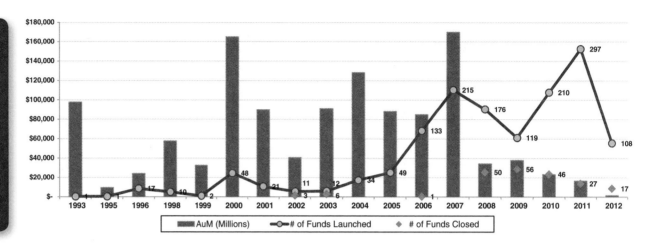

Exhibit 1.7 Funds Launched and Closed per Year and Current AuM

Source: Bloomberg, as of 5/15/12. Reprinted with permission from Bloomberg. Copyright 2012 Bloomberg L.P. All rights reserved.

capital. ETFs are outpacing them all. I think it is fair to say that ETFs as a category are not saturated and still growing in the form of issuance as well as user base.

ETF Closings

As in any rapid growth industry there is a risk that not all new entrants will succeed and some must close. In investment products this is not necessarily an indication of saturation or of general failure but a natural weeding out process by investors of investment themes and this does not present a danger to the product category. The process of building

an ETF, listing it on the exchange, and maintaining the infrastructure to keep that product properly managed is expensive. If a product grows in age without corresponding growth in assets, it becomes a burden that is simply not economical for a fund management company to maintain. There are many variables that determine the length of life of a fund with few assets. It is first and foremost a function of cost to run and maintain as an outstanding vehicle. Beyond that are considerations regarding the time in the market cycle and investor appetite. If the fund represents an asset class that has not normally been

Exhibit 1.8 Bloomberg Closed Funds Screen
Reprinted with permission from Bloomberg. Copyright 2012 Bloomberg L.P. All rights reserved.

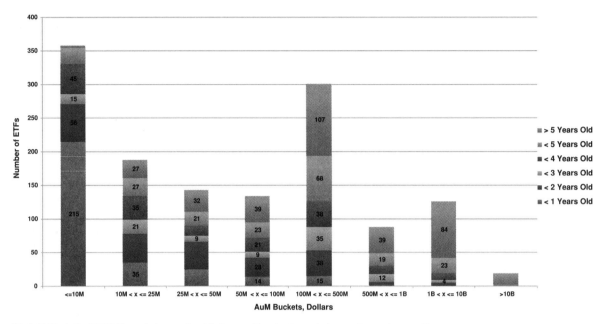

Exhibit 1.9 ETF Breakdown by Volume Bucket and Age since Inception
As of 12/31/2011. Reprinted with permission from Bloomberg. Copyright 2012 Bloomberg L.P. All rights reserved.

accessed via an equitized product, and if the fund company is large and can afford to keep a bigger stable of funds, then a small fund might have a longer life. A smaller, newer fund company will have less leeway in those situations.

As of June 6, 2012, there have been 212 funds closed in the U.S. markets. You can see a list of funds that were closed on Bloomberg by using the EXTF function as well. In Exhibit 1.8, you can see the most recently closed 17 funds, but you can also generate the full list and export it to Excel.

Exhibit 1.9 presents a look at exchange-traded products by assets broken out by age of funds. You can see that there are a significant number of funds, more than 350, with less than $10 million in AuM, and many of those funds, 215, are under a year old. There are a wide range of variables involved in making decisions about whether to keep funds open and for how long. From the chart, you might think that the older a fund is, the more assets it attracts, but that discounts the effects of some older funds that attracted few assets having been closed. There is survivor bias present in this chart. You might look at the upper categories of the left bars as indications of where fund closings may be imminent, but since there are so many other variables, that does not necessarily present the most accurate prediction.

Regarding fund closures, investors must remember that they occur with enough time lag for you to reallocate your exposure. You will be given the opportunity to trade out of your position or receive a net asset value (NAV) based redemption of either cash or shares. Although this will create a potentially taxable event in your own portfolio and generate some trading costs as you reallocate, there is no other loss associated with fund closings. This is a common event in all classes of investment funds, as product development teams try to ascertain where investor dollars will flow in the future.

Mutual Funds

Mutual funds are the largest group of investment company products by assets both in the United States and globally. There were $24.7 trillion in mutual funds worldwide as of the end of 2010. The United States represented just less than half that total with $11.9 trillion.[5]

Within the U.S. mutual fund product set, the asset class breakdown in Exhibit 1.10 shows that roughly 35 percent of the assets are in funds comprised of domestic equities. Equity-based funds (domestic and international) make up only about half of the mutual fund assets, with a relatively even split with fixed-income funds. There are essentially two types of mutual funds from a fund management perspective: actively managed or index linked. Actively managed funds represent a significant majority of the industry, with funds steered by portfolio managers whose aim is to guide the portfolio to generate alpha for investors.

Index funds, as the name implies, are funds benchmarked to indexes with a goal to just replicate them and so are passive in management nature. They are a small but growing portion of the U.S mutual fund market. According to the 2012 Investment Company Fact Book, index mutual funds manage nearly $1 trillion dollars in assets, or approximately 7.5 percent of the U.S. mutual fund market. This is similar in size to the overall ETF market.

The ETF market has evolved very differently, with a significant majority, more than 90 percent, of the outstanding funds index based and focused on equities. Perhaps the maturity of the mutual fund market and its breakdown gives some indication of where the growth will be in ETFs going forward. In the beginning, the ETF growth pattern was based less around investor demand and more around regulatory approval. Fixed-income funds came to market much later. They represent, however, a significant development in product structure and in certain ways a steeper learning curve for investors. They potentially provide a substantial growth opportunity.

Also, the majority of ETFs are index-linked funds. ETFs are only recently being allowed to pursue forms of actively managed portfolios. Investor preferences have changed, which is contributing to the growth of index-based funds both as a percent of the mutual fund market and as ETFs. But there are still a significant amount of actively managed assets in the mutual fund arena that could benefit from an ETF wrapper. We could see several paths of growth over coming years: the fixed-income ETF space, the actively managed space, and the alternatives space. Let's now examine some of the characteristics of mutual funds, especially as compared to ETFs.

Mutual funds offer several characteristics that investors have become comfortable with over the years. Most important, they have become entrenched in our investing culture. They have developed the distribution channels; they have created an entire ecosystem designed to funnel assets into the products in a painless way to investors.

The characteristics that investors are most familiar with:

- They can be purchased either directly from the mutual fund companies or from the product supermarkets.

- They offer a theoretically clear pricing scheme of publishing a NAV once daily.

- The NAV is the price at which investors can come into and out of the funds on a daily basis.

- Mutual fund purchases and redemptions take place in dollar amounts as opposed to trading in share amounts typical of ETFs.

- Mutual funds typically have multiple share classes per fund for different investors and from different distribution methods.

- They therefore have a wide spectrum of fee ranges beyond the actual management fee that investors can be subject to, based on how they came to invest in the fund.

- Since all trading takes place within the fund, mutual funds do not have the tax efficiency that many ETFs present.

- Since all trading takes place within the fund, all investors are subject to the costs of trading related to other investors entering and exiting the fund.

- Mutual funds are heavy users of 12b-1 fees. They use this to pay distributors for a variety of functions, including placing investors in the funds. This has driven a lot of investment over the years and possibly causes some advisors to continue funneling assets into those products.

As you review the list of characteristics, you can understand where ETFs stand out in stark contrast. With ETFs, uniquely, all investors interact on a level playing field with the same fees and the same information.

Although mutual funds have certainly provided investors with accessible investment vehicles over the years, it's now become clear that they have built up a huge infrastructure within the asset management business and defined the portfolio management and distribution groups that support it. Investors have paid for the development of this infrastructure, and its setup attracts star managers to run the funds as well as distributors to sell them. Mutual funds have become entrenched in the investing way of life and ETFs must continue to change that infrastructure in order to fit into more asset feeder structures that were designed to support mutual fund vehicles.

If you look at the hordes of slot machine players sitting for hours in extravagant gambling halls around the country, you can see evidence of Americans' ever present and strong desire to outperform. In many ways, actively managed investment funds cater to that inner desire to beat the averages or, in this case, the index. Unfortunately, sometimes the active managers are not providing better returns than an index-based fund. Numerous studies over the years have shown various ranges of underperformance by active managers. Yet a tremendous quantity of actively managed mutual fund products are available and demanded by investors. You can see the product numbers by type in Exhibit 1.11. You will notice that the number of outstanding mutual funds has been reasonably constant at approximately 8500 since 2001, while the number of ETFs has grown from 100 to 1000+ over that same time period. Both of these numbers include new fund openings and fund closures as well.

One of the most watched and discussed developments in the ETF industry was the introduction of actively managed ETFs in 2008. If there is an adoption of those products by the client base, then that will potentially open the floodgates to more actively managed products over the coming years. There will, however, have to be a resolution as to the best way to bring active products to market, either via fully transparent baskets or some form of screened holdings. The McKinsey report on ETFs[7] brings up a very interesting point in describing potential growth of active ETFs. It says that "if Active ETFs were to follow the same growth pattern that passive ETF products followed, they would constitute approximately 10 percent of all actively managed U.S. long-term mutual fund assets within a decade and exceed $1 trillion in AUM." Important to consider is that ETF companies have already been educating investors for almost 20 years about the structure, so a lot of the basic education has been done which will facilitate even faster adoption of new product styles like active ETFs. This would be a full-on challenge to the largest segment of mutual fund assets. Many in the industry are watching and preparing for this potential challenge to the long standing reign of the mutual fund.

Let's take a look at another cousin product, closed-end funds. It was the listed trading of this vehicle that served as a precursor to the listing of ETFs. There are

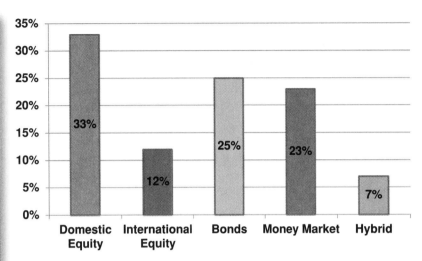

Exhibit 1.10 Breakdown of U.S. Mutual Fund Assets; Percentage by Type of Fund, Year-End 2011
Source: 2012 Investment Company Fact Book.

some very interesting and important differences between the products.

Closed-End Funds

In many of my comparisons and explanations of the ETF market, I reference them against mutual funds. That is where I see the largest shift of investment assets as a result of the growth of the more modern ETF structure. Mutual funds are related products and generally enter into the dialogue when people are making investment decisions. The conversation would not be

complete, however, without examining the closed-end fund segment of the market.

I am intimately familiar with closed-end funds, since before ETFs existed, I ran large CEF relative value portfolios. These portfolios typically ran to multiple hundreds of millions of dollars in long and short spread trades, taking advantage of discount anomalies in the products.

I've always been interested in investment products and how investors can use them to build optimal portfolios. I have never really understood how closed-end funds manage to continue to find initial investors in their IPOs when so much research details their move to a discount typically during the first 100 trading days. In the IPO process, you are actually purchasing the fund at a premium to the value of the assets.

It is the way that closed-end funds trade that is most relevant for a comparison with ETFs. This is where investors most often become confused. The critical difference is in the ETF creation and redemption feature and the fact that ETFs exhibit the trait of continuous issuance, while CEFs typically issue shares once only upon their IPO. The name itself explains that CEFs are closed-ended, meaning there are a fixed number of shares outstanding, while ETFs are considered to be open-ended like mutual funds.

In its simplest form, the fact is that you can buy an ETF share and sell its basket, and if you get to a large enough size, you can have an AP, exchange the two, creating perfect arbitrage. One asset equals the other, and therefore the trading of one, while separate, can definitely be economically related to the other. This consistently serves to narrow any discount that would potentially develop between the two assets. I discuss ETF discounts and premiums in the chapter focused on structure later in the book.

This ability does not exist in CEFs. It is not arbitrage when you are trading a closed-end fund versus its underlying basket, not that you really can trade it perfectly since the holdings of CEFs are only published periodically. There is no direct conversion of one for the other that would enable you to actually capture the spread. If a market anomaly causes an

ETF to trade away from its basket or there is a halt in the creation and redemption facility, then the investment community refers to the ETF as trading like a closed-end fund.

In standard practice, the discounts or premiums of a CEF are very different than those that might arise in an ETF. They are typically long-term and are more related to the nuances of the product structure and the supply and demand of the underlying asset class. There is little that the average investor can do about the discount or premium. Exhibit 1.12 shows you the long-term discount that might even dog the existence of a closed-end fund. In the bottom half of the chart, you can see the long-term discount averaging approximately 14.5 percent over the past five years in the fund. This is a stable discount with a low degree of volatility.

In Exhibit 1.13, you can see the keystrokes required to pull up the discount and/or premium chart for a CEF or ETF. For both products, you can graph the NAV of the fund, and it will also produce the discount or premium graph.

There are some discounts and premiums that move with a high degree of volatility. In Exhibit 1.14, I show an example of a fund that trades at a persistent premium over time. You can see the premium and discount chart for the closed-end fund over the past five years. The yellow highlights delineate periods of drastic swings. The left arrow is showing a move in the premium of the fund from above 80 to below 20 over a six-month period. Then the fund price moves back out to almost an 80 percent premium above NAV again,

STEP-BY-STEP

To bring up a chart that shows the discount or premium on funds:
1. Type in the ticker of the fund and the EQUITY button.
2. Then NAV <GO>.

	ETFs[1]	Mutual Funds[2]	CEFs	UITs	Total
1995	2	5,761	500	12,979	19,242
1996	19	6,293	497	11,764	18,573
1997	19	6,778	487	11,593	18,877
1998	29	7,489	492	10,966	18,976
1999	30	8,003	512	10,414	18,959
2000	80	8,370	482	10,072	19,004
2001	102	8,518	492	9,295	18,407
2002	113	8,511	545	8,303	17,472
2003	119	8,426	584	7,233	16,362
2004	152	8,415	619	6,499	15,685
2005	204	8,449	635	6,019	15,307
2006	359	8,721	647	5,907	15,634
2007	629	8,747	664	6,030	16,070
2008	743	8,884	643	5,984	16,254
2009	820	8,617	628	6,049	16,114
2010	950	8,545	624	5,971	16,090
2011	1,166	8,684	634	6,022	16,506

Exhibit 1.11 Number of Investment Companies by Type

[1] ETF data prior to 2001 were provided by Strategic Insight Simfund. ETF data include investment companies not registered under the Investment Company Act of 1940 and ETFs that invest primarily in other ETFs.

[2] Data include mutual funds that invest primarily in other mutual funds.

Source: Investment Company Institute Fact Book 2012.

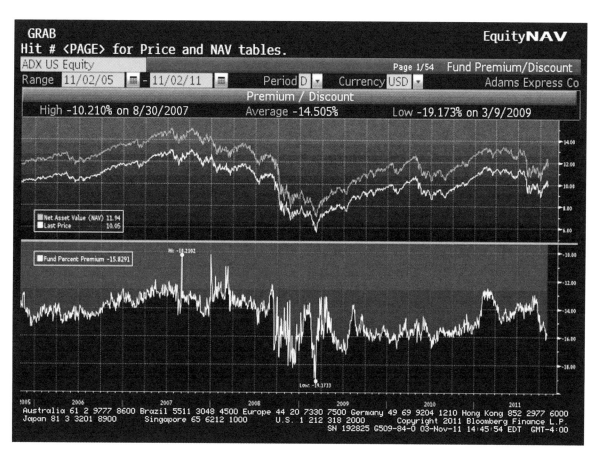

GRAB   Equity**NAV**

Hit # <PAGE> for Price and NAV tables.

ADX US Equity   Page 1/54   Fund Premium/Discount

Range 11/02/05 ▦ - 11/02/11 ▦   Period D ▼   Currency USD ▼   Adams Express Co

Premium / Discount

High -10.210% on 8/30/2007   Average -14.505%   Low -19.173% on 3/9/2009

■ Net Asset Value (NAV) 11.94
■ Last Price 10.05

■ Fund Percent Premium -15.8291

Hi: -10.2102

Low: -19.1733

2005   2006   2007   2008   2009   2010   2011

Australia 61 2 9777 8600 Brazil 5511 3048 4500 Europe 44 20 7330 7500 Germany 49 69 9204 1210 Hong Kong 852 2977 6000
Japan 81 3 3201 8900   Singapore 65 6212 1000   U.S. 1 212 318 2000   Copyright 2011 Bloomberg Finance L.P.
SN 192825 G509-84-0 03-Nov-11 14:45:54 EDT GMT-4:00

Exhibit 1.12 CEF Discount Chart (ADX NAV)

Exhibit 1.13 Bloomberg Typing Code—ADX NAV

and then in late 2008 it crashes down to almost a 20 percent discount to NAV, as highlighted by the yellow circle. The second arrow is highlighting another drastic move in the premium. What is interesting to think about in this example is that, instead of the fund being at a dramatic discount, it's actually at a dramatic premium. To clarify what that means, in the case of a fund having $10 worth of assets, it might be trading at $15 dollars in the secondary market (on the exchange). So an investor buying the fund is paying 50 percent more to buy the shares of the fund as opposed to buying its underlying basket of securities.

Some discounts seem to be reasonably stable and would therefore offer investors a small measure of comfort, except there are no structural measures to ensure the continuity of a discount or premium This is the greatest risk if you are attempting to take advantage of discount anomalies in CEFs: Something occurs in a fund, and a discount moves against you dramatically. In Exhibit 1.15, you can see a fund that traded at approximately a 10 percent discount for about two years. Then in late 2011, the fund moved from about

a 10 percent discount to more than 15 percent. If you had been long the fund and perhaps short some form of hedge that was designed to mimic the movements of the NAV of the fund, you would be losing significantly due to the underperformance of the fund price relative to its NAV. While CEFs might have been the exchange-listed precursor to the ETF, the ETF has made a giant product leap by combining the open ended attribute of a mutual fund, the exchange listing of a CEF and added its own touch of transparency to provide the investing community with an evolved and more flexible investing product.

Summary

The adoption and growing use of exchange-traded funds is revolutionary. They possess a clear set of characteristics that satisfy the modern tastes of today's investors. Their proliferation is evident in the institutional trading community, the retail community, and even the retirement savings community. Their use in 401(k)s and other plans are slowly being adopted.

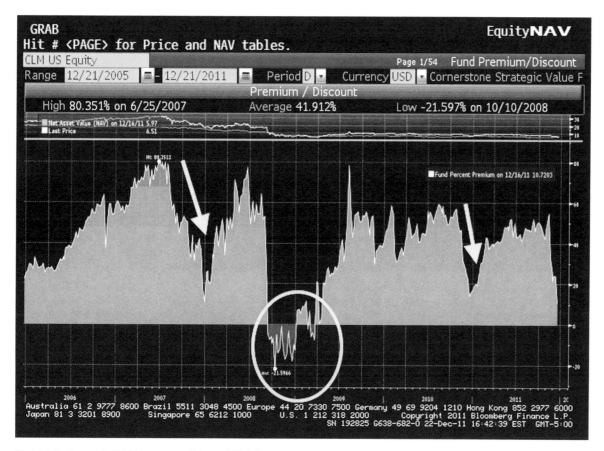

GRAB   Equity**NAV**

Hit # <PAGE> for Price and NAV tables.

CLM US Equity   Page 1/54   Fund Premium/Discount

Range 12/21/2005 ▦ - 12/21/2011 ▦   Period D ▼ Currency USD ▼ Cornerstone Strategic Value F

Premium / Discount

High 80.351% on 6/25/2007   Average 41.912%   Low -21.597% on 10/10/2008

■ Net Asset Value (NAV) on 12/16/11 5.97
■ Last Price   6.51

Ht: 80.3512

■ Fund Percent Premium on 12/16/11 10.7203

avg: -21.5966

2006   2007   2008   2009   2010   2011   2C
Australia 61 2 9777 8600 Brazil 5511 3048 4500 Europe 44 20 7330 7500 Germany 49 69 9204 1210 Hong Kong 852 2977 6000
Japan 81 3 3201 8900   Singapore 65 6212 1000   U.S. 1 212 318 2000   Copyright 2011 Bloomberg Finance L.P.
                                        SN 192825 G638-682-0 22-Dec-11 16:42:39 EST GMT-5:00

Exhibit 1.14 CEF Discount Chart (CLM)
Reprinted with permission from Bloomberg. Copyright 2012 Bloomberg L.P. All rights reserved.

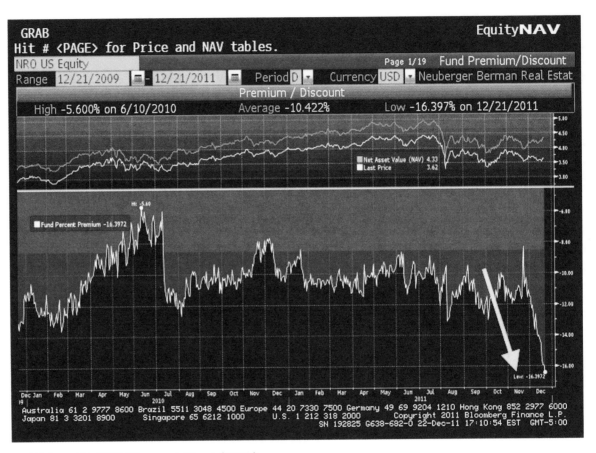

Exhibit 1.15 CEF Discount Chart (NRO)

Those plans have been slower in their adoption of ETFs due to legacy systems for recordkeeping, settlement, secondary market issues, and distribution fees. But the customer demand is pushing development, and use of ETFs is forcing the modernization of these systems. The desire of investors for transparency, lower fees, tax efficiency and standardization is obvious, and future growth will inevitably continue on a global basis as investor knowledge and facilitation systems continue to evolve. Understanding how these products work will be a crucial piece of investors' financial education now and for the future. The rest of the Visual Guide to ETFs provides a visual tour of how these products work, critical concepts and techniques for mastering ETF trading, and some sources for more information.

Notes

1. McKinsey and Company, "The Second Act Begins for ETFs: A Disruptive Investment Vehicle Vies for Center Stage in Asset Management." Financial Services Practice Research, August 2011, New York.

2. The ICI refers to the products as ETFs almost exclusively in the *2012 Investment Company Fact Book*. They state that ETF data in the book include investment companies not registered under the Investment Company Act of 1940 and exclude ETFs that invest primarily in other ETFs.

3. BlackRock iShares, "ETFs: A Call for Greater Transparency and Consistent Regulation," October 2011. BlackRock Research, New York.

4. The product numbers differ slightly because of differing inclusion of ETP, ETF, ETN, and ETC in the numbers between the ICI and BlackRock.

5. 2012 Investment Company Factbook. Investment Company Institute, Washington, DC.

6. Mutual Fund Fees and Expenses. www.sec.gov/answers/mffees.htm.

7. McKinsey & Company, "The Second Act Begins for ETFs: A Disruptive Investment Vehicle Vies for Center Stage in Asset Management." Financial Services Practice Research, August 2011, New York.

Test Yourself

1. Select three main characteristics of ETFs:
    a. Daily portfolio transparency
    b. Quarterly portfolio dissemination
    c. Limited shares outstanding
    d. Open-ended share issuance
    e. Exchange listing
    f. Regularly trade at significant discounts and premiums to NAV

2. If a retail investor is purchasing a product for cash at NAV, they are buying:
    a. A mutual fund
    b. A closed-end fund
    c. An ETF

3. ETFs get a significant portion of their tax efficiency from:
    a. Hiring better portfolio managers
    b. Trading more frequently
    c. The creation and redemption process

Answers: 1. a, d, e   2. a   3. c

CHAPTER 2

Understanding How ETF Portfolios Work

The Primary Markets

ETFs have the unique advantage of interacting in both the primary and the secondary markets daily. The primary market is where the funds undergo their process of creation and redemption. Everything that happens in the primary market is related to the actual underlying portfolio. Creations and redemptions generally take place at net asset value (NAV), and it is therefore important to understand this process to transact efficiently in the secondary market. In the secondary market, trading takes place separately from the underlying basket. The fund can trade at prices that are dictated by market forces, like great demand or even fear. The link between the two is the arbitrage functionality that is enabled by the open-ended issuance facilitated by creations and redemptions.

In this chapter, we'll take a look at the process of creation and redemption and how it works for a variety of different funds. We'll also look at creation units and how they relate to the actual portfolio of the ETF. In addition, we'll look at the various ways to see the fair value of an ETF and relate that to the actual price that you see trading in the market. Then, we'll discuss some features of the basket that have led to growth in the ETF product set, like stock loan and shorting. Once we have developed a firm understanding of what the fund is doing with its portfolio and how that changes, we'll move on to discuss secondary market trading of ETFs. This is a necessary step in understanding the entire lifecycle of an ETF.

The ETF Portfolio and Creation Units

The portfolio underlying an ETF is representative of what the fund holds. This is the actual assets under management of the fund. When you break the portfolio into smaller subsets representative of shares of ETFs, then you get what is referred to as the *creation unit*. The creation unit is the basket that the fund takes in when authorized participants (AP) are adding assets to the fund. As discussed in Chapter 1, this is how the fund will grow.

Generally, there is a direct translation from one to the other. In the screenshot, Exhibit 2.1, you can see the portfolio of an ETF.

You can see on the screenshot the name of the ETF, and you can see the holdings in descending order by market value in the portfolio. Exxon Mobil Corp. is the largest holding in the portfolio. You can see that there are 32,703 shares of XOM in the portfolio of the ETF. Those shares represent 4.727 percent of the assets of the fund. You can also see that in the red bar it says "97) View Creation Unit." Most ETFs publish a creation unit for which there is a basket available daily. These baskets are available on Bloomberg or via the other data sources.

The next screenshot, Exhibit 2.2, takes you into that screen to present a picture of the underlying creation unit of the ETF.

This is the creation unit of the same ETF. This list is also sorted in descending order by market value. Again you can see Exxon Mobil Corp. as the largest component of this creation unit. In this case, the position column is showing the shares of XOM in each creation unit, or 1,309. Let's take a look at how one translates into the other. On the top right of the screen, you can see that the creation unit size represents 50,000 shares of the ETF. That means that each lot of 50,000 ETF shares is composed of the displayed basket.

There is one other piece of information that you also require to run through this analysis demonstrating the relationship between the portfolio and the creation unit. To translate from the portfolio of the ETF to the creation unit, you need to know how many shares are outstanding in the fund. Every ETF provides a shares outstanding number daily.

This is a key piece of information about the size of the fund. It is interesting that when the products were developed, it seemed innocuous to provide the shares outstanding daily, but in practice, this has helped democratize the flow of information in the asset management industry.

The shares outstanding number enables us to determine how many units of a particular fund are outstanding.

If we take XOM shares per creation unit and multiply that by the units in the fund, we should get a reasonably close number of the shares in the portfolio.

It is important to understand the interconnectedness of the data being provided. The two numbers, however, are very rarely identical due to the actual real-world mechanics of running funds (including corporate actions, share dividends, round lots, and

GRAB

EquityMHD

EPS US Equity | 97) View Creation Unit | Page 1/28 Mutual Fund Holdings

WISDOMTREE EARNINGS 500 FUND — Portfolio Filing Date 7/5/2012

Fund Type ETF

Asset Class Equity — Creation/Redemption Fee 2500 USD

	Name	Ticker		Position	Value(USD)	Change	%Net
1)	Exxon Mobil Corp	XOM	US	32703	2.80M	unch	4.727
2)	Apple Inc	AAPL	US	4180	2.55M	unch	4.307
3)	Chevron Corp	CVX	US	16365	1.74M	unch	2.931
4)	Microsoft Corp	MSFT	US	55798	1.71M	unch	2.894
5)	JPMorgan Chase & Co	JPM	US	36211	1.24M	unch	2.103
6)	Wal-Mart Stores Inc	WMT	US	16636	1.18M	unch	1.997
7)	Wells Fargo & Co	WFC	US	34138	1.13M	unch	1.910
8)	AT&T Inc	T	US	26731	956.17k	unch	1.615
9)	International Business Machi	IBM	US	4853	947.74k	unch	1.601
10)	Intel Corp	INTC	US	33580	891.55k	unch	1.506
11)	General Electric Co	GE	US	39471	802.45k	unch	1.355
12)	Johnson & Johnson	JNJ	US	11411	773.44k	unch	1.306
13)	Pfizer Inc	PFE	US	33608	761.89k	unch	1.287
14)	Berkshire Hathaway Inc	BRK/B	US	9064	754.31k	unch	1.274
15)	Citigroup Inc	C	US	25538	685.44k	unch	1.158
16)	Coca-Cola Co/The	KO	US	8499	666.75k	unch	1.126
17)	Procter & Gamble Co/The	PG	US	10771	660.80k	unch	1.116
18)	Verizon Communications Inc	VZ	US	13819	620.33k	unch	1.048

Exhibit 2.1 ETF Holdings (MHD)

STEP-BY-STEP

How to pull up a creation unit on Bloomberg:

1. **Type the Ticker and the Equity button, then hit Go.**
2. **Type MHD Go.**
3. **Type 97 Go.**

```
GRAB                                                              EquityMHD
<Menu> to return to portfolio
EPS US Equity                                        Page 1/28  ETF Creation Unit
WISDOMTREE EARNINGS 500 FUND                         Creation Unit Size      50000
Fund Type        ETF                                    Cash Position   2.37k USD
Asset Class      Equity                          Creation/Redemption Fee   2500 USD
     Name                      Ticker          Position      Value(USD)       %Net
 1) Exxon Mobil Corp          XOM      US          1309     110424.494       4.729
 2) Apple Inc                 AAPL     US           167     100559.054       4.306
 3) Chevron Corp              CVX      US           655      68487.978       2.933
 4) Microsoft Corp            MSFT     US          2233      67112.816       2.874
 5) JPMorgan Chase & Co       JPM      US          1449      49179.058       2.106
 6) Wal-Mart Stores Inc       WMT      US           666      47352.934       2.028
 7) Wells Fargo & Co          WFC      US          1366      45064.342       1.930
 8) AT&T Inc                  T        US          1070      37835.201       1.620
 9) International Business Machine IBM US           194      36887.160       1.580
10) Intel Corp                INTC     US          1344      34906.368       1.495
11) General Electric Co       GE       US          1580      31647.401       1.355
12) Johnson & Johnson         JNJ      US           457      30838.588       1.321
13) Pfizer Inc                PFE      US          1345      30208.699       1.294
14) Berkshire Hathaway Inc    BRK/B    US           363      29889.419       1.280
15) Citigroup Inc             C        US          1022      26725.300       1.144
16) Coca-Cola Co/The          KO       US           340      26486.001       1.134
17) Procter & Gamble Co/The   PG       US           431      26355.651       1.129
18) Philip Morris International In PM   US           278      24847.639       1.064
Australia 61 2 9777 8600 Brazil 5511 3048 4500 Europe 44 20 7330 7500 Germany 49 69 9204 1210 Hong Kong 852 2977 6000
Japan 81 3 3201 8900    Singapore 65 6212 1000    U.S. 1 212 318 2000    Copyright 2012 Bloomberg Finance L.P.
                                                    SN 192825 G377-1429-0 06-Jul-12 14:17:30 EDT  GMT-4:00
```

Exhibit 2.2 ETF Creation Unit

Reprinted with permission from Bloomberg. Copyright 2012 Bloomberg L.P. All rights reserved.

other events). This demonstrates the creation unit relationship to the actual portfolio. There is also a cash number that will be the tie-in between the creation unit and the portfolio to account for rounding and other miscellaneous items.

Also, when portfolio managers of ETFs are trying to adjust positions in the course of maintaining the portfolio, you might see stocks in the creation unit that are different than some of those in the redemption unit. This adds to the efficiency of managing the portfolio by using the creation and redemption functionality instead of trading and generating taxable events.

Utilizing Shares Outstanding

The outstanding shares numbers that are provided for ETFs are a unique and important feature of the product. They can help to interpret the flow of assets into and out of funds. Interpreting what is happening in the fund by watching the shares outstanding number is an important skill to have when utilizing the products.

Shares Outstanding Can Help to Interpret Trading Activity

Let's go through a few examples of what you can learn from watching the shares outstanding numbers for your arsenal. We will learn that this can in no way be the only metric to monitor. If you see a very high trading volume in an ETF, it does not necessarily indicate that assets are flowing in one direction. If there is a high-frequency trading firm selling the ETF versus

some calculated hedge, and if, on the other side of the market, another high-frequency trading firm is buying the ETF versus some different calculated hedge, they may not be pushing assets. If, at the end of the day, the seller of the ETF has a creation done on its behalf, and the buyer has a redemption done on its behalf, then the net effect to the ETF would be zero change in assets. If you saw only volume, you might think that the high volumes indicated a shift of assets one way or the other, but since you can compare that high volume to a static shares outstanding figure, you can determine that the flow consisted of nondirectional buyers and sellers

As you can see in the chart in Exhibit 2.3, over a one-week period in November 2011, the ETF traded between 10 and 15 million shares daily, as indicated by the white line and dots showing daily volume. You can also see that from the 8th to the 9th, and then from the 10th to the 11th, there were no changes in the shares outstanding of the fund. This indicates that on those two days, even though a lot of volume traded on the exchanges, this did not translate back to a creation or redemption for the ETF. Then there was a large creation on the 10th as indicated by the jump in the shares outstanding number, but this is not clearly identifiable by the volume numbers.

Shares Outstanding Can Be a Misleading Indicator

It's not always clear that growth in shares outstanding is a bullish indicator. Therefore, if you see a significant change in the shares outstanding of an ETF, this

---

STEP-BY-STEP

Calculate the number of units outstanding in an ETF:

Shares Outstanding / Creation Unit = 1,300,000 / 50,000 = 26 Units

1. The Shares Outstanding = 1,300,000
2. Divided by the Creation Unit size = 50,000
3. Equals 26 units of the ETF outstanding

STEP-BY-STEP

Calculate the number of shares of XOM that should be in the ETF portfolio:

1. The XOM Shares per Creation Unit = 1,309
2. Multiplied by the Units = 26
3. 1,309 * 26 = 34,034
4. Actual number of XOM Shares in the Portfolio: 32,703

KEY POINT:

Every ETF provides two cash numbers on a daily basis. The estimated cash, represented on Bloomberg using EU appended to a ticker, shows the amount of cash that is expected to be in a given fund on the following day. This is a number that traders use when estimating fund fair value because it is forward looking. The total cash, represented on Bloomberg using TC appended to a ticker, shows the amount of cash that was in the portfolio for calculation of net asset value purposes as of the latest close of business.

KEY POINT:

The *shares outstanding* number enables you to watch the daily asset flows in and out of ETFs. This information was previously only available in a limited format to investors. You could have watched trading volumes only or watched shares outstanding only, but neither tells a complete story. In conjunction with other data, this number provides information on asset movements on an index level that was previously hard to access.

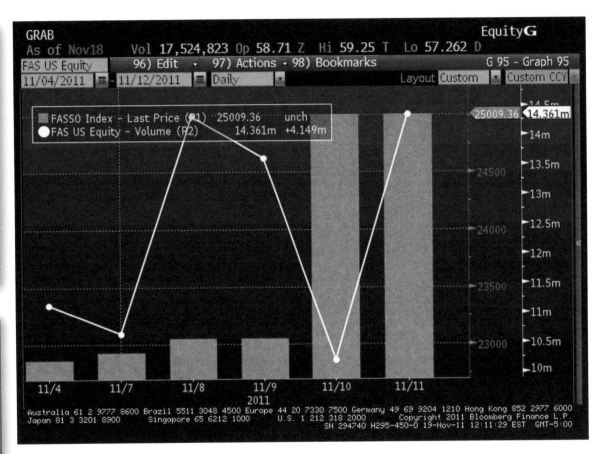

Exhibit 2.3 Shares Outstanding and Volume

Reprinted with permission from Bloomberg. Copyright 2012 Bloomberg L.P. All rights reserved.
Note: Blue bars are shares outstanding. White line is daily volume.

does not necessarily indicate a buying or selling opportunity. In Exhibit 2.4, there is a chart of the shares outstanding in XLF and the price of XLF from 2007 through 2009. If you were just watching the shares outstanding and you saw them spike in September 2008, and you were not watching price as well, you might think that a lot of assets are flowing into the fund, representing a buying opportunity. In this case, however, because of the market turmoil in the financial sector, portfolio managers were selling XLF as a means to hedge their long exposures and drive up demand for borrows. This, in turn, drove an increase in creations, as authorized participants with available balance sheet room created shares for inventory to lend by keeping a long ETF/short basket position on their books. If, on the other hand, you were watching only price, you might be surprised to learn that assets in the fund had increased drastically over that period. Thus it is important not to look at these indicators in isolation but understand that shares outstanding are available on a daily basis to help paint a more complete picture of market activity.

Shares Outstanding Revealing a Market Secret

As the trading volume of an ETF rises to levels that attract both buyers and sellers regularly, it is harder to predict AUM changes from volume levels and price changes. As we saw in Exhibit 2.3, an ETF can trade a lot without having subsequent creations or redemptions. In funds that are young or typically trade a lower

average daily volume, there can be a direct translation from a high-volume day to a creation or redemption. This can help to determine the direction of asset flows and market sentiment of that fund's benchmark. In Exhibit 2.5, you can see a fund that typically trades an average daily volume of 200,000 shares per day. The white line shows daily traded volume for a 10-day period in the end of October into November 2011. On November 1, the fund traded just more than a million shares, roughly five times its average daily volume. Then you can see that from 11/2 to 11/3, shares outstanding reported dropped by 850,000 shares. There is typically a one-day lag for reporting of the shares outstanding numbers.

Understanding the ETF Data

There are some standard steps that a diligent researcher might follow to decipher what is happening in particular funds. Let's take this example a little further and see if you might have been able to determine what had happened in the ETF on a standout high-volume day, given other pieces of data. You will see how the shares outstanding number becomes the key to the puzzle.

Starting from the beginning, on 11/1/11 there was an outlier high-volume day, as shown in Exhibit 2.6.

Next, take a look to see if any big blocks were traded on the day or, if not, where most of the volume took place. In Exhibit 2.7, you can see a screen showing average quote recap. This screen is sorted from largest

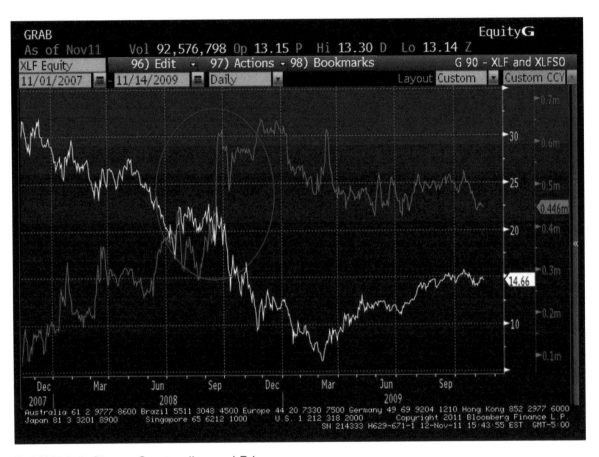

Exhibit 2.4 Shares Outstanding and Price
Reprinted with permission from Bloomberg. Copyright 2012 Bloomberg L.P. All rights reserved.

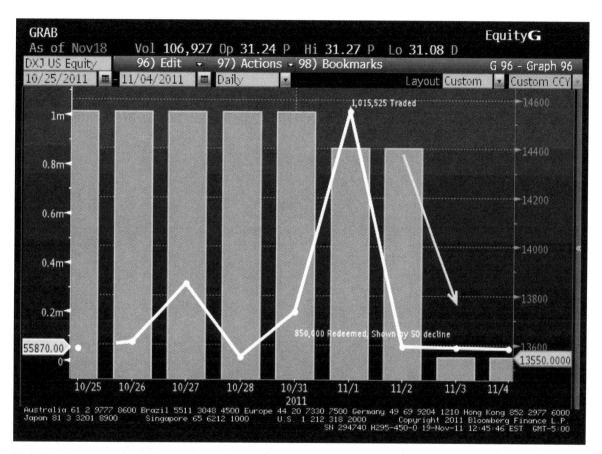

STEP-BY-STEP

Analyzing ETF trades:

1. Look at historical volume to isolate a day.
2. Look at block trades to see if anything extraordinary occurred.
3. Look at the trade summary to see if trading was lopsided.
4. Watch the shares outstanding for changes over the next few days.

Exhibit 2.5 Shares Outstanding and Redemption

Reprinted with permission from Bloomberg. Copyright 2012 Bloomberg L.P. All rights reserved.

KEY POINT:

Sometimes the creation unit will be different than the redemption unit. If there is a corporate action in a stock that the fund holds, this might necessitate the fund taking a position in a different stock. If there is time to adjust the portfolio, sometimes the fund can be delivering out the shares that it needs to get rid of via the redemption baskets, while taking in shares of a different stock via its creation basket. This sometimes enables the fund managers to manage the portfolio without creating taxable events for shareholders.

A significant trading day compared to the daily average volume of 194,703, as seen on the upper right.

DATE	PRICE	VOLUME	DATE	PRICE	VOLUME	DATE	PRICE	VOLUME
F 11/18	31.23	106927	F 10/28	33.03	19418	F 10/ 7	32.08	22579
T 11/17	31.09	170457	T 10/27	33.06	315221	T 10/ 6	32.275	61073
W 11/16 L	31.05	33505	W 10/26	32.10	76540	W 10/ 5	32.2072	102941
T 11/15	31.55	30461	T 10/25	31.96	51921	T 10/ 4	32.29	131406
M 11/14	31.58	42744	M 10/24	32.46	20502	M 10/ 3	32.07	121606
F 11/11	31.74	28699	F 10/21	32.29	59611	F 9/30	32.52	31803
T 11/10	31.67	61804	T 10/20	32.24	328509	T 9/29	33.10	75259
W 11/ 9	31.68	51052	W 10/19	32.27	33570	W 9/28	32.43	112304
T 11/ 8	32.26	34250	T 10/18	32.76	68352	T 9/27	32.58	544348
M 11/ 7	32.38	23916	M 10/17	32.48	93373	M 9/26	31.97	353888
F 11/ 4	32.14	55870	F 10/14	32.74	43775	F 9/23	31.83	150534
T 11/ 3	32.42	57748	T 10/13	32.65	50011	T 9/22	31.56	516154
W 11/ 2	31.99	61626	W 10/12	32.91	134244	W 9/21	32.22	80240
T 11/ 1	31.90	1015525	T 10/11	32.50	30639	T 9/20	32.25	37546
M 10/31	32.37	200137	M 10/10	32.78	6928	M 9/19	32.31	63120

GRAB   Equity**HP**

CLOSE/PRICE   Page 1/6   Historical Price Table

WISDOMTREE JAPAN HEDGED (DXJ US) PRICE 32.012 D $

High   41.21   on   2/17/11
Range 11/22/2010 – 11/18/2011   Period Daily   Avg   35.7272   Vol   194703
Currency USD   Market Trade   Low   31.05   on   11/16/11

Australia 61 2 9777 8600 Brazil 5511 3048 4500 Europe 44 20 7330 7500 Germany 49 69 9204 1210 Hong Kong 852 2977 6000
Japan 81 3 3201 8900   Singapore 65 6212 1000   U.S. 1 212 318 2000   Copyright 2012 Bloomberg Finance L.P.
SN 192825 G377-5266-0 10-Aug-12 7:58:49 EDT GMT-4:00

Exhibit 2.6 Looking at Historical Volume (HP)

block on the day to smallest. So a large block would show up on the top of the left-hand column. On 11/1/11, the largest block of DXJ traded at 13:52:17 in the afternoon, and it was only 21,000 shares. We know the fund traded 1,015,525 shares that day and can now see that one large block was not responsible for the increase in daily volume.

Next, we take a look at the trade matrix to see if we can determine whether the fund's traded volume was heavily skewed to the bid or ask side. You can look at the totals along the bottom of Exhibit 2.8 and see that there was more volume on the bid side (434,140 shares) as compared to the ask side (284,305), but this is not really a significant enough amount to provide clarity. A lot of the trading also took place at the mid-price, indicating that there was not really a heavy skew to the sell side. If you saw 950,000 shares traded on the bid side, you might be easily able to conclude that there was a large seller on the day when referencing that to the high volume number. But in this case, there is no extremely overweight traded volume on either side of the market so we must look for more data.

With the information gathered, it is hard to decipher if the abnormal trading volume was directionally skewed. We are then forced to wait a day or two to see if there is a significant change in the shares outstanding. If you refer back to Exhibit 2.5, you can see that the large redemption on 11/2/11 clarifies the story. The trading was done in a way that did not show an obvious trail, like a large block traded at a discount to the market spread or a heavy distinctive trading skew

to the bid side of the market during that day. But you can infer that there was a large seller of the fund, who sold to the liquidity providers, which then resulted in a redemption order by an authorized participant (AP) with the ETF issuer. Mystery solved.

Creation and Redemption

The Seeding and Launch of an ETF

A variety of processes are involved in the development of an ETF. Issuing firms speak with clients, they assess the markets, and they then devise creative concepts for exposures that they can wrap in an ETF structure. Part of the development process involves determining whether the fund will track an index or be actively managed. They decide whether the fund will use perfect replication or optimize its portfolio, and they obtain whatever regulatory approvals are necessary to bring the fund to market. Near the end of that process, they determine on which exchange they will list the fund's shares and whether the fund will have a lead market maker (LMM). Not all funds come to market with an LMM. We will learn more about that process in Chapter 4.

Typically, one of the final and necessary tasks before listing on the exchange is *seeding* the ETF. I actually do not like that term because it suggests that the process is different than the creation and redemption process, when, in fact, it is not. I prefer to call the first unit of assets into the product the *initial creation*. This term more sharply delineates what is happening. It clarifies the fact that it is not always a customer making an initial

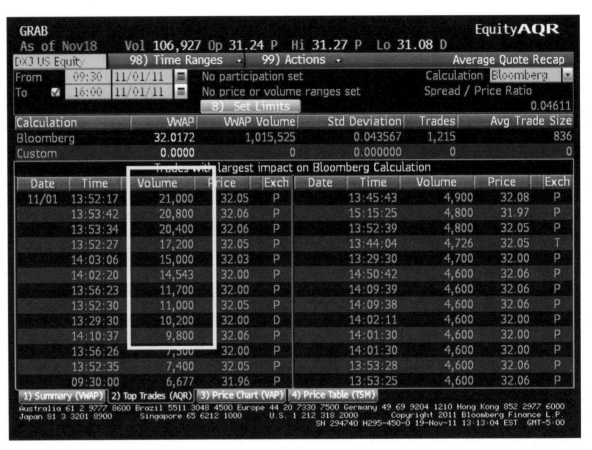

Exhibit 2.7 Looking at Large Trade Blocks (AQR)

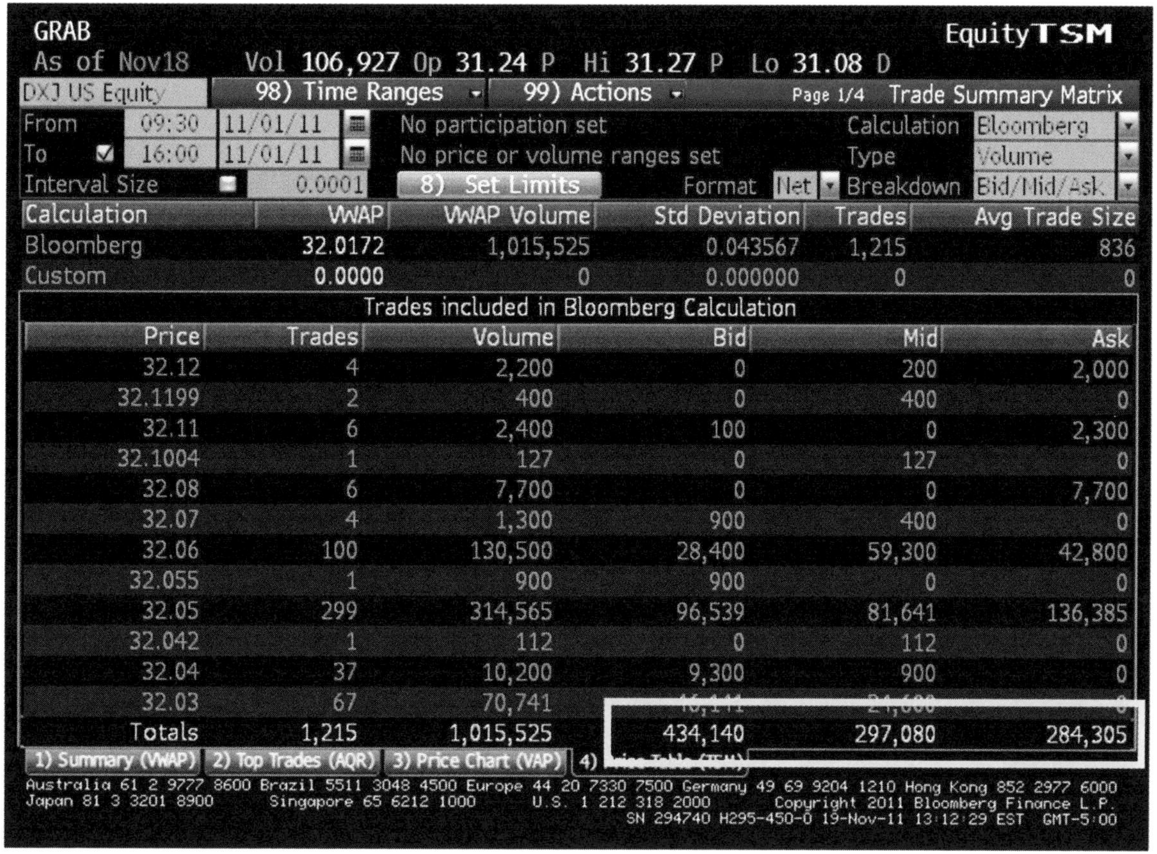

Exhibit 2.8 Looking at a Trade Summary (TSM)

investment into a fund but is the standard procedure of an authorized participant processing a creation. This is not to say that a customer, or anyone else, for that matter, cannot make the initial investment into an ETF, but it should be clear that this is done via the creation process and not a different seeding method. Typically, the initial creation is small, one or two units. The ETF starts with a small amount of assets and then grows from that base. This is different from a closed-end fund, which launches via an IPO at a premium to NAV to begin trading.

Visual Creation and Redemption

In a plain vanilla ETF, the standard creation process takes place as detailed in Exhibit 2.9.

The authorized participant will be delivering the basket stocks and any excess cash to the ETF sponsor. In exchange, the sponsor will deliver ETF shares.

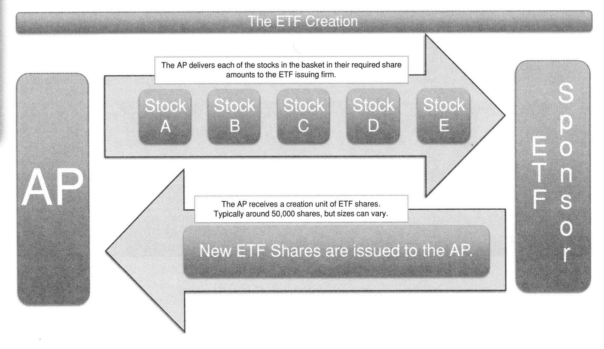

Exhibit 2.9 ETF Creation Process

This transaction takes place at NAV. Typically, the stocks will be marked at the closing price, and this, along with any cash, translates into the NAV price of the ETF. You can see from the diagram that the ETF portfolio manager in a standard creation is not going into the secondary markets and purchasing stocks. They are receiving them from the AP. What the AP has done to get those stocks is mostly irrelevant. The issuer does not know whether the stocks are borrowed or have been bought, as long as they are delivered in fully settled form. This works the same way as when you go into the markets and buy a stock, since there is no way for you to tell whether you are buying from someone who shorted the stock to you or from someone who sold the stock from their portfolio. The ETF issuer ensures that they have received the stock unencumbered, and they then issue new shares of the ETF to the AP. This is a primary market transaction that is not printed to the tape and is not considered to be a trade for tax purposes, as I discussed in Chapter 1.

The redemption process is the reverse situation. In the ETF redemption, the shares of the ETF are delivered from the AP to the ETF sponsor, and, in exchange, the basket is delivered out of the fund. You can see this clearly in Exhibit 2.10.

For the basic equity baskets, this is a very straightforward transaction. As ETFs expand into various different asset classes, the creation and redemption process has been expanded to enable cash delivery, adjustments for foreign currencies, and other elements. The costs and difficulties of acquiring and transferring the underlying baskets are translated into pricing of the ETF in the markets. Although the creation and redemptions are marked at NAV, there are sometimes additional costs involved to assemble or disassemble the basket. So a customer can trade through an authorized participant at NAV +/- costs. Let's go through some additional details about how the basic process works first, and then later, we'll navigate some of the twists.

The Initial Creation of an ETF

To detail the process of initial creation and the life cycle of an ETF, I will use my favorite simulated product, ticker ABS. ABS is a hypothetical exchange-traded fund that holds five stocks in equal weights: stock A, stock B, stock C, stock D, and stock E. They each trade on the exchange at the same time as the ETF, and they each trade 10 million shares per day. They each also trade at a price of $10 per share.

To bring the ETF to market, the ETF issuer determines the appropriate creation basket of the fund and how many ETF shares that will represent. The creation unit in this example represents 25,000 ABS shares and is as follows:

Stock	Shares
A	10,000
B	10,000
C	10,000
D	10,000
E	10,000

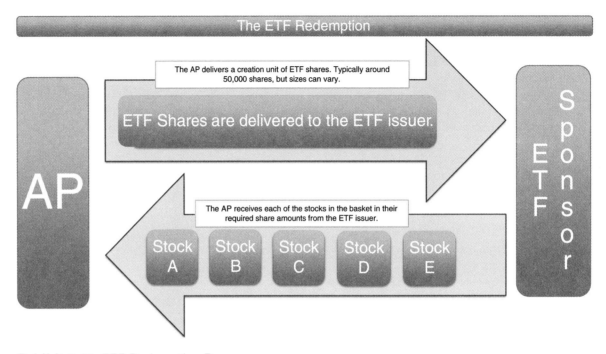

Exhibit 2.10 ETF Redemption Process

The issuer arranged with one of its authorized participants that it will be doing an initial creation in the fund ABS. This actual process involves the AP delivering the underlying shares in the basket to the issuer, and then new ABS shares will be issued. In this case, the AP theoretically goes into the market and buys 10,000 shares of each stock at as close to the closing price as possible. Remember, in a creation, the underlying shares are delivered to the issuing company at the closing price, and the ETF shares are delivered at NAV. In our example, these are going to be exactly the same because the fund does not yet have any assets or cash.

Right after the initial creation has taken place, the portfolio of ABS looks as follows:

This shows you that the fund has issued 25,000 shares because of its initial creation, and the fund holds positions of 10,000 shares in each of the five stocks. The total market value of the fund, also called

Ticker	Shares Outstanding	NAV	AUM
ABS	25,000	$20.00	$500,000

Ticker	Shares	Price	Market Value
A	10,000	$10.00	$100,000
B	10,000	$10.00	$100,000
C	10,000	$10.00	$100,000
D	10,000	$10.00	$100,000
E	10,000	$10.00	$100,000
Assets under Management			$500,000

assets under management, is equal to the value of the stocks in the basket, or $500,000. At this point, the AP is long the 25,000 shares of the ETF. See the Key Point for an understanding of the AP's position.

Let the Trading Begin

Now that there are shares outstanding in ABS, the fund can begin trading on the exchange. At the moment, there is only one shareholder, the AP. The AP will offer the shares out for sale to the market.

The entire ETF trading community and the customer base have the ability to trade the ETF. This enables the arbitrage mechanism to be working from the very first minute that an ETF is trading, which affords customer protection against the inappropriate pricing, premiums, or discounts usually seen in closed-end funds. A way to understand this is that if there are a lot of buyers in the ETF, and the seller (the initial AP) starts to move too far away from the fair value of the ETF, other market makers begin to offer the ETF cheaper. At this point in the life cycle of the fund, they will be shorting the ETF and probably buying the underlying basket to hedge their positions because they are trying to capture the arbitrage spread.

Then they will put in a creation to satisfy their settlement obligation because usually at the beginning of an ETF life, there are not a lot of shares available in the stock loan market to facilitate shorting. This will then drive more assets into the ETF.

Let's bring this back to our example.

Now that our ETF, ABS, is trading, a variety of customers are trying to buy the fund. The AP who did the initial creation has sold the entire position of 25,000 shares into the market and bought back the hedge, which is typically the underlying basket, and sees that there is still demand to buy shares. If the AP sees that there is liquidity in the underlying basket, they will offer the ETF, ABS, where they can buy the relative stocks in the creation unit. Typically, this is done simultaneously. Since they have just sold all 25,000 shares of the ETF, if they sell any more, a creation order will have to be put in so that more shares of the ETF can be issued. Say by the end of the day, the AP has sold a total of 50,000 ETF shares and bought 20,000 shares of each of the underlying stocks. The AP then does a creation for two units, equal to 50,000 shares of the ETF. To facilitate the creation, they deliver 20,000 shares of each stock to the issuer, and there are 50,000 shares more issued to the AP. At this time, the AP's position is long 25,000 shares of the ETF, and they are either short the basket or have hedged in another way.

The portfolio of the ETF looks as follows:

Ticker	Shares Outstanding	NAV	AUM
ABS	75,000	$20.00	$1,500,000

Ticker	Shares	Price	Market Value
A	30,000	$10.00	$ 300,000
B	30,000	$10.00	$ 300,000
C	30,000	$10.00	$ 300,000
D	30,000	$10.00	$ 300,000
E	30,000	$10.00	$ 300,000
Assets under Management			$1,500,000

Note that in this example so far, the prices of the underlying stocks did not move on the first day of trading. But the ETF traded 50,000 shares and processed a two-unit creation, effectively tripling the assets in the fund and the amount of shares outstanding.

Since the prices of the underlying stocks have not moved, the NAV of the ETF has not moved, either. For the purposes of the example, there is no daily management fee decrease of the NAV. In addition, because of the buyer interest and liquid underlying stocks, the arbitrage mechanism worked well and enabled the price of the ETF to stay right around NAV. You can also see that the ETF now has 30,000 shares of each of the underlying stocks representing its assets under management and corresponding to three units or 75,000 shares outstanding.

You should also notice that the AP, using the creation and redemption mechanism, is the conduit between the primary and secondary markets. As a customer buying the ETF shares, you are gaining exposure to the underlying assets. But it is the actual AP that is transferring them back and forth from the fund issuer. The customer transaction is separate, and the AP is acting in both the primary market (transaction with the issuer) and the secondary market (transaction with the customer), which highlights the distinction between the primary and secondary market nature of the products.

If market sentiment shifted the following day, and the investors decided they did not want the exposure to the underlying assets that are held by this ETF, customer selling would ensue. This reverse activity generally takes place where the liquidity providers will be buying ETF shares from the investor base, while at the same time selling the underlying assets to hedge their positions. If there is significant enough selling pressure, this will drive redemptions in the ETF as well.

Let's expand on our example to see what happens to the AP's position, as well that of the ETF. At this point, other liquidity providers have started trading the ETF beyond the initial AP. In the secondary market, customers are selling ETF shares to the liquidity providers. Say they sell 25,000 shares of the ETF to a liquidity provider. To hedge their position, the liquidity provider has gone into the markets and sold 10,000 shares of each of the stocks in the basket, A through E. The trading day ends. The liquidity provider now has a position of long 25,000 shares of the ETF ABS. They are short 10,000 shares of each of the stocks. They liaise with an AP to process a redemption order. In the redemption, they deliver the ETF shares to the issuer, and they receive 10,000 shares of each of the stocks. This action flattens their position, leaving their balance sheet free from that position and ready to provide more liquidity the next day. The assets of the ETF have also changed, as well as the shares outstanding. ETF issuers do not store ETF shares. When shares are redeemed during a redemption order, they are taken out of the public float of available shares. The shares outstanding number decreases, and astute investors will see ABSSO Index

Ticker	Shares Outstanding	NAV	AUM
ABS	50,000	$20.00	$1,000,000

Ticker	Shares	Price	Market Value
A	20,000	$10.00	$ 200,000
B	20,000	$10.00	$ 200,000
C	20,000	$10.00	$ 200,000
D	20,000	$10.00	$ 200,000
E	20,000	$10.00	$ 200,000
Assets under Management			$1,000,000

STEP-BY-STEP

Execution of an agency creation.

When a broker executes a creation on behalf of a client, there are several steps:

1. **The client gives the broker an order to buy the ETF at an implied price based on the value of the underlying basket.**
2. **The broker buys the basket.**
3. **The broker initiates a creation—delivering the underlying basket to the ETF issuer.**
4. **The broker receives ETF shares from the creation.**
5. **The broker then sells the ETF shares to the client at the implied NAV price minus any costs, which is printed to the tape.**

levels drop by 25,000 shares. The portfolio of the ETF now looks as follows:

As you can see, the assets in the fund have dropped by $500,000, not by price movements, but because the fund issuer delivered out 10,000 shares of each stock to satisfy the redemption. At the same time, the amount of shares outstanding declined by one unit, 25,000 shares. This process happens daily across the universe of ETFs, and millions of shares are created and redeemed regularly.

The Operational Nature of Creations and Redemptions

The creation and redemption functionality should be considered an operational function of the authorized participants. Too often, a customer will ask to have a creation or redemption done on their behalf. This statement leads to confusion. What the customer is actually trying to achieve is exposure to the ETF via someone trading the basket for them. Because the ETF trade at the end of that type of arrangement still has to be crossed on the exchange, the customer should understand that the trade is taking place in the secondary market, but at a price related to NAV.

What you really want as a customer is to have the ability to trade an ETF near fair value. However, you may also want a broker to go into the markets and buy the basket throughout the day to minimize impact and then turn around and sell you the ETF shares at the implied price. This order is being executed with fair value as the reference, and the customer is receiving the ETF at a price that is relative to the cost of buying the basket over the day. On the back end of that type of trade, the liquidity provider will have a position of long the basket and short the ETF shares, which they sold to the client. They will then process a creation to flatten out those shares versus the ETF issuer. The creation is effected at NAV, but the customer buys the ETF from the AP at the implied price of the executed basket.

Why is this important to understand? Because it should clarify that you don't have to qualify your counterparty as an authorized participant to handle these executions. They are mutually exclusive. Many liquidity providers can go out and execute a basket of stocks and, against that, can sell you ETF shares at the price as implied by that basket. They can then turn around and have the creation done for their own accounts. The major clearing firms are becoming authorized participants to be able to process these transactions. This is increasing the growth in the ETF trading industry, as the conduits in the primary market are growing beyond the standard big banks that were the original authorized participants.

One important aspect of this type of trading is that there are times when the actual ETF trade for the client does not need to be printed to the tape. If the creation or redemption is done directly into the client accounts, instead of into the accounts of the broker, then there is no necessity to cross the shares as a trade. This is a function of whether they clear at the AP, which can have ramifications in terms of giving larger customers the ability to enter and exit big positions without having to trade ETF shares on the exchange. This can offer them a certain degree of anonymity. If market participants are using volume flags as sentiment indicators without referencing shares outstanding changes, they might not notice changes from large creations or redemptions because the ETF volume will not spike. This is a process being adopted by larger institutions when moving positions between ETFs. It removes the risk from the broker dealer because they are doing an agency creation or redemption, but because it's done directly into the client accounts, it does not print to the tape. In effect, the AP is renting out its AP agreement to its prime brokerage customers, who can then transact in the primary market of the ETF without the involvement of the broker's trading desk.

Understanding ETF Values

Once you understand how the creation and redemption mechanism works, the next most important part of the process is to understand how to calculate the value of the ETF. The products have essentially four critical numbers that are important at various times throughout the valuation and execution process: the NAV (net asset value), the IV (indicative value, also known as the IOPV, indicative optimized portfolio value), the eNAV (estimated NAV), and the price.

Net Asset Value (NAV)

The NAV is a straightforward accounting of the actual assets of the fund.

$$NAV = (Assets - Liabilities) / Shares outstanding$$

The official NAV is published once daily by each ETF, a true similarity to their mutual fund cousins. It is calculated using the most recent closing price of each of the constituents in the portfolio. This is effectively a backward-looking number. It is not valuable for actually trading an ETF in the market because it represents the most recent closing prices, typically the previous trading day's closing value. It is the number, however, that is used for official performance statistics and other comparative analyses. This can lead to standardized comparisons of statistics that are incredibly valuable in the world of investment products. The NAV is also used as the pricing mark for valuation of many trading portfolios.

On a Bloomberg, you would find the NAV of an ETF by using the NV function. Typing ETFNV (where ETF is the ticker of any fund) Index <GO> would bring you to the NAV page of the fund. To see a historical perspective of the fund's NAV, you can use the HP function that you can see in Exhibit 2.11.

Indicative Value (IV)

The indicative value (IV) is the value that ETF issuers provide to offer a more real-time indication of the value of each ETF portfolio. It is also sometimes known as the indicative optimized portfolio value (IOPV) or intraday indicative value (IIV). Here is where the ETF structure stands apart from its mutual fund and closed-end fund cousins. No other listed investment vehicle provides an intraday indicative value of its portfolio based on market values of its constituents. This seemingly innocuous concept has aided in the development of a multibillion-dollar trading business around ETFs. The IV takes the most recent price of the portfolio of constituents in the market, adds whatever portfolio cash needs to be included, and produces a value for the ETF every 15 seconds. As a general guide, this number is very helpful to the client base to understand the value of the ETF at any given time, as well as use as a reference to base judgment of execution against. This is a major step up in transparency from quarterly portfolio releases or once daily NAVs.

In Exhibit 2.12, you can see the IV DES page for an ETF. It shows a variety of information calculated from the actual basket of the ETF. Note that this information is not adjusted for the costs of running a fund, trading corporate actions, or shares outstanding changes. So, in general, actual performance and dividend distributions are better taken from the fund description pages as opposed to the IV DES pages.

Utilizing the Indicative Value (IV) for Trading

Typically, ETF IVs are published on a 15-second lag. This lag may have been introduced as an economy because the funds were new and it was not clear how

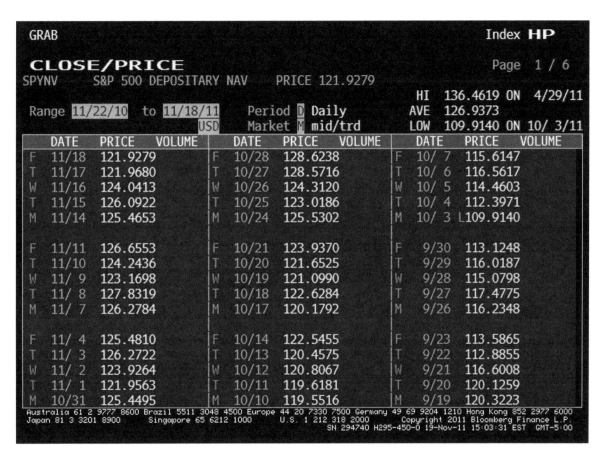

DEFINITION:
Indicative value (IV)

The most recent value of the ETF portfolio as calculated every 15 seconds. If the assets underlying the fund are closed, the closing price for those assets will be used for the calculation of IV.

| GRAB | | | | | | | | Index **HP** | |

CLOSE/PRICE   Page 1 / 6

SPYNV   S&P 500 DEPOSITARY NAV   PRICE 121.9279

| | | | | | | HI | 136.4619 | ON | 4/29/11 |

Range 11/22/10 to 11/18/11   Period D Daily   AVE 126.9373
                        USD   Market M mid/trd   LOW 109.9140 ON 10/ 3/11

	DATE	PRICE	VOLUME		DATE	PRICE	VOLUME		DATE	PRICE	VOLUME
F	11/18	121.9279		F	10/28	128.6238		F	10/ 7	115.6147	
T	11/17	121.9680		T	10/27	128.5716		T	10/ 6	116.5617	
W	11/16	124.0413		W	10/26	124.3120		W	10/ 5	114.4603	
T	11/15	126.0922		T	10/25	123.0186		T	10/ 4	112.3971	
M	11/14	125.4653		M	10/24	125.5302		M	10/ 3	L109.9140	
F	11/11	126.6553		F	10/21	123.9370		F	9/30	113.1248	
T	11/10	124.2436		T	10/20	121.6525		T	9/29	116.0187	
W	11/ 9	123.1698		W	10/19	121.0990		W	9/28	115.0798	
T	11/ 8	127.8319		T	10/18	122.6284		T	9/27	117.4775	
M	11/ 7	126.2784		M	10/17	120.1792		M	9/26	116.2348	
F	11/ 4	125.4810		F	10/14	122.5455		F	9/23	113.5865	
T	11/ 3	126.2722		T	10/13	120.4575		T	9/22	112.8855	
W	11/ 2	123.9264		W	10/12	120.8067		W	9/21	116.6008	
T	11/ 1	121.9563		T	10/11	119.6181		T	9/20	120.1259	
M	10/31	125.4495		M	10/10	119.5516		M	9/19	120.3223	

Australia 61 2 9777 8600 Brazil 5511 3048 4500 Europe 44 20 7330 7500 Germany 49 69 9204 1210 Hong Kong 852 2977 6000
Japan 81 3 3201 8900   Singapore 65 6212 1000   U.S. 1 212 318 2000   Copyright 2011 Bloomberg Finance L.P.
                        SN 294740 H295-450-0 19-Nov-11 15:03:31 EST GMT-5:00

Exhibit 2.11 Looking at Historical NAV (NV HP)

Reprinted with permission from Bloomberg. Copyright 2012 Bloomberg L.P. All rights reserved.

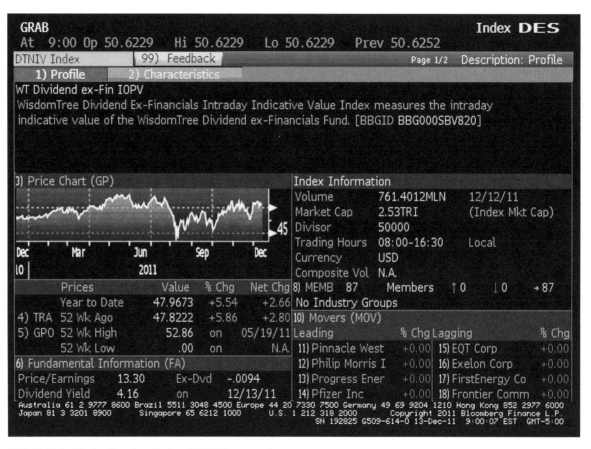

Exhibit 2.12 Indicative Value DES Screenshot

important an investment vehicle they would become. Real-time tick data are more expensive! Whatever the reason is, the IV is still published only every 15 seconds as opposed to in real time. There is not a trading desk in the world that would trade a product using a value that it calculated only every 15 seconds. Trading currently takes place in microseconds by some of the fastest participants, yet the fastest-growing investment product in history currently publishes portfolio valuations only every 15 seconds.

Savvy participants have been developing real-time pricing models for ETF valuation since the beginning of the structure in order to trade against the order flow. It has reached a point now in the markets that, because pricing is in real time and so many high-frequency traders are providing markets in ETFs, it sometimes makes more sense just to look at the automatically updating bid/ask to get an indication of ETF value, in conjunction with looking at the IV. This also provides another benefit: You can actually see a two-sided market that may give a better indication of where someone might trade.

Not only is the IV calculated every 15 seconds but also it is calculated using last price. Last price does not give an accurate indication of where you might be able to trade. It shows where things were on a historical basis (albeit very recent history). It would be much more valuable to show a bid and ask in real time of the calculated IV, so that at any given time you might be able to see the current value of the fund and place a bid or offer appropriately. It is this type of real-time

system that a liquidity provider will be using to determine where they would buy or sell a particular ETF.

Another concern with the IV is that it is really only close to real time for an ETF with a constituent basket that is trading at the exact same time as the fund. This leaves a giant swath of the market, those ETFs with international constituents, commodities that close earlier than 4 P.M., or illiquid bonds, where the IV is providing a value that has little relevance to the current trading price of the ETF. The IV then represents the most recent traded price of the underlying assets, so new market movements since the last traded price need to be added to that number to justify the current trading price of the ETF. Serious ETF traders have created their own estimated NAVs (eNAV) for trading purposes to overcome the 15-second lag and to approximate the values of those underlying assets whose prices are static.

Utilizing an Estimated NAV (eNAV)

In my view, an eNAV, which is the equivalent of a self-calculated fair value for an ETF, takes on value where IV stops. It is essentially an IV that is made real-time by calculating the basket value on every underlying tick (versus every 15 seconds) and by adjustments that account for updated market news. The magnitudes of these adjustments are subjective and usually are determined by proxy trading vehicles. These adjustments are used mainly with ETFs where the underlying assets trade in a different time zone, are halted, are difficult to trade, or don't have real-time ticks. A simple formula for calculating an eNAV would look as shown in Exhibit 2.13.

This formula is simply showing that you need to apply the most recent change in some proxy to the last value of the underlying assets, which is represented by the IV. You will come to a more representative valuation for the fund than if you were simply using the indicative value for a basket that has been closed for several hours.

A primary example of a subset of ETFs that can benefit from eNAV is the international ETF group with equities that don't trade at the same time as the ETF itself. While all professional traders currently calculate the fair value of ETFs for trading purposes, I expect more of the client base to begin utilizing an eNAV type of calculation to determine proper levels for pricing as the product proliferation continues. There are fee-based services that are starting to make real-time calculated eNAVs available to investors.

Let's look at eNAV on an international ETF, ETF-J, in more detail. We'll use the example of an ETF trading in the United States that holds a basket of Japanese stocks. For the purposes of the example, the Japanese stock market closes at 3 A.M. New York time. From 3 A.M. until 9 A.M., nothing happens in the news, so the U.S. futures have not moved since the close in

Japan, and the Japanese yen has not moved. At 9 A.M. New York time, the IV for ETF-J would be equal to the closing prices of the constituent stocks in Japan at the current yen rate, plus any excess cash in the fund. At 9:30, the markets open, and the price of ETF-J is trading right around the IV of ETF-J. At 9:45, there is a global market-moving event, and the U.S. market drops by 5 percent. The dollar stays stable, however, and the Japanese yen/USD pair does not move a tick. At this moment in time, the IV of ETF-J has not moved at all, and yet the bid/ask of ETF-J would have dropped about 5 percent in conjunction with the market-moving events taking place in the United States.

In the current conditions, it would appear that the price of ETF-J is trading at a 5 percent discount to its calculated indicative value. But what has really happened is that the community of traders has calculated an eNAV that tells them that if the U.S. markets are down 5 percent, so also should the Japanese markets. They have adjusted their calculated fair values down by that percentage. Assume that ETF-J trades at the moment at the middle of the bid/ask spread. What is the last traded price of ETF-J telling you? Is it saying that ETF-J is trading cheaply? Not as far as the market is concerned. The people on either side of the trading have differing opinions of values for the fund and

Exhibit 2.13 Simplified eNAV Calculation

different amounts of capital to risk. Therefore, ETF-J is acting like a price discovery vehicle for where investors think the underlying basket of constituents will be trading when that market next opens. This is a critical point to understand when you are looking at IV values in relation to prices in the next section.

In this situation, the IV will be reflecting any move in the currency. Let's add to our example: At 10 A.M., an event weakens the Japanese yen by 5 percent versus the U.S. dollar, but this has no effect on the U.S. stock market. What will happen is that the IV will also represent a decrease in value due to the yen drop. The trading price of ETF-J should then drop by about another 5 percent to represent this move. So now, the IV of ETF-J is down 5 percent, the U.S. market is trading down 5 percent, and ETF-J is trading down 10 percent on the day. Even now the fund is not necessarily cheap, although it appears to be trading at a 5 percent discount to IV.

When developing an eNAV for determining a fair value for an ETF, you would try to incorporate any market-related events into determining a value for where the actual assets of the fund should be trading. Once this is done, you can compare the eNAV to the trading price of the fund to determine a measure of cheapness or richness, called a *discount* or *premium.*

This concept of developing a personal fair value, or eNAV, is behind the giant trading volumes in the ETF market. Market participants have any number of variables incorporated into their trading strategies relating to various financing rates, different estimations of

beta to the market, and various spreads and hedges they use to determine how much and at what level they should trade a specific ETF.

ETFs and their subjective eNAVs have brought together many different types of market participants who are trying to profit from high-speed arbitrage of these products and their underlying assets. If the ETF consists of a domestic equity basket, then the perfect hedge is obviously the basket itself. The arbitrage then becomes a game of speed of execution and financing rates, and this is aided by colocation of servers and the proliferation of the high-frequency trading in the ETF product. However, if the basket of an ETF is not accessible at the same time as the ETF, as is the case with most international ETFs, the trading strategies calculate an eNAV that tries to look for a bid/offer in the market of someone with a different opinion. That is, since each eNAV in this case will be slightly different, increased trading volumes can ensue. Investors should be aware of the subjective nature of ETF valuations during times when the underlying assets are not trading and understand that some ETFs will trade at perceived premiums or discounts because of legitimate time lags in their published NAVs.

The Best Trading Indicators

To assess an ETF's actual fair value without calculating your own eNAV, the bid/ask or last price of an ETF will be the most accurate representation of the trading communities' eNAV versus the level of the IV.

In the most liquid ETFs, for example, where the ETF spread is actually tighter than the basket, and the ETF is trading much more rapidly than every 15 seconds, the bid and ask and last price will provide a more valuable indicator of where the ETF should be trading than the IV, even though the basket is trading at the same time as the fund. This is because the market makers and other fund liquidity providers with real-time systems are providing quotes to trade, and these quotes are being refreshed at a faster rate than the IV. In this case, the last price will almost always be within the bid and ask, and it will provide an indicator as to whether the ETF is trading on the bid side or ask side of the spread.

In an ETF that does not trade very frequently, even though the basket is trading at the same time, the bid and ask would be more valuable. In this scenario, the last price could be showing a trade that occurred at some time in the past and is not updating to the current value of the fund. The market makers and liquidity providers will, however, be updating their spread quotes, so those would be most valuable in determining current fair value. In this case, the IV is also somewhat valuable but will still be on a 15-second delay. The community of traders will be updating their bid and ask quotes in real time, so you can expect to see the IV producing a value for the fund, but on a slight delay to the actual spread. So it is important to get a time reference of the last price to determine how valuable it is in assessing the fair value.

In an ETF that has underlying assets that are not trading at the same time as the ETF, the bid and ask quotes will be your most valuable guide in determining fund fair value. This number should be a close approximation of your calculated eNAV. This is because the community of market makers and liquidity providers will be providing quotes in the ETFs based on their own eNAV, and they will be providing those quotes in real time. Depending on the volume of the ETF, the last price will be more valuable for high-volume funds, and less so as frequency of trading diminishes.

Funds with Difficult-to-Trade Underlying Baskets

This valuation technique is also the same for funds where the underlying basket may be less liquid, like those of some bond or commodity funds. These funds work in a similar manner as if the basket was not trading at the same time as the fund. The IV may not always be a good indicator of fair value. The ETF bid and ask should always reflect the costs involved in trading the underlying basket as calculated by a liquidity provider. If there is a lot of slippage expected in trading the actual basket, as would be the case in pricing bonds in an over-the-counter (OTC) market versus an equity on a transparent exchange, then you will see wider spreads as well.

ETF Spreads and Prices in the Market

The market price and spreads on ETFs are mysterious to many market participants. They really should not be. They are a function of the costs to trade the underlying basket and the risk premium associated with a particular trade. Wider bid/ask spreads on an ETF are an indicator of a fund with low intraday customer activity, unrelated to asset levels in the fund. For example, if the fund has a domestic basket that is 4 cents wide in ETF terms, but the fund trades only 25,000 shares daily and the spread on the fund is 10 cents wide, then the spread is providing an indication of cost to access the fund when trading in small size. The ETF bid and ask are providing an assessment of the costs of creating/redeeming and holding a small position in the basket over some time period. This is because, in funds that don't trade many shares on a daily basis, the market-making community will have to hold positions in the ETF until they are able to build up enough size to equal a creation unit, so their position can be flattened using the creation and redemption process. For example, if they are only able to trade 3,000 shares of the fund on a daily basis, and the fund has a 50,000 share creation unit size, it might take them 16 trading days to get a large enough position, so they would have to account for financing on that smaller position over the time period. This is why you will encounter spreads for large blocks being tighter than market spreads.

In Exhibit 2.14, you can see the bid and ask spread with the various components that go into those prices. The quoted spread of most ETFs will trade outside the spread of the underlying basket to account for the various fees and difficulties in trading those baskets. A few highest-volume ETFs will trade inside those spreads

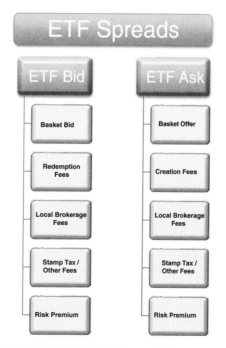

Exhibit 2.14 ETF Spread Components

because of the extreme number of participants and their different valuation methods for trading those products, as well as excess shares outstanding to accommodate all the loan demand of the short interest.

When you understand the various components that will be included in the spread on an ETF, then you can understand its market width. As you can see, the creation and redemption fee for an ETF is embedded in its spread. As the volume of an ETF increases, there is more of a probability that the liquidity provider can unwind the ETF trade in the secondary market and therefore not have to go into the primary market to do a creation or redemption. Therefore, as volumes increase, the costs to create and redeem ETFs become a smaller amount of the spread. I discuss the intricacies of creation and redemption fees as a part of spreads in more detail in *The ETF Handbook* (John Wiley & Sons, 2010).

For a plain vanilla domestic ETF, the fees in general are very small. There are no stamps or other taxes, there is no currency to hedge, and local brokerage on equity baskets is extremely low, so all the spreads in these ETFs become a function of volume and the liquidity premium. It becomes important to understand the nuances of calculating fair values in ETFs because you can then judge the spread that you may be seeing on a screen and assess if you really want to do a trade.

As I mentioned, there are occasions where the spread on an ETF in the market will be tighter than the actual spread of the underlying basket. The broad emerging market ETFs are an example of this phenomenon. While a variety of things are happening in the fixed-income funds, you will also encounter tighter spreads and even more liquidity than would be presented by the underlying baskets because of the growth and diversity of the market participants.

Summary

The primary market, where ETF shares are issued and redeemed, is the key to this novel structure. It enables open-ended issuance and facilitates arbitrage between the basket and the ETF. If you can understand how this works, then you can unlock the keys to utilizing these products advantageously in your portfolios. There is a wealth of information now being provided to investors about what is going on inside these funds and how that is affected by trading on the exchanges. It is easy to get tripped up and misunderstand some of the information, which we have seen from both novices and professionals, but we must remember that ETFs issued under the Investment Company Act of 1940 are some of the most transparent investment vehicles ever developed. This adds to their simplicity and inherent safety for investors. In the following chapters, we'll take a look at what is happening in the secondary market when ETFs are trading on the exchanges. And then we'll look at processes for execution and other techniques for using the products.

Test Yourself

1. True or false—An authorized participant has a distinct advantage over all other market participants in trading ETFs.

2. Select three items built into the ETF bid-and-ask spread:
   a. Risk premium
   b. 12B-1 Fee
   c. Creation or redemption fee
   d. Management fees
   e. Basket value

3. True or false—If the last price of a Japanese equity ETF is 2 percent below the indicative value, then it is clear that the fund is trading cheaply.

Answers: 1. False   2. a, c, e   3. False

CHAPTER 3

Understanding the Short Interest of ETFs

Short selling ranks high on the list of misunderstood facets of the ETF structure. What is short selling, and why is it prevalent in the U.S. markets, particularly in ETFs? According to the Division of Market Regulation, "a short sale is generally the sale of a stock that you do not own (or that you will borrow for delivery). Short-sellers believe the price of the stock will fall, or are seeking to hedge against potential price volatility in securities that they own."[1] The main reasons detailed for shorting are "to profit from an expected downward price movement, to provide liquidity in response to unanticipated buyer demand, or to hedge the risk of a long position in the same security or related security."[2] These reasons for short selling correlate with certain functions of the ETF product, which is well suited for use as hedges against general market moves, as when trying to isolate alpha (i.e.,

market outperformance) within a portfolio or trying to capture spreads between two fungible vehicles, the ETF and its underlying basket.

Although short selling does have its merit and use in trading strategies, following the numbers of investors who go short relative to shares outstanding is another telling indicator of market sentiment. Short interest is a figure that is tracked by most stock exchanges to quantify the amount of short investors per listed security. Of the more than 1,000 U.S.-listed exchange-traded products (ETPs), which include the subset of ETFs, 7 had higher short interest than shares outstanding as of July 2, 2012. Those funds totaled up to approximately $17 billion in assets, with about 90 percent of that number in the largest fund. Although a large number of assets, this is still a small fraction of the ETF industry as a whole. These funds can be seen in the list of the top 20 ETPs in Exhibit 3.1, sorted by the ratio of short interest to shares outstanding as of 7/2/2012.

Beyond the top seven in Exhibit 3.1, the remainder of all other listed ETPs in the United States had short interest less than their number of outstanding shares as of that date. This is more in line with the typical statistics of single-stock equities that average investors are accustomed to trading.[3]

High short interest in certain ETFs warrants examination to understand how the arbitrage mechanism enables this to happen more cost-effectively than in a standard equity. It is also imperative to understand why this cannot lead to a situation where an ETF provider would not have enough assets to meet redemption requests. In addition, I'll examine whether the risk presented by a large short position in an ETF creates any further risk to an investor, as compared to the risks that arise when trading any stock, trusting that collateral and the centralized clearing system of the U.S. markets, through which all shares match, are sufficient.

The Bloomberg data system provides very detailed information on the short interest of every ETF. By utilizing the short interest (SI) function you can see a graphical representation of short interest, as can be seen in Exhibit 3.2. You can see the middle white line showing a graph of actual shares short over time. And you can see the short interest ratio represented by the green line in the top chart, which is a representation of the shares short divided by the average daily volume.

The Lending Tree of Short Positions

The first step in understanding high short interest is to understand the process of the lending tree in U.S. equities and ETFs. Given that an investor cannot short-sell a security without first locating and borrowing it, a basic formula must hold true.

Number of outstanding shares + Number of open interest shares held short = Number of open interest shares held long.

For example, imagine that a particular ETF has only 100 shares in existence, all owned by investor A, who has a lending agreement in place with his or her custodian. Investor B, who is interested in shorting these shares, borrows them from investor A and provides cash collateral from the sale of these securities. Investor B sells these shares (taking an effective short position) to investor C, who is now long 100 shares. Separately, investor D wants to short-sell this security. D must locate the shares held long by investor C, must post the cash collateral, and may then sell these securities to investor E. To review, there were only 100 ETF shares outstanding (and consequently only enough underlying securities to constitute these 100 shares). A is long 100 shares, B is short 100, C is long 100, D is short 100, and E is long 100, so:

100 Shares outstanding + 200 Shares in open short interest = 300 Shares in open long interest.

Shares outstanding in an ETF could be considered a theoretical short position of the issuer,

	Ticker	Name	Inception Date	Market Capitalization	30 Day Average Daily Volume	Short Interest	Shares Outstanding	Short Interest / Shares Outstanding
1	RTH US	MARKET VECTORS RETAIL ETF	12/21/2011	$ 19,959,908	89,317	1,952,644	471,530	4.14
2	XRT US	SPDR S&P RETAIL ETF	6/19/2006	$ 730,664,734	7,672,886	41,485,941	12,200,110	3.40
3	RKH US	MARKET VECTORS BANK AND BROK	12/21/2011	$ 18,450,129	16,927	1,122,094	481,220	2.33
4	FXE US	CURRENCYSHARES EURO TRUST	12/12/2005	$ 238,317,001	1,409,564	4,349,149	1,900,000	2.29
5	XOP US	SPDR S&P OIL & GAS EXP & PR	6/19/2006	$ 900,936,035	5,714,340	34,377,348	17,200,000	2.00
6	KCE US	SPDR S&P CAPITAL MARKETS ETF	11/8/2005	$ 23,610,001	11,665	1,158,616	750,000	1.54
7	IWM US	ISHARES RUSSELL 2000	5/26/2000	$ 15,714,907,227	54,462,800	205,120,745	192,750,000	1.06
8	RYH US	GUGGENHEIM S&P 500 EQUAL WEI	11/7/2006	$ 67,014,000	21,861	894,279	900,000	0.99
9	KBWR US	POWERSHARES KBW REGIONAL BAN	11/1/2011	$ 22,456,028	30,105	580,216	800,000	0.73
10	CVOL US	CĐTRACKS ETN VOLATILITY INDE	11/15/2010	$ 6,427,500	42,302	535,781	750,000	0.71
11	TMF US	DIREXION DLY 20+Y T BULL 3X	4/15/2009	$ 23,696,999	140,354	204,163	300,000	0.68
12	DRV US	DIREXION DLY REAL EST BEAR 3X	7/16/2009	$ 18,620,474	178,053	565,745	833,870	0.68
13	FXY US	CURRENCYSHARES JAPANESE YEN	2/13/2007	$ 190,712,006	207,387	1,030,960	1,550,000	0.67
14	DUST US	DIREXION GOLD MINERS BEAR 3X	12/8/2010	$ 20,680,042	486,547	325,020	500,000	0.65
15	VZZB US	IPATH LE S&P 500 VIX MID	7/8/2011	$ 2,001,547	4,082	51,834	79,930	0.65
16	KRE US	SPDR S&P REGIONAL BANKING	6/19/2006	$ 1,186,277,832	2,408,668	27,676,955	42,702,580	0.65
17	SVXY US	PROSHARES SHORT VIX ST FUTUR	10/4/2011	$ 14,615,475	428,672	96,066	150,010	0.64
18	UNG US	US NATURAL GAS FUND LP	4/18/2007	$ 1,180,017,578	12,413,479	37,249,629	60,266,480	0.62
19	XME US	SPDR S&P METALS & MINING ETF	6/19/2006	$ 798,772,949	3,604,018	11,275,658	18,550,230	0.61
20	TLT US	ISHARES BARCLAYS 20+ YEAR TR	7/26/2002	$ 3,732,449,951	11,134,373	15,916,167	29,800,000	0.53

$ 24,910,587,414

Exhibit 3.1 Table of Short Interest in ETFs: Twenty ETPs with Highest Ratio of Short Interest to Shares Outstanding
As of 7/2/2012. Reprinted with permission from Bloomberg. Copyright 2012 Bloomberg L.P. All rights reserved.

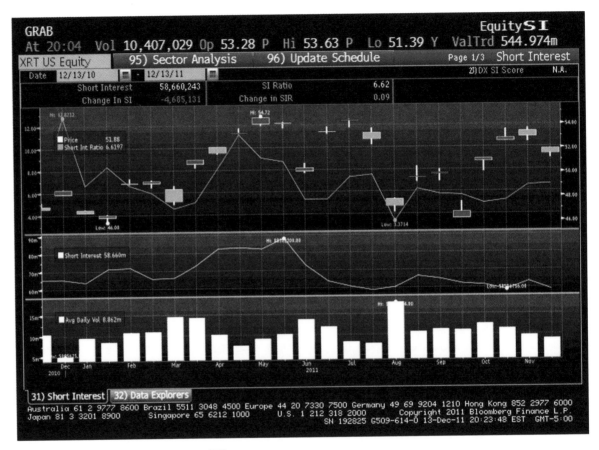

Exhibit 3.2 ETF Short Interest (SI)

Issued: 100 Units Long 100 Units	Borrows: 100 Units Short 100 Units	Buys: 100 Units Long 100 Units	Borrows: 100 Units Short 100 Units	Buys: 100 Units Long 100 Units
Long Position: 100 Units	Short Position: 100 Units	Long Position: 200 Units	Short Position: 200 Units	Long Position: 300 Units

Exhibit 3.3 The Lending Tree: An Example of the ETF Shareholder Chain

leading to an even more simplified 300 shares short (B, D, issuer) = 300 shares long (A, C, E). Furthermore, although there are only 100 shares with physical backing in existence, recall that investors B and D both were required to post cash collateral (at least on the order of 100 percent, if not greater). Effectively, 300 shares worth of the ETF are now in existence, 100 in physical securities, and 200 shares in posted cash collateral. This can be seen in Exhibit 3.3.

Now let us address what will happen when A, who is long 100 shares but has lent out his securities, decides to change his position. If A decides to sell his shares, it will be incumbent upon the stock-lending group of the clearing firm at which those shares are kept to borrow more shares or recall the loan. This can be a big investment bank or even one of the prime brokers for advisor and retail businesses. Because most shares are not segregated but kept in one theoretical custody box with the shares of other investors, there is no additional risk presented to A upon selling his shares.

One investor's shares are typically commingled with the shares of other investors at the settlement and firm position levels. Investor A can sell those upon immediate decision without having to locate the lent shares and coercing the borrower to give them back. It is the responsibility of the lending agent to either bring back the shares so the sale can settle or locate other shares to cover the outstanding loan. Most of the time, this process happens beyond the knowledge of investors, during back-office procedures.

In the single-stock world, the stock loan desk has only the finite number of shares outstanding issued during their respective IPOs to use in their process of lending and covering. However, with an ETF, the process for the stock-lending desk contains an additional option: creation and redemption. Remember that ETFs are open-ended funds in a state of continuous issuance.

A significant number of ETF shares are sitting in ETF stock-lending portfolios designed to facilitate the borrowing and short sale of ETFs. That is, there are traders with balance sheets whose job is to create ETF shares, hedge with either the short basket or other proxy hedge, and maintain that position so as to add shares to the lending market. The economics of this trade are simple: The costs involved in being long an ETF and collecting a fee for lending your ETF shares must outweigh the cost of being short the underlying basket to hedge your market exposure.[4] So the stock-lending desk will be analyzing its necessary short coverage positions against the economics of creating new ETF shares, recalling lent shares, or utilizing other long positions to cover client changes in positions. All of this is done seamlessly via position management systems designed to manage stock-lending processes so that the client base sees its positions trading and settling properly.

Another important point to understand is that the cost of borrowing an ETF should be directly tied to the cost of borrowing the underlying assets or hedging with a proxy vehicle if the underlying basket is not viable to short. There are two main forms of arbitrage in the ETF market. The arbitrage available when trading a basket or future versus an ETF is the most prevalent. However, there are also arbitrageurs who analyze the cost of borrowing an ETF and the cost of borrowing the underlying basket and position one against the other when profitable. This helps to facilitate the higher shorting levels in ETFs versus regular equities. If there is a high demand to borrow an ETF, and a trader can borrow the basket cheaply, he or she may be able to capture a rate-spread profit. It all boils down to the cost of borrowing those underlying securities. As the rate to borrow an underlying basket increases because the securities are becoming harder to locate, the price to borrow the corresponding ETF also increases. However, with the availability of futures and other derivatives that are highly correlated to the underlying basket of an ETF, there are other avenues to finance an ETF position that may even make borrowing the ETF cheaper than actually borrowing the basket of stocks. This can also help to facilitate high amounts of shorting. Many institutional users of the products are now beginning to analyze and capture the revenue streams associated with long positions in ETFs within their portfolios. This is happening as the opacity of stock borrow fees becomes even more transparent.

Short Scenario 1: Short Covering

In this scenario, a theoretical short squeeze situation is examined. Because of the continuous issuance functionality realized in the creation and redemption process, there can never be a traditional short squeeze in an ETF. When you examine the process of what happens in an ETF in which the underlying basket is rising rapidly and the shorts begin to cover, you can see how this functionality removes that risk. Using the lending tree example, if investor A sells his position in the market, then investor B (the borrower) potentially needs to find a new borrow for the short or close out the position. There are several options in this scenario:

- The stock loan desk that first found the borrow will be able to borrow the same ETF from another available long position on its books.
- The stock loan desk will be able to locate shares for loan at one of the other clearinghouses on the street and borrow those shares.
- The stock loan desk will be able to create shares for loan to the client.

Note here that all stock-lending arrangements are based on market borrow rates. If the underlying basket of an ETF becomes more difficult to borrow, then the rates for borrowing increase, which will be reflected in the borrow rate of the ETF. To further clarify, technically, an ETF cannot itself become hard to borrow, because of the open-ended issuance functionality. It is a function of being able to attain a stock-borrow on the underlying basket. If the basket cannot be borrowed, then the position of being long the ETF is much more difficult to hedge, adding to the cost to maintain the ETF position and thus making the ETF more expensive and harder to borrow, with fewer shares in the lending market. This highlights the transference mechanism of the economics of the underlying basket passing through the ETF wrapper to the end investor. As the cost of borrowing a specific basket of stocks increases, this naturally translates into a higher cost to borrow for the particular ETF containing those stocks in its basket.

ETF Borrow Rates Are a Function of the Underlying Basket

A closer inspection of the underlying basket of an ETF with high short interest sheds some light on this process. Let's look at an analysis of the underlying basket stocks in the required weights to create shares in the SPDR S&P Retail ETF, XRT. On 3/31/11, there were 19.8 million shares outstanding in the fund, meaning that the fund had shares of the underlying basket representing those 19.8 million shares. And on 3/31/11, there were 73,022,120 shares shorted of the fund.[5] The creation unit of the fund is 50,000 shares, meaning that there were 396 units outstanding and 1,460 units short. Calculations on the underlying basket showing the implied percentage of shares held by the fund and the implied percentage of shares needed for the shorts are shown in Exhibit 3.4. What you can see is that to represent every share short in the SPDR S&P Retail, you would still only be utilizing approximately 10 percent of the shares outstanding in TLB, Talbots Inc. This is the stock with the largest percentage weight in the basket. It is a very small percentage of the outstanding shares that would be required if creations were done to facilitate all shorts; therefore, the risk of a major short squeeze in the underlying remains muted. This is why facilitating the high degree of shorting in the SPDR S&P Retail ETF is possible, because at these percentages of available shares outstanding, the costs of borrowing the underlying stocks are not going to increase drastically.

	Stock Symbol	Shares per Creation Unit	Shares Outstanding	Implied Held Based on Shares Outstanding	% of Shares Outstanding Held by XRT	Implied Held Based on Short Interest	% of Shares Shorts Require
1	TLB	4,806	69,905,980	961,200	1.37%	7,018,886	10.04%
2	WTSLA	6,647	101,434,500	1,329,400	1.31%	9,707,561	9.57%
3	SAH	1,899	40,760,970	379,800	0.93%	2,773,380	6.80%
4	PBY	2,374	52,633,030	474,800	0.90%	3,467,090	6.59%
5	BWS	1,786	43,924,340	357,200	0.81%	2,608,350	5.94%
6	DSW	675	16,812,220	135,000	0.80%	985,799	5.86%
7	BKS	2,379	60,247,770	475,800	0.79%	3,474,392	5.77%
8	NILE	525	14,573,160	105,000	0.72%	766,732	5.26%
9	ZUMZ	1,066	30,989,620	213,200	0.69%	1,556,832	5.02%
10	ABG	1,101	32,817,180	220,200	0.67%	1,607,947	4.90%

Exhibit 3.4 Table Showing Percent of Stock Float Held by an ETF
Source: Bloomberg, as of 3/31/11. Reprinted with permission from Bloomberg. Copyright 2012 Bloomberg L.P. All rights reserved.

If, for some reason, the ETF basket has become impossible to borrow and some ETF shares are redeemed and taken out of the lending market, then the short holder will be forced to buy back the ETF short position or they will be bought in, in which case the shares will be bought at the market using the posted collateral. If there is a rush of ETF short holders to buy back their ETFs, the market makers will be selling ETF shares (providing liquidity) and buying shares in the underlying baskets. There is a robust community of ETF market makers who are pursuing arbitrage between the underlying basket and the ETF. To facilitate their trading, they are continuously borrowing underlying shares and ETF shares. This selling of the ETF and buying of the basket by the market makers will potentially drive the prices of the underlying basket stocks higher, but, because of the transference mechanism, the ETF will not trade a large premium or discount to its NAV. At the end of the trading session, the ETF market makers will have positions of short ETF shares and long ETF baskets, which they will then either exchange with the issuer in the form of a creation or use other hedging techniques to flatten their balance sheets.

Creations will cause the ETF issuer to issue new shares, driving availability higher, which will act as a release valve on those remaining shorts that need to locate borrows for their positions.

Short Scenario 2: Redemption en Masse

The misconception in this scenario is that when there are more shares short than outstanding in an ETF, there can be a redemption, which would cause the closing of the ETF, thus wiping out shareholders who have positions in the fund.

In this theoretical case, all long investors attempt to redeem their shares with the ETF issuer at once. The ETF issuer will accept shares for redemption only if those shares have not been lent out. Shares submitted for redemption must be unencumbered.

As a reminder, in the simplified example described previously, any of the long investors may redeem their shares if they are fully settled by their prime broker; otherwise, the underlying securities will be purchased by the agent with posted cash collateral or, if that is unavailable, the cash amount of the securities are returned to the investor. As described in the example of the lending tree, there can be more open long interest in an ETF than there are actual shares outstanding in the fund. In this case, it is not relevant how many shares are in issuance because market moves will cause all open positions, both long and short, to move in concert.

There is the potential for an investor not to engage in securities lending and consequently not to lend any shares and thus potentially collect all the outstanding shares in an ETF. At this point, the ETF would, in effect, not be trading in the marketplace because there would be no shares left to trade. The investor could then request an authorized participant to perform a redemption and effectively close the ETF (unless the ETF issuer was able to arrange another creation to keep shares trading in the marketplace). But in this case, all other investors would have previously exited their positions in the fund because they would have either sold their longs or had their borrows called back, so they would have had to cover their short positions. Typically, however, ETF shares are so widely held by a variety of investors that collecting all outstanding shares would be a fruitless endeavor with no economic benefit, as no greater arbitrage potential or economic benefit would be achieved.

Finally, if an investor tried to redeem the only existing shares of the ETF or even a significant fraction, the ETF issuer would be able to refuse, as delineated by the prospectus. See, for example, the excerpt from the iShares Russell 2000 Index Fund prospectus:

If the Trust determines, based on information available to the Trust when a redemption request is submitted by an Authorized Participant, that (i) the short interest of the Fund in the marketplace is greater than or equal to 150% and (ii) the orders in the aggregate from all Authorized Participants redeeming Fund shares on such Business Day represent 25% or more of the outstanding shares of the Fund, such Authorized Participant will be required to verify to the Trust the accuracy of its deemed representations. If, after receiving notice of the verification requirement, the Authorized Participant does not verify the accuracy of its deemed representations in accordance with this requirement, its redemption request will be considered not to have been timely and received in proper form.[6]

Similarly, in the statement of additional information of the SPDR Series Trust, you can read:

An Authorized Participant submitting a redemption request is deemed to represent to the Trust that it (or its client) (i) owns outright or has full legal authority and legal beneficial right to tender for redemption the requisite number of Shares to be redeemed and can receive the entire proceeds of the redemption, and (ii) the Shares to be redeemed have not been loaned or pledged to another party nor are they the subject of a repurchase agreement, securities lending agreement or such other arrangement which would preclude the delivery of such Shares to the Trust. The Trust reserves the right to verify these representations at its discretion, but will typically require verification with respect to a redemption request from a Fund in connection with higher levels of redemption activity and/or short interest in the Fund. If the Authorized Participant, upon receipt of a verification request, does not provide sufficient

verification of its representations as determined by the Trust, the redemption request will not be considered to have been received in proper form and may be rejected by the Trust.[7]

These examples explain how high short interest in certain ETFs is not a risk to the funds or their investors. It also becomes pretty clear that if the stock loan arena became more transparent, the costs for borrowing ETFs would probably decline, providing a direct benefit to investors. Let's take a look at a widely held ETF and some short positions of the fund.

Understanding Short Interest in a Popular ETF

IWM, the iShares Russell 2000 Index fund, is undoubtedly a very popular ETF. As of 11/4/11, the fund was the 10th largest ETF by AUM, with approximately $17 billion under management. If you look at it from a volume perspective, on the same day, the average daily volume of the fund ranked fourth among all ETPs at approximately 84 million shares trading per day.

The short interest in this fund is very high. As of October 20, 2011, there were 184.1 million shares outstanding in the fund and short interest of 277,134,414, as per Bloomberg. This indicates that more shares were short in the ETF than there were shares outstanding on this date. And as has been explained previously, this can take place in a normally functioning ETF environment.

In October 2011, a U.S. Senate subcommittee held an informational hearing on ETFs. The witnesses submitted written testimony, as well as providing some summarizing verbal comments. Some comments provided by one of the witnesses provide an ample opportunity for further clarification of how the ETF structure works. The comment that I focus on regarding short interest was written as follows: "A cursory analysis of trading volumes in IWM component securities indicates it would take more than 180 trading days, or more than six months, trading at 10% of each stock's volume every day, to offset reported short interest in that ETF."[8]

I provide a few studies to try to understand what is meant in that statement. First, I attempted to recreate their number to develop a base for the assertion. To do this, I took the creation basket for IWM as of 10/20/11 as my base basket. I then calculated, based on the number of shares outstanding, how many units of IWM are in existence and therefore how many shares of each stock the portfolio theoretically holds. This will be slightly different than the actual portfolio holdings of the ETF, but I consider it to be more representative of what will have to be traded in simulating scenarios of short covering. If I take the shares outstanding number and divide by the creation unit size of 50,000 shares, I see that there are 3,682 units outstanding of IWM. I then multiply the shares per creation unit by the number of units to come up to a theoretical position held by the ETF in each stock. In the table in

Exhibit 3.5, I present the top 20 names in the portfolio as sorted by my calculation of number of days to cover all theoretically short shares while trading only 10 percent of the ADV each day.

The first name on the list is CFNB. You can see that the six-month average daily trading volume is 2,540 shares per day. It is a very low-volume stock. Correspondingly, the IWM creation unit requires only seven shares of CFNB for every unit of 50,000 ETF shares. I then calculated two columns of shares required. One represents how many shares of CFNB the ETF should hold based on the shares outstanding:

$$7 \text{ Shares per creation unit} \times 3,683 \text{ Units}$$
$$= 25,774 \text{ Shares of CFNB required}$$

The next column calculates a similar number of required shares, but this is inferred from the short interest in the ETF. Based on the short interest in the ETF, first I infer a number of theoretical outstanding units:

$$\frac{277,134,414 \text{ ETF shares short}}{50,000 \text{ ETF shares per C.U.}} = 5,542.69 \text{ Implied units outstanding}$$

From this new unit number, I can infer how many shares of each stock in the basket should be held, based on the shares of short interest. In this case:

7 Shares per creation unit * 5,542.69 Theoretical units = 38,799 Implied shares of CFNB required

Then I infer how many days of trading at 10 percent of the average daily volume this would take me to acquire. That calculation looks as follows:

$$\frac{38{,}799 \text{ Inferred shares needed}}{2{,}540 \text{ ADV} \times 0.10} = \frac{152.75 \text{ Days to purchase the theoretical shares needed}}{}$$

This number then becomes the constraint in terms of number of days required to trade the basket. This number is approximately 18 percent lower than was represented to the U.S. Senate. In addition, if you calculate the number of shares needed to buy, as inferred by the short interest, you are ignoring the fact that the ETF portfolio actually holds a significant number of the underlying shares. What must be ascertained is the shares that need be purchased to bring the IWM portfolio up to 1:1 with the short interest in the ETF. In this case, you are going to calculate the difference in the number of shares held by the fund versus those represented by the short interest.

In Exhibit 3.6, you can see a similar table with the addition of a column showing the difference between the shares held by the fund and the shares required to represent the excess shares short.

The column highlighted on the right shows the shares that you would be required to buy if you were looking to bring the basket up to a 1:1 ratio of shares held by the fund to shares represented by shorts. As you can see, it would take approximately 50 trading days at 10 percent of the average daily volume to bring the position into line.

This may not be the optimal number, but it is only approximately a third of what was represented to the U.S. Senate in the hearings! In addition, using 10 percent of the average daily volume is arbitrarily low, as you can potentially trade a much higher percentage of the ADV without an impact on pricing.

Another interesting point to ponder, when examining what it might take to potentially trade the shares as required, is to see what they represent of the float of each stock. I demonstrated how the float is important earlier in the chapter when we were speaking about XRT and saw how small a percentage of the float of each underlying stock was represented by the short shares. In Exhibit 3.7, you can see the same underlying basket with a sort applied to percentage of float. Again, I show only the top 20 worst offenders.

The stock represented by ticker ARX is where the fund would theoretically hold the largest percentage of outstanding float. The number is only 7.96 percent of the float when we look at all the shares that would be required, based on short interest. This is a reasonably small number. One of the problems in the argument was that it posited that an ETF showing as a top holder of a stock was a negative thing. In reality, this is an irrelevant number because the ETF is representing the behavior of potentially thousands (or more) holders in one line. It's much more relevant to look at holdings as a percentage of float. An ETF holding all the shares of a particular stock might become a

	Ticker	Shares per Creation Unit	Six-Month Average Daily Volume	Equity Float	Shares Theoretically Held by IWM (per Shares Outstanding)	% of Float	Shares Required to Represent Short Interest	% of Float	Excess Shares to Bring Shares Outstanding Equal to Short Interest	Number of Days Trading to Buy All Theoretical Short Shares
1	CFNB	7	2,540	1,747,930	25,774	1.47%	38,799	2.22%	13,025	152.75
2	ATLO	27	11,599	8,387,083	99,414	1.19%	149,653	1.78%	50,239	129.02
3	WEYS	24	11,855	6,714,611	88,368	1.32%	133,025	1.98%	44,657	112.21
4	BWINB	28	14,012	7,630,381	103,096	1.35%	155,195	2.03%	52,099	110.76
5	CNBKA	11	5,571	3,363,215	40,502	1.20%	60,970	1.81%	20,468	109.43
6	CSBK	29	14,931	8,539,348	106,778	1.25%	160,738	1.88%	53,960	107.65
7	NKSH	23	11,857	6,484,470	84,686	1.31%	127,482	1.97%	42,796	107.52
8	ESBF	41	21,443	10,126,869	150,962	1.49%	227,250	2.24%	76,288	105.98
9	EBTX	28	14,806	7,048,403	103,096	1.46%	155,195	2.20%	52,099	104.82
10	GABC	43	22,931	10,199,950	158,326	1.55%	238,336	2.34%	80,010	103.94
11	BSRR	39	20,986	12,032,785	143,598	1.19%	216,165	1.80%	72,567	103.00
12	BFIN	69	37,373	17,855,965	254,058	1.42%	382,445	2.14%	128,387	102.33
13	CAC	26	14,462	7,331,836	95,732	1.31%	144,110	1.97%	48,378	99.65
14	FNLC	29	16,142	8,709,442	106,778	1.23%	160,738	1.85%	53,960	99.58
15	HTLF	44	25,400	13,858,264	162,008	1.17%	243,878	1.76%	81,870	96.01
16	CCNE	41	23,780	10,916,826	150,962	1.38%	227,250	2.08%	76,288	95.56
17	GRIF	8	4,641	4,062,637	29,456	0.73%	44,342	1.09%	14,886	95.54
18	ODC	17	9,928	5,011,121	62,594	1.25%	94,226	1.88%	31,632	94.91
19	WHG	21	12,325	6,184,106	77,322	1.25%	116,396	1.88%	39,074	94.44
20	HOME	55	32,329	13,882,069	202,510	1.46%	304,848	2.20%	102,338	94.30

Exhibit 3.5 Days to Cover Short Interest—All Shares
As of 10/20/11. Reprinted with permission from Bloomberg. Copyright 2012 Bloomberg L.P. All rights reserved.

	Ticker	Shares per Creation Unit	Six-Month Average Daily Volume	Equity Float	Shares Theoretically Held by IWM (per Shares Outstanding)	% of Float	Shares Required to Represent Short Interest	% of Float	Excess Shares to Bring Shares Outstanding Equal to Short Interest	Number of Days Trading to Buy Basket Shares at 10% ADV
1	CFNB	7	2,540	1,747,930	25,774	1.47%	38,799	2.22%	13,025	51.28
2	ATLO	27	11,599	8,387,083	99,414	1.19%	149,653	1.78%	50,239	43.31
3	WEYS	24	11,855	6,714,611	88,368	1.32%	133,025	1.98%	44,657	37.67
4	BWINB	28	14,012	7,630,381	103,096	1.35%	155,195	2.03%	52,099	37.18
5	CNBKA	11	5,571	3,363,215	40,502	1.20%	60,970	1.81%	20,468	36.74
6	CSBK	29	14,931	8,539,348	106,778	1.25%	160,738	1.88%	53,960	36.14
7	NKSH	23	11,857	6,484,470	84,686	1.31%	127,482	1.97%	42,796	36.09
8	ESBF	41	21,443	10,126,869	150,962	1.49%	227,250	2.24%	76,288	35.58
9	EBTX	28	14,806	7,048,403	103,096	1.46%	155,195	2.20%	52,099	35.19
10	GABC	43	22,931	10,199,950	158,326	1.55%	238,336	2.34%	80,010	34.89
11	BSRR	39	20,986	12,032,785	143,598	1.19%	216,165	1.80%	72,567	34.58
12	BFIN	69	37,373	17,855,965	254,058	1.42%	382,445	2.14%	128,387	34.35
13	CAC	26	14,462	7,331,836	95,732	1.31%	144,110	1.97%	48,378	33.45
14	FNLC	29	16,142	8,709,442	106,778	1.23%	160,738	1.85%	53,960	33.43
15	HTLF	44	25,400	13,858,264	162,008	1.17%	243,878	1.76%	81,870	32.23
16	CCNE	41	23,780	10,916,826	150,962	1.38%	227,250	2.08%	76,288	32.08
17	GRIF	8	4,641	4,062,637	29,456	0.73%	44,342	1.09%	14,886	32.07
18	ODC	17	9,928	5,011,121	62,594	1.25%	94,226	1.88%	31,632	31.86
19	WHG	21	12,325	6,184,106	77,322	1.25%	116,396	1.88%	39,074	31.70
20	HOME	55	32,329	13,882,069	202,510	1.46%	304,848	2.20%	102,338	31.66

Exhibit 3.6 Days to Cover Short Interest–Excess Shares Only
As of 10/20/11. Reprinted with permission from Bloomberg. Copyright 2012 Bloomberg L.P. All rights reserved.

	Ticker	Shares per Creation Unit	Six-Month Average Daily Volume	Equity Float	Shares Theoretically Held by IWM (per Shares Outstanding)	% of Float	Shares Required to Represent Short Interest	% of Float	Excess Shares to Bring Shares Outstanding Equal to Short Interest	Number of Days Trading to Buy Basket Shares at 10% ADV
1	ARX	66	226,342	4,593,930	243,012	5.29%	365,817	7.96%	122,805	5.43
2	HEI	139	172,622	11,872,727	511,798	4.31%	770,434	6.49%	258,636	1 4.98
3	CARB	24	111,210	2,652,072	88,368	3.33%	133,025	5.02%	44,657	4.02
4	KIOR	36	162,202	4,065,996	132,552	3.26%	199,537	4.91%	66,985	4.13
5	DFR	39	33,460	4,468,443	143,598	3.21%	216,165	4.84%	72,567	2 1.69
6	RCKB	100	108,635	12,159,984	368,200	3.03%	554,269	4.56%	186,069	1 7.13
7	ABCD	54	54,874	7,217,447	198,828	2.75%	299,305	4.15%	100,477	1 8.31
8	LAWS	12	16,177	1,620,220	44,184	2.73%	6 6,512	4.11%	22,328	1 3.80
9	STAG	52	110,805	8,222,580	191,464	2.33%	288,220	3.51%	96,756	8.73
10	MEDH	106	297,842	18,300,755	390,292	2.13%	587,525	3.21%	197,233	6.62
11	BNHNA	44	6 4,135	7,762,527	162,008	2.09%	243,878	3.14%	81,870	1 2.77
12	INFI	63	78,306	11,878,653	231,966	1.95%	349,189	2.94%	117,223	1 4.97
13	AMRC	58	215,037	11,152,501	213,556	1.91%	321,476	2.88%	107,920	5.02
14	SLTM	199	230,964	38,476,971	732,718	1.90%	1,102,995	2.87%	370,277	1 6.03
15	BSFT	76	754,010	14,863,369	279,832	1.88%	421,244	2.83%	141,412	1.88
16	GBL	23	19,824	4,624,359	84,686	1.83%	127,482	2.76%	42,796	2 1.59
17	AUMN	93	180,290	19,094,978	342,426	1.79%	515,470	2.70%	173,044	9.60
18	HEV	240	2,490,410	49,607,178	883,680	1.78%	1,330,245	2.68%	446,565	1.79
19	NYMX	64	72,042	13,453,334	235,648	1.75%	354,732	2.64%	119,084	1 6.53
20	CALX	125	469,318	26,489,487	460,250	1.74%	692,836	2.62%	232,586	4.96

Exhibit 3.7 Percent of Float

As of 10/20/11. Reprinted with permission from Bloomberg. Copyright 2012 Bloomberg L.P. All rights reserved.

situation worthy of investigation. But if you go back through the information presented earlier, that scenario would also affect the cost to borrow the ETF and the ability of people to trade the ETF because of trouble accessing some of the underlying. This would assuredly cause the positions to be closed before the holdings became so high. We can see there is a natural self-leveling mechanism built into the structure to prevent this type of behavior.

Summary

How ETF short interest relates back to the basket is a difficult subject that can confuse even the most astute market veterans. It's important to distill the ETF back to the underlying basket. When that basket is cheap and liquid, then that should translate into cheap and liquid stock loan availability in the ETF. There are a wide variety of users of the ETF product set, and when it gets expensive to borrow an underlying basket, the costs for some participants will go higher than they are willing to pay. This will start a process of unwinding short positions. Thanks to the open-ended issuance function, the added availability of newly created shares and the redemption of excess shares act as a release valve on any pressure that may build up in the system.

Notes

1. SEC Division of Market Regulation, "Key Points about Regulation," SHO 2/24/11.

2. Ibid.

3. Bloomberg, as of 1/31/11.

4. David Abner, *The ETF Handbook* (Hoboken, NJ: John Wiley & Sons, 2010), 212, "Exhibit 12.3 Cash Flows of a Long ETF and a Short Basket Position."

5. Shares outstanding and short interest from Bloomberg. Holdings file from National Securities Clearing Corp.

6. 2010 Prospectus to Shareholders, iShares Russell 2000 Index Fund, August 1, 2010.

7. www.spdrs.com/library-content/public/SPDR Series Trust SAI.pdf.

8. "ETFs and the Present Danger to Capital Formation," testimony by Harold Bradley and Robert E. Litan before the Subcommittee on Securities, Insurance, and Investments of the Senate Banking Committee, 12. October 19, 2011.

Test Yourself

1. True or false—The short interest in an ETF can be higher than the shares outstanding of that ETF.

2. True or false—The cost to borrow a basket of stocks will be reflected in the cost to borrow an ETF that holds that basket.

3. True or false—Selling short is the practice of heinous individuals trying to unravel the financial system.

Answers: 1. True 2. True 3. False

CHAPTER 4

Trading and Liquidity of the ETF Markets

The Secondary Markets

One of the most prominent aspects of the ETF structure is its exchange listing and intraday trading. The fact that the funds trade in a standardized format on an exchange all day is a major benefit to long-term investors and more active traders alike. Investors need to learn the skill of ETF execution to be efficient users of the product. One would be surprised at the educational curve that still needs to be climbed. There is a tremendous need for more education about the different techniques of executing order flow in ETFs. I have participated in roughly 300 meetings per year for the last several years with institutional-size users of ETFs, and almost all of them have revolved around the nuances of trading the products. It is important to understand how to value the ETFs and how to best trade them, especially in larger sizes. An investor in ETFs must also be aware how the trading community operates and know that traders that commit risk on block-size trades look to make revenue from the trading spread as well as from the commission. In addition, the major execution platforms that handle order flow for the many thousands of advisors who have rapidly adopted ETFs are not as robust as they could be to properly give their clients the complete information needed to make the best ETF trading decisions. Many trading platforms still treat ETF execution like that of single stocks, without acknowledging the wide differences. It would be beneficial to investors to have a trading platform that values the ETF and stress tests hypothetical executions. Investors need to be able to easily visualize and understand the various methods of achieving liquidity and evaluate them. Currently, trading platforms are lagging behind and, in many ways, have become a bottleneck to broader growth in the industry.

I remember my own experience. One day, years ago, I had an aha! moment in trading as I was facilitating ETF order flow for hedge funds and other institutions. I suddenly realized that some of my clients were paying me 3 cents a share for an execution they could do on their own electronically for less than a penny. I realized this was unsustainable. I foresaw that my days facilitating this type of flow should be numbered. I was correct; new methods were adopted, and competition increased for that client segment. I was wrong, however, in not anticipating the new client segment that would come behind them, clamoring for even greater liquidity in more exotic ETFs. This demand, as well as the need for block trading, continues to drive the brokerage trading side of the business.

I strongly support the trading community and the liquidity provision that has been the lifeblood of this industry's growth. But at heart, I'm still an investor who wants to be able to use the products efficiently and be equipped when interacting with liquidity providers to have a good overall ETF experience. This will require sharing information about calculating fair values, broadening ways to provide liquidity in a transparent manner, and a client-broker partnership that is based on strong service for clear commissions.

In this chapter, I'll discuss methods of execution for both institutional-style users and the average investor using a discount brokerage account. I'll present examples and suggest ways to develop partnerships in which both parties can succeed without one squeezing the other until no business is left. I'll discuss some of the details regarding the future execution of ETFs, both in 401(k)s and other retirement accounts. We'll start by looking at what an exchange-based market is, the lack of value of the bid and ask in an ETF market, the disappearance of depth of book, and how trading a fund will impact its market.

Looking at the Market

Level I Quotes

The first thing you will do upon deciding that you are going to buy or sell an ETF will be to pull up a quote. There are several important pieces of information embedded in any quote line that provide a quick, yet cursory, glance at the data of the related fund. You can see the ticker, the last price, the bid and the ask, the sizes of the bid and ask, and the volume number.

When you look at a quote on an ETF, the quoted market that you see, bid/ask, bid size/ask size, is typically referred to as the inside market, also called the national best bid offer (NBBO). This is the best bid, or the highest price that people are willing to pay to a seller. The bid size is how many shares they are willing to buy. The ask is the lowest price at which people are

Ticker	Last Price	Bid/Ask	Bid Size/Ask Size	Volume
ETF	$10.00	$10.05/$10.10	3,000/6,000	500,323

willing to sell shares of the ETF, and the ask size is the size that is for sale.

The last price, bid, ask, and volume are all available in historical format so that you can see them over some time span, as represented by the extensive graphing functionality of the Bloomberg or other charting services. You can easily produce a chart of the volume in a particular ETF over time, like you see in Exhibit 4.1. This shows the growth in daily trading volume over time of a popular Indian equity ETF.

An Example of Speaking to an ETF Trader

Think about this hypothetical example: I'm a market maker in ETFs, and you're my client. I know that if you ask me for a market in an ETF, and I am more than 10 cents wide (*wide* meaning distance between the bid and offer), you won't trade with me, and I will lose the commission. So you call up and ask me for a two-way market in an ETF. I know the fair value spread that I have in the ETF is 4 cents wide at .04 at .08, and I am apprehensive that the markets are very strong and will continue running before I can get my hedge on, so I skew my two-way market higher because I would rather buy than sell. So the market I make is .04 at .14. Looking at that market, I have no potential spread versus my hedge if you are a seller, but that is acceptable because I'm more worried about missing out on my hedge. But if you are a buyer, I have a full 6 cents of spread versus my hedge.

On the other hand, if you call me up and we have an established and trusting relationship, you might say to me, "Can you give me an offer in an ETF?" You have now given me a clearer indication that I will be the seller, and I can make a reasonable assessment of the market and may be willing to make you an offer that is tighter than my two-way would have been. Now I might offer you the ETF at .11. This leaves some room to get my hedge on (risk premium), while being 50 percent tighter than it would be in a two-way market situation. To clarify, however, I might also use this knowledge against you and make you an offer at .16, saying that my two-way would have been .06 to .16, but only because I knew I wouldn't be buying anything.

You always have the ability to ask a liquidity provider for a two-way market or for whichever side of the market you are interested in. You also need to understand the market environment in which the market is being made. See Chapter 5 regarding the flash crash later in this chapter for another example of what can happen in a market during a moment of extreme volatility. But you must understand that market makers will assess the market condition and make a price based on where they think they can get a hedge on without losing any of the commission.

KEY POINT:

Ticker is the three- or four-letter code that is used to represent the fund or company on an exchange. A mutual fund typically has a five-letter ticker.

Last Price is the price at which the ETF most recently traded.

The Bid is the level at which people in the marketplace are willing to buy the ETF.

The Ask is the level at which people in the marketplace are offering the ETF for sale.

The Size is shown for both sides of the market (bid and ask). This is a display of how many shares are wanted to buy (bid for) and how many shares are offered for sale (at the ask).

The Volume is a measure of how many shares of the ETF have traded so far in the market. When the volume is shown in a quote, it is typically the volume for the day.

KEY POINT:

Someone *makes a market* when he is showing a two-sided price (bid and ask) on which you can trade. He is also showing the size at which he's willing to trade. If you have a good relationship with your trader, you can ask for either an offer or a bid and show your direction. This takes away some risk and can enable the market maker to be tighter than if they were required to quote a two-sided market.

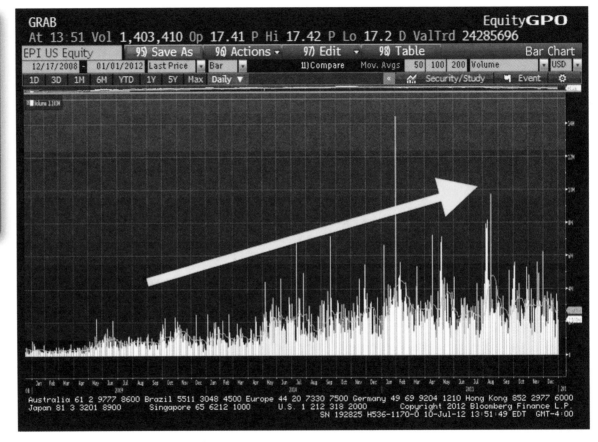

Exhibit 4.1 ETF Volume (GPO)

Chart reprinted with permission from Bloomberg. Copyright 2012 Bloomberg L.P. All rights reserved.

When looking at a graph like this, it is also important to notice the volume spikes that are showing extremely high-volume days as compared to the average, which you can see depicted by the green line.

You can also watch the bid and ask (called the spread) throughout the trading day and see stock trades as they happen. This is very useful for determining what is happening in the market at a given time, as we'll discuss later in the chapter. In Exhibit 4.2, you can see one-second intervals during the trading day with a streaming bid and ask spread and also a size register. You can see the size of the spread and the size of trades throughout the trading day.

Displayed Bid and Ask Have Lost Relevance in ETFs

The technological revolution in the markets has diminished the value of the NBBO. The visible bid and ask prices in today's markets are no longer accurately representative of the best prices at which parties are willing to trade. It's very easy to electronically place orders that are pegged to the bid or ask. This functionality enables an order to move freely up or down as prices change while always showing only on the bid side, if the order is a buy. It is also soon going to be possible to submit orders that are pegged to the indicative value of domestic ETFs. Decimalization has also caused a movement of many displayed spreads toward a penny wide because it becomes cost-efficient to bid in front of someone else on the exchange. This positioning enables a trader to potentially obscure larger orders behind it on the order book and to gain potentially valuable trading information, like where there are potential buyers or sellers, for little cost.

These are some easy-to-understand reasons that ETF price spreads move rapidly toward 1 cent when an ETF becomes popular. In the ETF market, there is the additional complexity that spreads are a function of both investor interest and the underlying assets. You saw this in Chapter 1, where I highlighted an ETF with a tighter spread than its actual basket. You can also see this in an Indian equity ETF. This fund trades at a 1-cent-wide spread in the U.S. market, which is much tighter than the standard spread of its basket in India. This has important ramifications for U.S. investors. In particular, small investors gain the benefits of being able to trade small size on a very tight spread. For larger investors, however, the spread has diminished as a vehicle to determine where larger trading size might be attained. The fact that many market participants calculate a wide variety of ETF fair values is what keeps some of these spreads pegged at 1 cent wide.

In ETFs that trade lower volumes and have baskets that are not as easy to trade, the spread is based on customer interest and model values, both of which are somewhat subjective and easily changed. Because there are not a lot of buyers and sellers congregating in this market, the NBBO will be just a starting point of indication for small size. If you are going to trade a block in an ETF, it shouldn't actually matter whether a spread is 30 cents wide or 3 cents wide because the ETF can and should be traded around the actual or

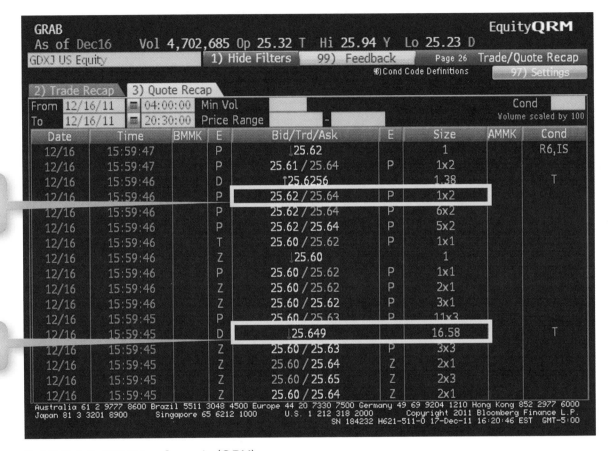

This is an example of a current market that is .02 wide, with a size of 100 shares bid for and 200 shares offered.

This is an example of a trade of 1,658 shares taking place at $25.649.

Exhibit 4.2 ETF Price Spreads (QRM)

Chart reprinted with permission from Bloomberg. Copyright 2012 Bloomberg L.P. All rights reserved.

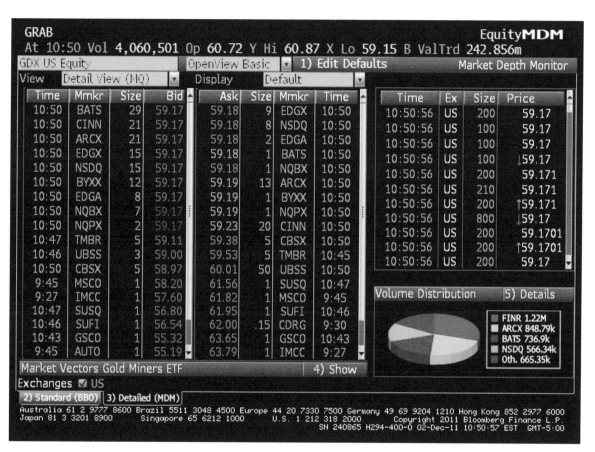

Exhibit 4.3 Level II Quote Screen (MDM)

model fair value. I discussed this in detail in Chapter 2, but because of this, the actual value of the displayed quote has diminished for this type of order flow.

Displayed Size Has Lost Relevance in ETFs

This is true for displayed size as well. In the current market regulatory and high-speed trading environment, there is no advantage to showing your hand by displaying the whole size that you want to buy or sell on the screens. The advent of nondisplayed size order types makes it difficult to see what might be available to buy or sell when you look up an order book. When you look at the quote size and you see a bid for 100 shares, that can easily be a buyer who has 100,000 share bid but is only displaying 100 shares

The SEC discovered that ETF order books are less populated than in single stocks. They discussed this finding in their report on the flash crash that you will read about in Chapter 5. The displayed bid/ask size is also less revealing because an ETF has the structural advantage of open-ended issuance of new shares. When larger size is needed, clients can always call up a liquidity provider and ask for a market. The size they will be able to trade is tied more to the volume available in the underlying basket than the actual ETF itself. It is important to understand that most liquidity providers do not display full sizes of ETF shares that they are willing to buy or sell to customers publicly on the exchanges but will selectively show size markets when asked by the customers of their firm.

How does the lack of sizable electronic quotes affect investors who trade ETFs electronically? For the purposes of looking at a quote, the bid and ask that you will see are the most recent data for people willing to trade electronically. The sizes that you see are the best representations that participants are willing to display electronically at those prices. When you are trading in small sizes—that is, those representing less than or equal to what you see as the sizes on the bid or ask—this will be enough information to take action in the marketplace. Large sizes can also be easily traded, but your due diligence will help determine how you will rise above your competition. This is addressed in detail later in the chapter.

Level II Quotes

The level two quote screens available on Bloomberg and elsewhere try to provide more information about market participants, representing what is known as the depth of the market. The depth of the market is beyond what is shown as the NBBO, representing what else might be available and at what prices. In Exhibit 4.3, you can see the depth of book for the Gold Miners ETF. What is interesting is that you can see the multitude of quotes on both sides of the inside market, 59.17 to 59.18. There are approximately seven bids on different exchanges and five offers. The depth of the book that you see even for an ETF like this, which trades more than 10 million shares per day on average, is very thin. In this screenshot, you can see only 11,600 shares offered up to 60.01. Looking at the screen, you

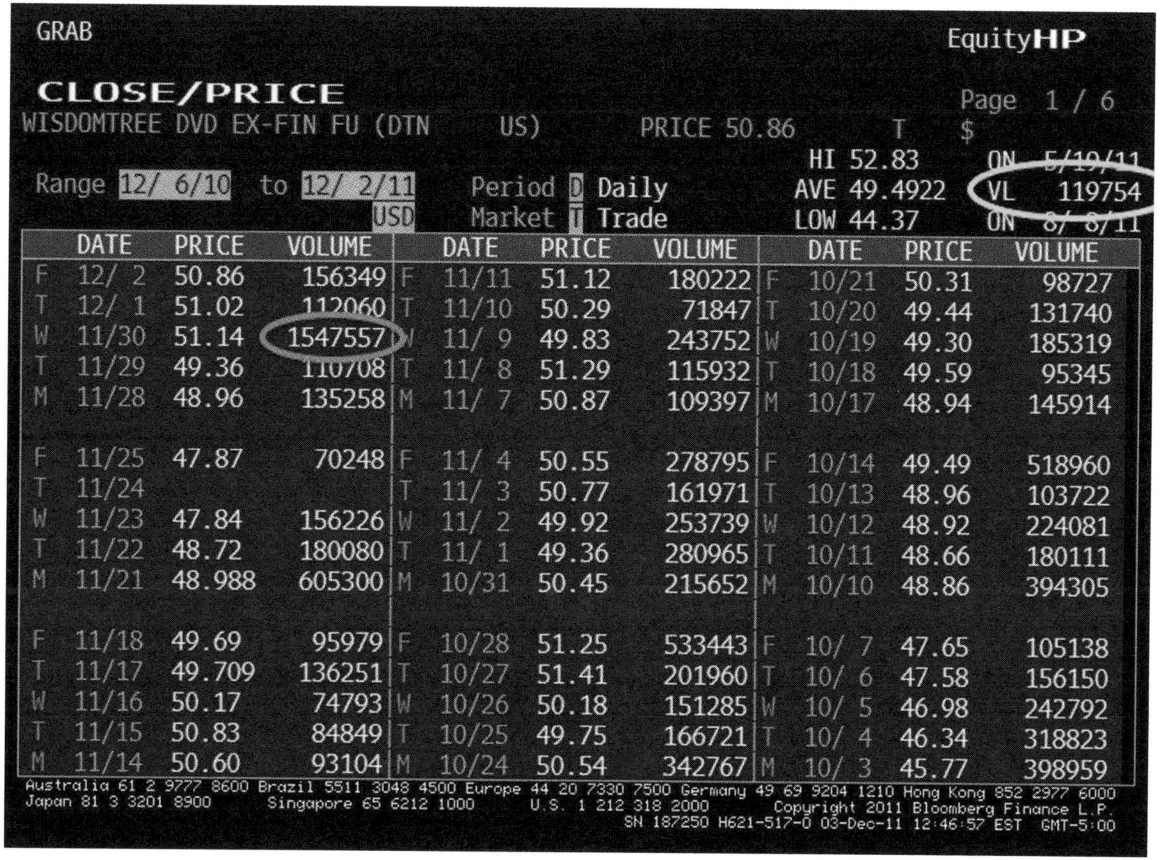

GRAB Equity HP

CLOSE/PRICE Page 1 / 6

WISDOMTREE DVD EX-FIN FU (DTN US) PRICE 50.86 T $

Range 12/ 6/10 to 12/ 2/11 USD Period D Daily Market T Trade

HI 52.83 ON 5/19/11
AVE 49.4922 VL 119754
LOW 44.37 ON 8/ 8/11

	DATE	PRICE	VOLUME		DATE	PRICE	VOLUME		DATE	PRICE	VOLUME
F	12/ 2	50.86	156349	F	11/11	51.12	180222	F	10/21	50.31	98727
T	12/ 1	51.02	112060	T	11/10	50.29	71847	T	10/20	49.44	131740
W	11/30	51.14	1547557	W	11/ 9	49.83	243752	W	10/19	49.30	185319
T	11/29	49.36	110708	T	11/ 8	51.29	115932	T	10/18	49.59	95345
M	11/28	48.96	135258	M	11/ 7	50.87	109397	M	10/17	48.94	145914
F	11/25	47.87	70248	F	11/ 4	50.55	278795	F	10/14	49.49	518960
T	11/24			T	11/ 3	50.77	161971	T	10/13	48.96	103722
W	11/23	47.84	156226	W	11/ 2	49.92	253739	W	10/12	48.92	224081
T	11/22	48.72	180080	T	11/ 1	49.36	280965	T	10/11	48.66	180111
M	11/21	48.988	605300	M	10/31	50.45	215652	M	10/10	48.86	394305
F	11/18	49.69	95979	F	10/28	51.25	533443	F	10/ 7	47.65	105138
T	11/17	49.709	136251	T	10/27	51.41	201960	T	10/ 6	47.58	156150
W	11/16	50.17	74793	W	10/26	50.18	151285	W	10/ 5	46.98	242792
T	11/15	50.83	84849	T	10/25	49.75	166721	T	10/ 4	46.34	318823
M	11/14	50.60	93104	M	10/24	50.54	342767	M	10/ 3	45.77	398959

Australia 61 2 9777 8600 Brazil 5511 3048 4500 Europe 44 20 7330 7500 Germany 49 69 9204 1210 Hong Kong 852 2977 6000
Japan 81 3 3201 8900 Singapore 65 6212 1000 U.S. 1 212 318 2000 Copyright 2011 Bloomberg Finance L.P.
SN 187250 H621-517-0 03-Dec-11 12:46:57 EST GMT-5:00

Exhibit 4.4 ETF Volume–Domestic (HP)

Chart reprinted with permission from Bloomberg. Copyright 2012 Bloomberg L.P. All rights reserved.

might think that you would move the ETF price by approximately 1.4 percent to buy even 25,000 shares and might only be half filled. In reality, you can buy many hundreds of thousands or even millions of shares right around that inside quote by getting in touch with an ETF liquidity provider.

When looking at the Level II quote, you can see the whole book, all the bids and orders that are displayed. This does not show nondisplayed quotes. In today's electronic marketplace, the fear of gaming causes market participants to be reluctant to show their full size. Therefore, a significant portion of ETF large-size order flow takes place via phone call to liquidity providers, with trades then printed to the exchanges.

The ETF market has led to a democratization of portfolio tools. Or it may be more likely that the era of electronic trading has led to the proliferation of tools like the ETF for developing and managing investment portfolios. Due to its listed format, an ETF appears very similar to its single-stock equity cousins, but it is actually a very different animal. The arbitrage mechanism that exists between an ETF and its constituents changes the nature of ETF trading. The growth of ETFs has potentially changed the nature of stock trading as well. Some in the marketplace argue that as ETFs grow, a larger percentage of single-stock equity volume is a result, not of buyers or sellers in that actual stock, but of people trading the stock to hedge or perform arbitrage on ETF positions. There are quite a few unfounded claims that the ETF product has distorted the trading of markets in general. None of them has ever produced quantifiable evidence to back up the assertions.

It is important to understand here that there are several reasons that someone may be bidding a particular price in an ETF. The first reason is that they are a believer in the growth story of whatever is contained in the constituent basket and wish to be long. This is typical of any investment. The second reason may be that the ETF fits into a particular trading strategy. This can be high-frequency, merger arbitrage, or any variety, but also, specific to the ETF, it could be arbitrage against the constituent basket itself. Whatever the reason, the numerous trading strategies the ETF product supports benefits the end investor with greater trading liquidity and lower trading costs.

The bid or ask level of an ETF not only represents the price someone is willing to pay for or to sell an ETF but also represents what the marketplace considers to be fair value at that exact moment in time. The underlying constituents of an ETF will give an actual fair value or implied fair value if the latest prices of the basket available are not current. You need to be able to view and compare the fair value and bid/ask of the ETF when making investment decisions.

Video:
ETF Liquidity

www.wiley.com/go/abnervg

Understanding ETF Liquidity

The most misunderstood function in the entire ETF industry is trading volume. The discussion around trading volume and potential liquidity has hamstrung many clients. The lack of understanding of how trading volume and underlying liquidity relate has been one of the biggest roadblocks to ETF asset growth in a more widely distributed manner across the product set. It has worked to keep ETF assets concentrated in a smaller number of funds. Product use is now expanding as the investing public becomes more educated about how to access products with lower perceived liquidity.

ETF trading volume does not equal ETF liquidity. The trading volume of an ETF is a number that shows, over some time period in the past, how many shares have traded of that particular ETF. ETF liquidity is a measure of how many shares of an ETF can be potentially traded in some future time period. The impact on the market of achieving that liquidity is discussed later in the chapter. In Exhibit 4.4, you can see the HP screen of an ETF. The green circle highlights that the average daily volume (ADV) is 119,754. In the red circle, you can see that the ETF traded 1,547,557 on 11/30/11, more than 10 times its average daily volume. If you had been using the ADV number to assess how many shares of the ETF you could possibly trade, then you might never have imagined you could trade that many shares in a day.

The liquidity of an ETF is a function of a much greater group of variables than just the historical trading volume. Taking the average daily volume of an ETF itself as a benchmark for how many ETF shares can be traded without impact is a big mistake that clients make, causing them to limit themselves to only a small percentage of the available fund universe. Technology has not yet progressed to the level where every end investor can access the liquidity of the underlying basket without an intervening liquidity provider. But there are a series of systems being introduced that are helping to solve this problem.

Most descriptions of the ETF product that I have seen explain that ETF liquidity is a function of the underlying basket. The underlying basket is really only one piece of overall ETF liquidity. For example, if the underlying basket is closed in the Hong Kong ETF, then the basket is not providing any of the liquidity for intraday trading in the United States. Yet, as you can see in Exhibit 4.5, the fund trades approximately 6 million shares per day (green circle).

You can also see that the fund traded more than 30 million shares on 11/1/11, during the U.S. trading day, while the basket of stocks listed in Hong Kong was closed. So clearly liquidity was created through means other than the basket.

In Exhibit 4.6, I present a diagram of the liquidity function of an ETF. In it, you can see that the liquidity of an ETF is made up of the IDTS (Implied Daily Tradable Shares) from the basket, plus the average daily trading volume, plus additional liquidity that may be achieved by accessing the derivatives markets, plus any other highly correlated products or

```
GRAB                                                              EquityHP

CLOSE/PRICE                                               Page  1 / 6
ISHARES MSCI HONG KONG I (EWH    US)        PRICE 15.79      D    $
                                                    HI 19.97      ON  1/12/11
Range 12/ 6/10  to  12/ 2/11   Period D Daily       AVE 17.9717   VL  5700666
                       USD      Market T Trade       LOW 13.86      ON 10/ 4/11
   DATE   PRICE  VOLUME     DATE   PRICE  VOLUME       DATE   PRICE  VOLUME
F  12/ 2  15.79  3585514 F  11/11  16.15  4665655 F   10/21  15.71  11526229
T  12/ 1  15.96  4611013 T  11/10  16.08  4107489 T   10/20  15.26   4963887
W  11/30  15.99  9818174 W  11/ 9  15.98 23501818 W   10/19  15.40   3625028
T  11/29  15.36  6934851 T  11/ 8  16.87 11897218 T   10/18  15.62   5344889
M  11/28  15.42  3177324 M  11/ 7  16.75  4410304 M   10/17  15.63   9537712

F  11/25  15.01  1556984 F  11/ 4  16.48  9291485 F   10/14  16.05   5447782
T  11/24                 T  11/ 3  16.74 13633131 T   10/13  15.88   5366305
W  11/23  15.01  4064513 W  11/ 2  16.75  8896102 W   10/12  15.99   7629333
T  11/22  15.22  4243678 T  11/ 1  16.35 31110491 T   10/11  15.56   6459769
M  11/21  15.09  5518789 M  10/31  16.19  5264095 M   10/10  15.49   6668696

F  11/18  15.47  2334882 F  10/28  16.86  6449091 F   10/ 7  14.89   8823032
T  11/17  15.37  4535803 T  10/27  16.77 12917011 T   10/ 6  14.68   6893015
W  11/16  15.64  4003692 W  10/26  16.11  8134037 W   10/ 5  14.27  28996755
T  11/15  16.11  3496596 T  10/25  15.82  4293285 T   10/ 4 L13.86  15026217
M  11/14  15.96  2977320 M  10/24  16.10 10714364 M   10/ 3  13.93   5787121
Australia 61 2 9777 8600 Brazil 5511 3048 4500 Europe 44 20 7330 7500 Germany 49 69 9204 1210 Hong Kong 852 2977 6000
Japan 81 3 3201 8900      Singapore 65 6212 1000    U.S. 1 212 318 2000     Copyright 2011 Bloomberg Finance L.P.
                                                    SN 187250 H621-517-0 03-Dec-11 12:57:56 EST  GMT-5:00
```

Exhibit 4.5 ETF Volume–International (HP)
Chart reprinted with permission from Bloomberg. Copyright 2012 Bloomberg L.P. All rights reserved.

baskets that can be used to offset positions in the ETF itself.

In Chapter 1, I explained that the spread of an S&P 500 ETF, at .01, is tighter than the actual basket spread that is .04 wide. This is made possible by the additional sources of good hedges such as S&P futures, enabling liquidity providers to be able to trade the ETF and efficiently hedge their portfolio. If an ETF has multiple

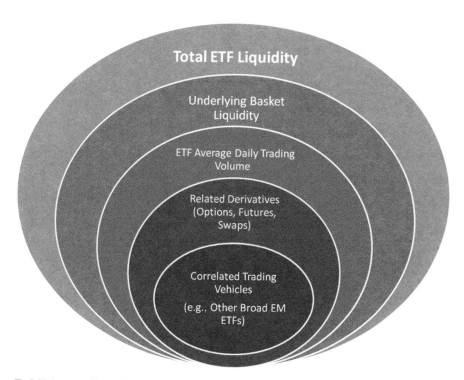

Total ETF Liquidity

Underlying Basket
Liquidity

ETF Average Daily Trading
Volume

Related Derivatives
(Options, Futures,
Swaps)

Correlated Trading
Vehicles

(e.g., Other Broad EM
ETFs)

Exhibit 4.6 The Components of ETF Liquidity

liquid alternate hedges in addition to its basket, then it will have an easier time attracting assets and have a much better chance to thrive in the ETF landscape.

The basket will, however, be one of the main sources of liquidity. Everything will eventually funnel down to trading the actual basket because that is what drives creations and redemptions in the funds. This makes it imperative that, as a starting point, you understand the liquidity of a fund as implied by its underlying shares. To do this, you need to understand the components of ETF liquidity and, in particular, the implied daily tradable shares (IDTS).

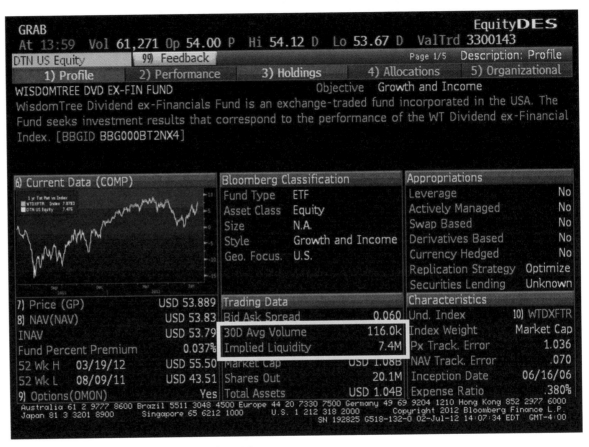

Exhibit 4.7 ETF Implied Liquidity (IDTS)

Components of ETF Liquidity

Since the introduction of the product, it has been said that the liquidity of an ETF is based on its underlying basket. Although this is not the only component of ETF liquidity, it is one of the most important. Four components of ETF liquidity work in conjunction to equal total ETF liquidity:

1. The liquidity of the underlying basket (as determined by IDTS)
2. The average daily volume (ADV) of the ETF
3. Derivatives based on the ETF
4. Correlated, but different, trading vehicles

To understand the importance of both the underlying basket liquidity and the total liquidity picture, let us first look at the various components.

Average Daily Trading Volume of an ETF

The average daily trading volume of an ETF takes the amount of shares that an ETF has traded over some time period in the past and calculates an average of the volume for each of those days. In an ETF with rapidly growing assets, this average will be lower than its more recent trading volumes, since it includes what has happened in the past. If the average is very low, and there are some very high volume days, then a new investor is given an idea of what could potentially happen in the fund. Because this is based only on actual ETF trading volume and not the underlying basket, however, it does not provide a representation of the liquidity of the underlying basket itself. A high trading volume in an ETF, resulting in a high ADV, can be incorporated into the liquidity picture of the ETF, but it is not its only component.

Related Derivatives for Providing ETF Liquidity

The most common derivatives that help market makers provide liquidity in ETFs are options and futures. On a product where there is a very liquid futures market, many participants can trade the ETF versus the corresponding future. This will, in essence, supplement the underlying basket as a source of liquidity. Since the listed futures market is reasonably thin in terms of diversity of product, only the main indexes are involved. The S&P 500 Index against the ETF SPY, the Nasdaq 100 Index against QQQ, and the Russell 2000 Index against the IWM are frequently traded examples.

In addition, a liquid options market in the contracts of an ETF can lead to greater ETF liquidity as people trade the options against the ETF shares for various strategies.

Correlated Trading Vehicles for Providing ETF Liquidity

When there are products that correlate very well to each other, participants can trade them against each other, thus driving trading volumes in each. The broad-based emerging markets funds are an example of this type of trading. Even though the underlying baskets are closed during the U.S. trading day, traders have developed trading relationships between EEM and VWO and DEM and trade those three products against each other. In addition, they have found ways to formulate baskets of other ETFs that also correlate well for strategies. This, in turn, drives volumes in the ETFs as traders pursue various strategies against each other, even though the underlying basket is not presenting any liquidity at the moment of trading.

ETF Basket Liquidity: Implied Daily Tradable Shares

Understanding the liquidity of an ETF has proven to be a challenging endeavor for market participants. There is a field available on Bloomberg terminals called ETF Implied Liquidity that is designed to explain a piece of the ETF liquidity function. This field is based around the calculation of the implied daily tradable shares (IDTS) of an ETF. This is a novel way of looking at the liquidity of an ETF based on its underlying basket to assess whether the ETF might be appropriate for your intended investment or trade size. This calculation has never before been available on a broad scale.

In Exhibit 4.7, you can see the field displaying the ETF Implied Liquidity for the ETF and, above it, the actual 30-Day Average Volume. As you will come to understand, the two fields are quite different.

Until now, there has not been a number available for investors that represents the volume that can potentially be traded in an ETF based on the underlying basket. The IDTS looks at the average daily trading volume of each of the underlying components of the ETF and calculates how many ETF shares can be traded based on those volumes. This should be the greatest source of liquidity for an ETF because all trading in the ETF eventually distills down to the actual basket of underlying holdings.

What the ETF Implied Liquidity Field Is Showing

If we look again at the example in Exhibit 4.7, we can see that the ADV of the fund is 116,000 shares, but the implied liquidity of the ETF is 7.4 million shares. This indicates that the ETF holdings are composed of a very liquid basket of stocks. If you were trading only a small percentage[1] of them in the proper sizes to make up the basket, then you could potentially trade a huge number of implied ETF shares. If you were a portfolio manager who wanted to invest roughly $53 million in the ETF (1 million shares * $53 share price), you might be hesitant at first because the fund only trades approximately $6 million notional per day (116,000 shares * $53 share price). But if you looked at the underlying basket, you would see that it could possibly trade almost $400 million notional daily (7.4 million shares * $53 share price).

Investors can now see the potential liquidity of the baskets on a large range of products. Those products might have seemed impractical for use because of a low average daily volume, but investors can now see the liquidity of the underlying basket. That, coupled with the understanding of how to get that volume by

	Ticker	Name	Inception Date	ETF Implied Liquidity (IDTS)	30-Day Average Daily Volume
1	EUSA US	ISHARES MSCI USA INDEX FUND	5/7/2010	274,182,574	25,407
2	SCHX US	SCHWAB US LARGE-CAP ETF	11/3/2009	201,000,000	216,611
3	MGC US	VANGUARD MEGA CAP 300 ETF	12/21/2007	193,280,629	57,627
4	IWL US	ISHARES RUSSELL TOP 200 INDE	9/25/2009	188,431,496	188,244
5	VOO US	VANGUARD S&P 500 ETF	9/9/2010	184,042,641	727,284
6	SCHV US	SCHWAB US LARGE-CAP VALUE	12/11/2009	155,237,500	73,392
7	PXLV US	POWERSHARES FUNDAMENTAL PURE	6/16/2011	137,880,774	2,800
8	FLG US	FOCUS MORNINGSTAR LARGE CAP	3/30/2011	135,440,277	2,667
9	IWY US	ISHARES RUSSELL TOP 200 GROW	9/25/2009	129,161,248	36,428
10	MGV US	VANGUARD MEGA CAP 300 VALUE	12/21/2007	120,622,056	28,999

Exhibit 4.8 Table of Funds with High ETF Implied Liquidity
As of 7/2/2012. Reprinted with permission from Bloomberg. Copyright 2012 Bloomberg L.P. All rights reserved.

having the underlying basket traded on their behalf and interpolated into ETF shares, broadly expands the universe of investable products.

Exhibit 4.8 shows a table of 10 funds with very high ETF implied liquidity and their 30-day ADV. You can see that the funds typically trade low volumes on a daily basis, but their baskets are extremely liquid.

The Calculation

It is simple to calculate ETF implied liquidity, but it can be resource intensive because it requires knowing all of the components of each ETF and the average daily volume for each as well.

The formula:

$$\text{IDTS} = ((\text{30-day ADV} \times \text{VP}) / \text{Constituent Shares per Unit}) \times \text{Creation Unit Size}$$

Where:

30-Day ADV = the average daily volume over 30 days
VP = variable percentage (defaulted to 25%)[2]
Constituent shares per CU = number of shares of each stock required in the basket
Creation unit = Number of ETF shares for each basket of stocks

	Ticker	Shares per Creation Unit	30-Day Average Daily Volume	Implied Daily Tradable Shares (IDTS)	Weight in Basket
1	FTR US	19,986	11,805,090	7,383,350	2.85%
2	SCCO US	2,320	1,784,614	9,615,374	2.72%
3	POM US	2,105	1,790,314	10,631,321	1.53%
4	MWV US	888	1,104,324	15,545,107	0.95%
5	AEE US	1,112	1,683,501	18,924,251	1.39%
6	WIN US	5,584	8,740,177	19,565,224	2.01%
7	ETR US	497	1,036,151	26,060,130	1.26%
8	HRB US	1,843	4,076,931	27,651,457	1.10%
9	HAS US	737	1,662,685	28,200,225	0.93%
10	AVP US	2,361	5,476,549	28,994,857	1.42%

Exhibit 4.9 The Lowest IDTS Numbers for an ETF
As of 7/2/2012. Reprinted with permission from Bloomberg. Copyright 2012 Bloomberg L.P. All rights reserved.

The smallest IDTS becomes the constraint on how many shares can potentially be traded and is therefore the ETF implied liquidity.

An Example

In Exhibit 4.9, you can see the 10 lowest IDTS numbers calculated for the basket of an ETF. The implied basket liquidity of the ETF is 7.4 million shares per day (as was seen in Exhibit 4.7), which is represented by the lowest IDTS of 7,383,350 for stock FTR. This means that for every basket of 50,000 shares of the ETF, you are required to have 19,986 shares of FTR to do a creation. The formula would look as follows:

$$IDTS = ((11,805,090 \times .25) / 19,986) \times 50,000$$

Where:

Creation unit size = 50,000 shares

The process entails calculating the IDTS for each stock in the ETF basket and then sorting to find the smallest constraints. Note that the constraint is not simply the stock in the basket with the lowest average daily volume. It is a function of the weight of each of the stocks in the basket and their corresponding average volumes. The variable percentage is the amount of the daily average volume that you are comfortable trading. On Bloomberg screens they are using a fixed number of 25% of the ADV of each constituent. This number was chosen because it allows the trader to be a large enough piece of the volume while having no effect on the price of the underlying instrument. If you want to assume a more aggressive trading stance you can adjust that percentage which would cause liquidity to reflect higher as well.

Some Considerations When Utilizing IDTS

There are some things to consider when using the implied ETF liquidity number. It identifies a large group of potentially very liquid ETFs that investors can utilize. If there were a smooth and efficient way for investors to access that liquidity electronically, ETF use would spread to more of these products. If an ETF shows an implied liquidity of millions of shares, yet it is trading only a few thousand shares per day, it may be because it has not been easy to see and quantify that potential liquidity previously. Indeed, it is still not that easy to access it. The brokerage community is working on methods of having clients enter ETF orders and, when possible, having the system go out and execute in the underlying basket. Most large-block ETF trading still takes place on an upstairs basis, where a customer calls a trader and asks for a market. The market makers are utilizing the underlying liquidity pool and translating that into ETF liquidity.

Another concept to understand when using the IDTS is that its best application is on ETFs that hold an actual underlying basket of stocks. Although this is where the majority of assets are in the industry, there are a lot of newer products that do not hold the actual basket. This makes it harder to determine the potential liquidity of the product.

Exhibit 4.10 is an example of where the ETF implied liquidity field fits into the overall liquidity function of an ETF. You can see the DES page for the SPDR S&P 500 ETF Trust, the ETF with the highest average daily trading volume. You can see the ADV of 178.6 million shares, and you can see the ETF implied liquidity of only 55.5 million shares daily. The ETF implied liquidity, based on the basket, is only about 31 percent of the total overall volume. It is thus a lower percentage of the overall ETF liquidity function than in other ETFs. Since there is such a liquid futures and options market surrounding this product, there are multiple ways for market participants to trade the ETF. This drives daily trading volumes even higher than would be implied by the underlying basket.

There are a variety of reasons that an ETF can trade many more shares than would be shown by the ETF implied liquidity field. When that is the case, the field is displaying potential liquidity based on

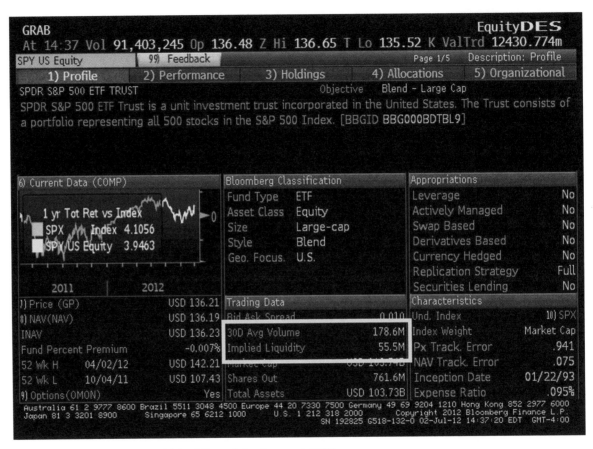

Exhibit 4.10 The Implied Liquidity of the Largest ETF

Reprinted with permission from Bloomberg. Copyright 2012 Bloomberg L.P. All rights reserved.

ETF	Ticker	Name	Shares per Creation Unit	30-Day Average Daily Volume	Implied Daily Tradable Shares (IDTS)	Implied Daily Tradable Dollars (IDT$)
VOO	BF/B	Brown-Forman Corp. COM B USD 0.15	25	211,516	105,758,234	$6,538,619,110
VOO	BRK/B	Berkshire Hathaway Inc COM B USD 0.0033	447	4,610,223	128,921,211	$7,970,695,596
VOO	PM	Philip Morris International Inc COM USD NPV	434	5,444,806	156,820,449	$9,695,596,686

ETF	Ticker	Name	Shares per Creation Unit	30-Day Average Daily Volume	Implied Daily Tradable Shares (IDTS)	Implied Daily Tradable Dollars (IDT$)
IVV	BF/B	Brown-Forman Corp. COM B USD 0.15	55	211,516	48,071,925	$6,523,389,378
IVV	BRK/B	Berkshire Hathaway Inc COM B USD 0.0033	979	4,610,223	58,863,924	$7,987,870,187
IVV	PM	Philip Morris International Inc COM USD NPV	949	5,444,806	71,717,677	$9,732,132,255

ETF	Ticker	Name	Shares per Creation Unit	30-Day Average Daily Volume	Implied Daily Tradable Shares (IDTS)	Implied Daily Tradable Dollars (IDT$)
SPY	BF/B	Brown-Forman Corp. COM B USD 0.15	55	211,516	48,071,925	$6,497,314,965
SPY	BRK/B	Berkshire Hathaway Inc COM B USD 0.0033	973	4,610,223	59,226,908	$8,005,002,429
SPY	PM	Philip Morris International Inc COM USD NPV	943	5,444,806	72,173,993	$9,754,907,149

Exhibit 4.11 Implied Liquidity for Three Comparable ETFs

trading the exact basket and does not account for optimizing the trading basket or a variety of other trading strategies.

The function is extremely helpful when looking at an ETF that is not trading a high average daily volume to assess its suitability for investment. As was seen in Exhibit 4.7, the low-volume ETF with a very high implied liquidity presents an opportunity for investment that might have been ignored when ADV was used as the measurement metric. This reinforces the concept that average daily volume is not a valuable measure of how many shares can be traded in an ETF on a particular day. This has been seen with many examples of ETFs with low ADVs trading large blocks much more than what might have been expected.

Video:
EBILS

www.wiley.com/go/abnervg

The ETF Basket Implied Liquidity Scale (EBILS)

The implied daily tradable shares (IDTS) available on Bloomberg provides a clear and quantifiable number of shares that can potentially be traded in an ETF. Investors need to go further to assess where that number fits within the product universe. Many portfolio managers look at positions in dollar terms, potentially

asking, "Can I invest $25 million in a particular ETF in a day?" So some would prefer to look at the implied daily tradable dollars (IDT$), which is a representation of potential liquidity of the basket in dollar terms. This will be important when you are comparing multiple ETFs at different prices and attempting to determine what liquidity may be available in each.

In Exhibit 4.11, you can see the three names that constrain basket liquidity for each of the three main S&P 500 Index ETFs. If you compare them based on implied daily tradable shares, then it would seem as if the first is twice as liquid as the others. The difference is actually due to the price point of the ETF rather than the actual basket. When you look at the three funds in dollar terms, you can see that they all present similar implied daily tradable dollars (IDT$), representing a similar amount of liquidity.

The next step would be to try to gain an understanding of where these implied liquidity numbers fit relative to each other. I have developed a scale of ETFs to make it easy to identify whether the ETF you are interested in fits within your liquidity parameters. The ETF basket implied liquidity scale (EBILS) gives the underlying basket of each ETF a rating as follows:

EBILS—ETF Basket Implied Liquidity Scale
  A—Extremely liquid basket
  B—Very high basket liquidity
  C—Good basket liquidity
  D—Low basket liquidity
  E—Very low basket liquidity

EBILS - ETF Basket Implied Liquidity Scale

ETF Basket Implied Liquidity Scale - Dollars

Data as of 7/2/2012

Rating	Implied Daily Tradable Dollars (IDT$)	# of ETFs	% of ETFs	Liquidity Level	Interpretation
A	More than $1,000,000,000	73	9%	Extremely Liquid Basket	The underlying basket trades very easily
B	$1,000,000,000 > x > $100,000,000	231	29%	Very Liquid Basket	You can trade up to $1 Billion dollars notional of this fund on a given day
C	$100,000,000 > x > $10,000,000	287	37%	Good Basket Liquidity	This fund will trade with average liquidity
D	$10,000,000 > x > $1,000,000	146	19%	Low Basket Liquidity	The basket implies less than a $10 Million Dollars Notional Liquidity daily
E	Less than $1,000,000	47	6%	Very Low Basket Liquidity	The fund basket is difficult to trade

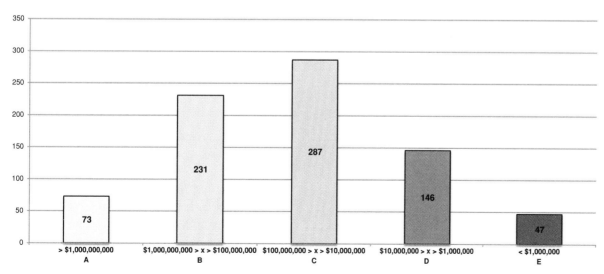

Exhibit 4.12 ETF Basket Implied Liquidity Scale–Dollars

Each of these levels corresponds to a dollar-based implied daily tradable dollar level and is then cross-referenced to an implied daily tradable shares level on a grid.

The dollar trading amounts of each liquidity rating correspond as follows:

EBILS—Implied Daily Tradable Dollars (IDT$)
A— > $1 billion
B— $1 billion > x > $100 million
C— $100 million > x > $10 million
D— $10 million > x > $1 million
E— < $1 million

These numbers represent the dollar notional amount of the ETF that could possibly be traded, while constrained to a maximum of 25 percent of the average daily volume of each of the stocks, in the proper weights within the basket. The IDT$ is presented in dollars of ETFs. As an example, an ETF with an A rating has a basket in which you could easily trade more than a billion dollars' worth of the ETF in a day, while being no more than 25 percent of the volume of any stock in the basket. This is a very liquid basket. On the other end of the spectrum, a fund with an E rating means that you will be able to trade less than 1 million dollars' worth of ETF notional via the basket on a given day. This is also while being no more than 25 percent of the volume of any of the underlying stocks. This is a fund with very low dollar liquidity as implied by the basket.

In Exhibit 4.12, you can see the breakdown of funds by number and percent of the five EBILS ratings. There are more than 500 ETFs with ratings of C or higher. These ETFs represent funds with baskets that can be traded and implied into more than $10 million per day in each of the funds. On the extreme high end, 9 percent of the funds have baskets that could be traded to imply $1 billion of liquidity in the ETF on any given day. These ratings correspond to the IDT$.

It is also important to understand these numbers in share amounts. Although most ETFs with very high dollar notional liquidity have very liquid baskets in share terms, there are differing levels within each dollar liquidity rating. So within each EBILS letter rating, there is a number level that corresponds to each particular ETF. This number is the implied daily tradable shares numbers broken down to five levels as follows:

EBILS—Implied Daily Tradable Shares (IDTS)
1— > 100 million
2— 100 million > x > 10 million
3— 10 million > x > 1 million
4— 1 million > x > 250,000
5— < 250,000

Using these numbers, an ETF in level 1 can potentially trade more than 100 million shares daily based on the basket. A fund considered to be level 5 implies that less than 250,000 shares of the fund could be interpolated from the basket in a day. This would be considered a basket that is difficult to trade. In Exhibit 4.13, you can see the breakdown of how funds fit into the EBILS parameters based on implied daily tradable shares.

It is easier to think of the rating scale as a grid where each ETF fits in a particular box corresponding to both a dollar and a share amount of implied liquidity. In Exhibit 4.14, you can see the EBILS grid for the currently available universe of equity ETFs with an implied liquidity number as per Bloomberg. The empty spaces represent areas where it is unlikely than an ETF will fall. For example, in the space on the grid corresponding to rating A level 4 (A4), the ETF would have a basket that presents liquidity of more than a billion dollars notional but in share terms less than a million shares per day. This is a highly unlikely scenario. You can also see that a significant amount of funds are rated either B or C, presenting good to very liquid baskets, and have a level 3 IDTS, amounting to more than a million shares of implied liquidity available daily.

Exhibit 4.15 shows the same EBIL scale in list form. As you can see, for each EBIL rating, A thru E, there are five sublevels representing different potential implied daily tradable share quantities.

How to Think about EBILS Ratings

If you were a portfolio manager running a multibillion-dollar portfolio where every position you took in an ETF averaged $30 million in notional, you might consider using only funds that have a rating of C or higher, whereas if you were managing a smaller portfolio and your typical position sizes were about $1 million each, you might expand your range of ETFs that you would use to include funds with a D rating or higher. This gives you a universe of 737 of 783 rated ETFs. That is almost 94 percent of the rated ETFs with sufficient liquidity available via the underlying basket.

These ratings do not include ETNs. If you were using average daily volumes and you restricted yourself to funds that trade more than 100,000 shares per day, you would be limited to 194 of 783, only 25 percent of the available product universe. Understanding an ETF liquidity scale, like the EBILS, enables you to broaden the universe of products that you can position within your portfolio. This is a critical factor in building ETF portfolios.

Summary

In summary, ETFs trade intraday on an exchange and are in a state of continuous issuance. These characteristics set ETFs apart and serve to give the investors more control over their execution, as well as more access to liquidity. Control over execution is a responsibility for product users. Investors need to understand the trading community they trade against, as well as how to value any ETF they want to position. Technology and trading platforms do not offer all the necessary information in one neat package, but all the data are publicly available. It is hoped that as the ETF industry continues to grow, so will those businesses servicing them.

The introduction of the ETF implied liquidity function and the ETF basket implied liquidity scale (EBILS) greatly expands the public's knowledge about underlying liquidity in an ETF. It will take the focus off average daily volume because, for risk management purposes, it provides a much clearer indication of what potential liquidity can be in an ETF. It will also become a very valuable

EBILS - ETF Basket Implied Liquidity Scale

ETF Basket Implied Liquidity Scale - Shares

Data as of 7/2/2012

Level	Implied Daily Tradable Shares (IDTS)	# of ETFs	% of ETFs	Liquidity Level	Interpretation
1	More than 100,000,000	15	2%	Extremely Liquid Basket	The underlying basket trades very easily
2	100,000,000 > x > 10,000,000	136	17%	Very Liquid Basket	You can trade up to 100,000,000 shares of the ETF on a given day
3	10,000,000 > x > 1,000,000	302	39%	Good Basket Liquidity	This fund will trade with average liquidity
4	1,000,000 > x > 250,000	185	24%	Low Basket Liquidity	The basket implies less than a million shares interpolated volume daily
5	Less than 250,000	146	19%	Very Low Basket Liquidity	The fund basket is difficult to trade

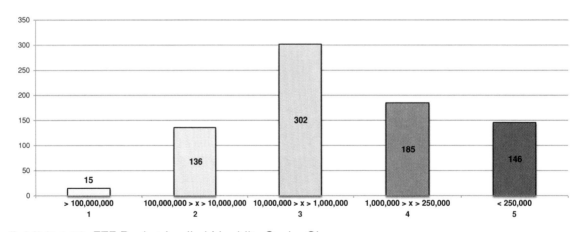

Exhibit 4.13 ETF Basket Implied Liquidity Scale–Shares

		A	B	C	D	E
		Extremely Liquid	**Very Liquid**	**Good Liquidity**	**Low Liquidity**	**Very Low Liquidity**
		Implied Daily Tradable Dollars (IDT$) Rating				
		> $1,000,000,000	$1,000,000,000 > x > $100,000,000	$100,000,000 > x > $10,000,000	$10,000,000 > x > $1,000,000	< $1,000,000
1	> 100,000,000	A1 = 15 / 2%				
2	100,000,000 > x > 10,000,000	A2 = 57 / 7%	B2 = 79 / 10%			
3	10,000,000 > x > 1,000,000	A3 = 1 / .5%	B3 = 152 / 19%	C3 = 147 / 19%	D3 = 1 / .5%	
4	1,000,000 > x > 250,000			C4 = 134 / 17%	D4 = 51 / 7%	
5	< 250,000			C5 = 6 / 1%	D5 = 94 / 12%	E5 = 46 / 6%

Implied Daily Tradable Shares (IDTS) Level

Exhibit 4.14 EBILS Rating Grid

tool for issuers to explain to clients what the underlying liquidity picture looks like in their funds. It will provide a deeper measure of confidence to portfolio managers for building portfolios and managing risk in those portfolios. It should drive demand for easier and more transparent liquidity transfer between ETFs and their underlying baskets. It will certainly broaden the horizons of investors who may have been unsure about expanding beyond the most highly traded ETFs into those that present with highly liquid underlying baskets.

Notes

1. The default is 25 percent of the average daily volume in each of the components. This is based on the assumption that at only a quarter of the volume, trading will not have an impact upon market price.

2. The variable percentage is defaulted to 25 percent of the average daily volume of each of the underlying so you can get a perspective of how many ETF shares can be traded without having an impact on the price of each underlying stock. You would want to adjust upward to be more aggressive, which would reflect higher liquidity, or lower to be more constrained.

EBIL Rating	Level	# of ETFs	% of ETFs	Implied Daily Tradable Shares (IDTS)	Implied Daily Tradable Dollars (IDT$)	Basket Liquidity Levels
A	1	15	2%	> 100,000,000	> $1,000,000,000	Extremely Liquid Baskets
	2	57	7%	100,000,000 > x > 10,000,000	> $1,000,000,000	Extremely Liquid Baskets
	3	1	0%	10,000,000 > x > 1,000,000	> $1,000,000,000	Extremely Liquid Baskets
	4			1,000,000 > x > 250,000	> $1,000,000,000	Extremely Liquid Baskets
	5			< 250,000	> $1,000,000,000	Extremely Liquid Baskets
B	1			> 100,000,000	$1,000,000,000 > x > $100,000,000	Very High Basket Liquidity
	2	79	10%	100,000,000 > x > 10,000,000	$1,000,000,000 > x > $100,000,000	Very High Basket Liquidity
	3	152	19%	10,000,000 > x > 1,000,000	$1,000,000,000 > x > $100,000,000	Very High Basket Liquidity
	4			1,000,000 > x > 250,000	$1,000,000,000 > x > $100,000,000	Very High Basket Liquidity
	5			< 250,000	$1,000,000,000 > x > $100,000,000	Very High Basket Liquidity
C	1			> 100,000,000	$100,000,000 > x > $10,000,000	Good Basket Liquidity
	2			100,000,000 > x > 10,000,000	$100,000,000 > x > $10,000,000	Good Basket Liquidity
	3	147	19%	10,000,000 > x > 1,000,000	$100,000,000 > x > $10,000,000	Good Basket Liquidity
	4	134	17%	1,000,000 > x > 250,000	$100,000,000 > x > $10,000,000	Good Basket Liquidity
	5	6	1%	< 250,000	$100,000,000 > x > $10,000,000	Good Basket Liquidity
D	1			> 100,000,000	$10,000,000 > x > $1,000,000	Low Basket Liquidity
	2			100,000,000 > x > 10,000,000	$10,000,000 > x > $1,000,000	Low Basket Liquidity
	3	1	0%	10,000,000 > x > 1,000,000	$10,000,000 > x > $1,000,000	Low Basket Liquidity
	4	51	7%	1,000,000 > x > 250,000	$10,000,000 > x > $1,000,000	Low Basket Liquidity
	5	94	12%	< 250,000	$10,000,000 > x > $1,000,000	Low Basket Liquidity
E	1			> 100,000,000	< $1,000,000	Very Low Basket Liquidity
	2	46	6%	100,000,000 > x > 10,000,000	< $1,000,000	Very Low Basket Liquidity
	3			10,000,000 > x > 1,000,000	< $1,000,000	Very Low Basket Liquidity
	4			1,000,000 > x > 250,000	< $1,000,000	Very Low Basket Liquidity
	5			< 250,000	< $1,000,000	Very Low Basket Liquidity

Exhibit 4.15 EBILS Rating Listing

Test Yourself

1. True or false—Looking at the average daily volume (ADV) of an ETF will give you a complete picture of how many shares of an ETF you can possibly trade in a day.

2. True or false—If you see a 15-cent-wide spread in an ETF on your quote screen, there is no way that you would be able to trade a block of that ETF inside those two prices.

3. IDTS stands for:
   a. I Don't Trade Shares
   b. Implied Daily Tradable Shares
   c. I Don't Take Sugar
   d. Improbably Domestic Trading Scheme

Answers: 1. False　2. False　3. b.

CHAPTER 5

ETFs and the Flash Crash

For a period of approximately 15 minutes on May 6, 2010, markets appeared to behave abnormally, as many equity and ETF securities saw trades occur at prices in the range of 40 percent or more down from their most recent prior trade prices. Nothing about these corporations or the ETF fund structure containing the equity in these corporations had materially changed over that 15-minute period to warrant such excessive drops in valuation. Why did this happen, and why hadn't it occurred before? What has been done to prevent it from occurring in the future? This chapter goes through the details of how ETFs were affected.

Why Did ETF Pricing Seem to Stray?

After the events of May 6, 2010, there was no shortage of theories and assumptions attempting to explain their true cause. It took the SEC and the Commodity Fu-

tures Trading Commission (CFTC) until September 30, 2010, however, to release their official findings.[1] The almost five-month delay by a governing regulatory body displays the complexity of the inner workings of the various exchanges and the markets in general.

Regarding ETFs, secondary market trading and pricing is based on several factors; two of the most important are the underlying basket and the proxy hedge vehicle. ETFs trade differently than single-stock equities. A significant portion of ETF trading typically takes place between a customer and a professional trader or liquidity provider. Very rarely are two customers trading with each other. This becomes more pronounced as you get beyond the top 30 highest-volume ETFs, as can be seen from the inverse correlation between NYSE Arca Lead Market Maker (LMM) participation rates and volume.[2] In many cases, a seller in an ETF is making a sale to an ETF liquidity provider or market maker, who is pricing the bid level based on where the underlying basket is expected to sell at the same time, or a proxy hedge, to lock in some arbitrage-style spread. Let us start the analysis with ETFs with domestic equities in the basket. If you are a market maker pricing your bid based on where the underlying basket is trading, then your price is almost completely dependent on current and accurate pricing in those underlying stocks.

The public now knows that on the day of the flash crash, the NASDAQ and other exchanges had declared self-help against NYSE Arca, indicating detection of some form of pricing discrepancy on U.S. equities, and that several stocks had entered slow mode in the period just before the market dislocation. Both of these events would cause a distortion in the calculation of fair value for an ETF, which would, in turn, cause a market maker or other liquidity provider to widen its bid-offer spread to move away from the inside market until a fair price could be determined. A simple thought process tells us that, in an ETF with a domestic underlying basket, if you cannot price the underlying basket, then you cannot price the ETF. This is not an ETF structural problem but a real-time data problem: An ETF is simply a wrapper whose value is derived from the value of its underlying basket of securities, and if you cannot gather accurate data on the underlying, you cannot assess the value of the ETF. At that moment in time, for example, if a mutual fund had been offering real-time NAV calculation (something ETFs are known for), it also potentially would not have had a good or valid valuation. Furthermore, had the 15-minute price dislocation occurred

between 3:45 P.M. and the 4:00 P.M. close, many mutual fund NAVs would potentially have also been struck far below their actual fair value. The valuation process is the same for both types of funds, but one product provides a mechanism for real-time pricing and trading of the actual fund (ETFs), and the other product does not (mutual funds). In essence, the price dislocations affected every equity product that trades intraday.

Volume is another parameter that can cause an ETF market maker to move away from the inside market to reevaluate the fair value calculation. While the markets work in millisecond time frames (or faster), volume spikes in extremely short periods can be used as an indicator of underlying market events worthy of attention. In Exhibit 5.1, you can see a chart of one of the most highly traded U.S.-listed ETFs. The chart shows the price of the fund (top) and the volume traded (bottom) over five-minute periods throughout May 6, 2010. It is clear that volume started to increase dramatically in percentage terms between 2:00 P.M. and 2:30 P.M., and then in the five-minute periods approaching (and at) 2:45 P.M., volume spiked drastically. If the ETF typically trades approximately 5 million shares every five minutes and then for two periods that volume spikes to 25 and then 30 million shares per period, the trading community would naturally reassess risk parameters and pricing verification. When the volume spikes occurred at the exact same time as pricing discrepancies between the exchanges, causing price verification problems, withdrawal of liquidity providers from the market to check their quoting

Exhibit 5.1 SPY ETF Trade Price and Volume on May 6, 2010

system was a natural reaction. You can see from the dramatic price rebound that day that as soon as price verification was determined, market participants were able to reenter the market and bring ETF prices back in line. One critical point to realize is that during the market dislocation, when several equity prices were in slow quoting mode, volume swung to the ETF market as the proxy. The overall volume traded in ETFs for the days of May 6 and May 7 were the third and fifth highest, respectively, in volume history.[3] This clearly demonstrates that ETFs have a role in the investing world and that there are enough participants who believe in the merits of the product. It confirms their natural use for myriad purposes, from positioning to hedging and beyond, especially during times of market duress.

Closer Look at the SEC-CFTC Report Findings

Some very important features of the September 30, 2010, SEC report can shed some further light on what happened regarding ETFs. On page 39 of the report, we read, "A large majority of ETF market makers with whom we spoke, and particularly those that value underlying stocks as part of their normal market making activities, paused their market making for considerable periods of time starting at 2:45 P.M on May 6. We believe that this is one of the reasons equity-based ETFs were disproportionately affected by the extreme price volatilities of that afternoon."[4]

One notable aspect of what happened is described at the very beginning of the report. On page 4, as part of the executive summary, the report describes trading pauses undertaken by many automated trading systems in response to extreme and sudden price declines.

A trading pause is a logical function embedded into an automated trading system to allow participants to assess market situations. "Participants reported that these assessments include the following factors: whether observed severe price moves could be an artifact of erroneous data; the impact of such moves on risk and position limits; impacts on intraday profit and loss (P&L); the potential for trades to be broken, leaving their firms inadvertently long or short on one side of the market; and the ability of their systems to handle the very high volume of trades and orders they were processing that day."[5] There can be either data integrity pauses, based around price moves, or feed-driven integrity pauses, based around quote latency, that will cause a trading system to stop trading to determine whether the calculated fair value is reasonable before continuing to trade.

It is also important to understand the use of what are termed *stub quotes* in this context and how they relate to a pause in market-making activities. On page 38 of the same report, we read, "In order to comply with their obligation to maintain continuous two-sided quotations, market makers utilize stub quotes if they choose to discontinue actively quoting."[6] Thus, on May 6, while in the process of reassessing whether to reenter the market, some market maker quotations had extended

The Timetable of What Happened on May 6, 2010

2:05 p.m. On May 6, 2010, due to increasingly violent protests in Athens over the Greek debt crisis, the euro fell sharply.
2:23 p.m. The NASDAQ exchange issued alerts of unusual price movements.
2:32 p.m. Some high-frequency trading (HFT) models began betting that there would be continued price declines by increasing short positions on S&P 500 E-Mini futures contracts.
2:36 p.m. Due to the massive number of orders, the exchanges were unable to comply with the terms of Regulation NMS,[6] leading to pricing discrepancies across exchanges.
2:37 p.m. Therefore, the NASDAQ, CBOE, and BATS exchanges enabled a self-help function and stopped routing orders to Arca, the electronic trading platform of the NYSE.
2:40 p.m. Several trading firms pulled out of the market because of the high degree of uncertainty, leading to a dearth of buyers and sellers.
2:44 p.m. Volume in S&P 500 E-Mini futures contracts had spiked up to six times the usual volume.
2:45 p.m. The E-Mini futures contracts plunged in value in a very short period. This triggered a CME circuit breaker to halt trading for five seconds.
2:47 p.m. The S&P 500 hit its low point of the day, a 9.1 percent loss off the intraday high. Shares of many equity and ETF securities traded as low as a penny and as high as $100,000.
3:01 p.m. NASDAQ revoked self-help and resumed sending orders to Arca for price matching.

to stub quote spreads; for market makers on NASDAQ or NYSE Arca, such stub quotes could be automatically generated upon a market maker's withdrawal from the market. When a market maker is unable to determine a fair value for an ETF because of some form of system or quoting issue, they may step back from their inside quote to assess the market. Their system can automatically generate a stub quote (not intended to be traded against) while they are developing a valid fair value for the ETF. They are still, technically, making a market in a security and fulfilling their obligation, but the bid and offer is so unreasonably wide that no one would normally trade there.

Then, more conclusively, on page 40 we read, "Therefore, when professionals pulled out because of data integrity concerns, ETFs may not have had the same level of resting liquidity far from the mid-quote as did large-cap stocks, allowing a disproportionate number of ETF orders to hit stub-quote levels."[7] Market makers were not sure of pricing, so they moved out to stub levels, expecting not to trade, but were getting executed against because of market orders that were fired off and low levels of bids and offers on the books to accommodate those orders

Another reason a market maker might not be confident of its quote is if an NYSE liquidity replenishment point (LRP) has been hit.[8] On page 68 of the report, we can read, "A LRP may be triggered even when there is additional interest on NYSE's order book beyond the LRP price point. In these cases NYSE will suspend automated quotations in the security, and will identify its quote on the consolidated tape with a 'non-firm' indicator. This is referred to as a 'slow market' or 'going slow' in the security."[10] In the case where two competing quoting systems are being used, as a main and a backup, and they begin to show different prices because one has gone slow, you would move away from the inside market until you can determine which price is truly indicative of where the market is trading. This process can cause problems for market makers in ETFs whose systems are pricing the ETF off the underlying basket because their valuation quotes can be affected by stocks in slow mode.

Although the events of May 6, 2010, are widely known, pricing discrepancies, as well as the declaration of the self-help rule, have occurred numerous times before and continue to occur quite frequently. The BATS Exchange provides a feed for when the exchange has declared self-help and consequently revoked this declaration (at http://batstrading.com/alerts/). Many of the declarations last no longer than a minute (and many are even shorter than that).

To summarize, ETF market makers widened their quotes, causing a liquidity vacuum. As the markets kept falling, they triggered an avalanche of stop orders, which became market sell orders that swept down the order books. This explains why we see executions at random levels and not all at $0.01. Some executions happened at $0.15, and some occurred at various other prices along the spectrum. ETFs with many client buyers in the systems were able to absorb the selling, while others with fewer buyers were trading all the way down to $0.01, which is the level to which many market makers had moved their quotes (stub quotes).

Can This Happen Again?

The SEC made several recommendations based on conclusions drawn from the events of May 6, 2010.

- The first move, and probably the one with the most impact on the markets, was the implementation of a volatility-based trading pause program on stocks and ETFs.[10] The SEC has piloted a program aimed at stemming a recurrence of these events. The pilot was meant to last only through December 2011 but has been extended several times. It will work as follows:

  - For stocks that are subject to the circuit breaker program, trades will be broken at specified levels, depending on the stock price, between 9:45 a.m. and 3:35 P.M.

- For stocks priced at $25 or less, trades will be broken if the trades are at least 10 percent away from the circuit breaker trigger price.

- For stocks priced between $25 and $50, trades will be broken if they are 5 percent away from the circuit breaker trigger price.

- For stocks priced at more than $50, the trades will be broken if they are 3 percent away from the circuit breaker trigger price.

- Where circuit breakers are not applicable, the exchanges and the Financial Industry Regulatory Authority (FINRA) will break trades at specified levels for events involving multiple stocks, depending on how many stocks are involved:

  - For events involving between 5 and 20 stocks, trades will be broken that are at least 10 percent away from the reference price, typically the last sale before pricing was disrupted.

  - For events involving more than 20 stocks, trades will be broken that are at least 30 percent away from the reference price.

- The SEC-CFTC acknowledges the greater interconnections of equities and derivatives markets. We would stress that this has become more pronounced as the futures markets are often used to facilitate the arbitrage functionality of some of the largest and highest-volume ETFs. This

should drive a more unified rules system between the two markets to eliminate any potential for inconsistencies.

- The report acknowledges that there were inconsistencies in the regulations regarding broken trades, leading to uncertainty, and endeavors to clean up this process.

- Although the report notes in many places the importance, speed, and advanced technology of many market participants, it does not acknowledge that the continued adherence of the NYSE to a process of slowing down markets to allow for human intervention can cause unintended problems in the highly automated trading environment of modern markets. We should endeavor to adopt a fully automated system by all players on all exchanges, as a human-in-the-loop model is simply incapable of keeping up with current trading speeds.

- Another crucial acknowledgment is that many market participants will employ their own, often harsher, volatility-based system integrity checks and pauses. This should lead us to consider the proliferation of ETF use among investors and how liquidity is provided in those products. It is understood from the report, as well as from common sense, that in many ETFs, resting orders in the order book provide less liquidity, while liquidity typically comes from interaction with a professional market participant. What is not clarified in the report but should become the subject of study is the relationship between the issuers of ETFs and the market-making community. Currently, there are no formalized relationships and, therefore, no incentives in place to protect quotes to the benefit of investors. Current regulations,[11] which were created many years ago, prohibit any formalized economic relationship between the issuer of an ETF and its market makers. These regulations were developed before these newer fund-type investment products were traded on exchanges, and it was not anticipated that new products would actually benefit from the provision of liquidity in a more formalized manner. It may be determined through further research that finding a way for the issuer community to provide a backstop to liquidity providers to assure participation during extreme market volatility would benefit investors. This is the rationale behind the market quality programs currently being studied.

Summary

It seems clear from my research, and from that of the regulatory bodies, that ETFs were not the cause of the flash crash. The day of the event and the following day were actually some of the highest-volume trading days for the products, at least until we encountered the volatility from the current ongoing financial crisis. This shows that investors' faith may have been damaged in regard to the overall market, but their faith in the product continued, and they used the products in a time of market duress to manage portfolio volatility. The massive amounts of structural change that the markets are undergoing are not going to be without events that are unintended consequences, but it seems clear that ETFs will be the tools that will help investors navigate these periods.

Notes

1. Findings Regarding the Market Events of May 6, 2010. Report of the staffs of the CFTC and the SEC to the Joint Advisory Committee on Emerging Regulatory Issues. Published September 30, 2010.

2. NYSE Arca CADV Buckets/LMM Participation rates, Jan–April 2011: less than 10,000/16.58 percent; 10,000–50,000/11.44 percent; 50,000–100,000/8.47 percent; 1,000,000–5,000,000/7.56 percent; greater than 5,000,000/7.19 percent. Data supplied by NYSE Arca. (CADV = composite average daily volume.)

3. The top five highest days by shares volume of ETFs in order: 9/18/2008, 10/10/2008, 5/6/2010, 11/20/2008, 5/7/2010. Credit Suisse AES Analysis.

4. Findings Regarding the Market Events of May 6, 2010.

5. Findings Regarding the Market Events of May 6, 2010.

6. "Stub quotes are quotes at unrealistically low or high prices that fulfill a market maker's obligation to provide continuous bids and offers, but at levels that the market maker does not expect to be reached under ordinary market conditions." SEC-CFTC Report, 38.

7. Findings Regarding the Market Events of May 6, 2010.

8. "LRPs are intended to act as a 'speed bump' and to dampen volatility in a given stock by temporarily converting from an automated market to a manual auction market when a price movement of sufficient size is reached. In such a case, trading on NYSE in that stock will 'go slow' and automatic executions will cease for a period ranging from a fraction of a second to a minute or two to allow the Designated Market Maker to solicit and/or contribute additional liquidity before returning to an automated market." SEC-CFTC Report, 68.

9. Ibid.

10. Rule 80C—Trading pauses in individual securities due to extraordinary market volatility. This rule was adopted on June 10, 2010.

11. Finra Rule 5250, Payments for market making.

12. NYSE-Arca informational document.

Test Yourself

1. True or false—If you are a liquidity provider in ETFs and you are unable to calculate fair value for the funds you trade, you will naturally increase the size you are trading and tighten your spreads.

2. True or false—In an ETF with a domestic underlying basket, if three stocks in the basket all halt trading because of news, then the indicative value for that fund will still be a good indication of the value of the ETF.

3. True or false—Since the flash crash, investors have stopped using ETFs for positioning within their portfolios.

Answers: 1. False   2. False   3. False

CHAPTER 6

How to Execute Orders in ETFs

There are so many uses for ETFs within portfolios that they have become tools for a wide variety of investors. The average investor is using them in small trading accounts and personal investment portfolios. Smaller money managers and financial advisors are moving client assets into the funds for directional exposure or hedging that would have been costlier to access prior to the products. At the same time, some of the largest institutions—hedge funds, registered investment advisors, asset management firms, pensions, endowments, and family offices—are managing large portfolios of ETFs and using them for risk management, directional exposures, and trading strategies based purely around select ETFs. This diverse investor base uses ETFs in many different ways, each requiring its own unique strategy for best execution. If you are managing portfolios of ETFs with millions or more in client assets, mastering execution can distinguish you from the competition and save your firm and your clients a significant amount of money.

If your firm is not yet a model of trading efficiency, there are tools and market participants available to help you. The fact that you are using ETFs as compared to stocks is working to your advantage. I have discussed that ETFs trade very differently than stocks. In short, they trade better, typically with tighter spreads and larger size on the BBO than ordinary equities. According to a recent article from *Automated Trader* magazine, "an ETF with ADV below 200,000 shares typically had a best bid or offer (BBO) spread of 20 bps—less than half the spread size of a stock of comparable liquidity."[1] This percentage difference stays relatively consistent as you move up the volume curve as well. As can be seen in Exhibit 6.1, however, there is a very long tail of products in the ETF market that do not trade anywhere near where the higher-volume products trade. According to the chart, as of July 2012, only 114 products traded more than a million shares per day on average. This is only 7 percent of the outstanding products. On the

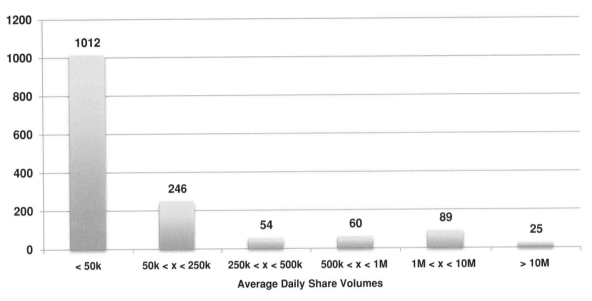

Exhibit 6.1 The Long Tail of ETF Volumes
Reprinted with permission from Bloomberg. Copyright 2012 Bloomberg L.P. All rights reserved.

other end of the spectrum, more than 1,000 trade less than 50,000 shares per day.

If a product is trading more than a million shares a day, it's reasonably easy to use any electronic trading system to trade smaller blocks in the ETF or to use algorithms if you are a reasonably small percent of the ADV. However, a tremendous number of compelling products trade less than a million shares per day; this is the sweet spot of products that I focus on in my work. These are products that provide all the benefits of the ETF structure and yet require a certain amount of trading savvy for efficient use. You can certainly go out and trade them like almost any equity, but by understanding the differences in how ETFs and equities trade, you will be able to add significant value to your portfolios.

Along with the client base becoming more sophisticated traders, the trading community is developing methods for providing more liquidity. The cohort of money managers who are managing portfolios of ETFs has grown alongside the ETFs and, in some ways, has inspired growth in the industry. The breadth and depth of the ETF product offerings enable these portfolio managers to create diverse portfolios with various risk parameters and a broad array of asset classes more efficiently, with less trading complexity and cost. Some of these asset management firms have now grown so big and so savvy in their ETF use that they are driving a need for greater risk tolerance and more sophisticated trading among the liquidity-providing community. In the following sections, we will discuss how markets are made in ETFs, who is making those markets, and procedures for executing large orders efficiently.

A Story about Large Block Trading

In June 2003, I was an ETF liquidity provider on the Bear Stearns derivatives trading desk. In that business, we were providing liquidity in ETFs to the firm's institutional clients. Most users of ETFs at that time were hedge funds using them to hedge their portfolios or play intraday volatility. We had developed what seemed at that time to be a forward-thinking system in which we could utilize basket trading to trade all the underlying components

of an ETF in the proper sizes. We could also trade futures (if they existed for that particular underlying index) and consolidate all the implied positions to give us a clear picture of our risk in real time. This enabled us to make some large markets very quickly, and on the street, we were considered an aggressive desk. This meant that our markets were tight as far as our competitors were concerned, and we were willing and able to trade in large size. Typically back then, *large size* meant 200,000 to 500,000 shares at a time, although a handful of very large hedge funds would want us to be able to trade in 1 to 2 million share blocks. It was considered to be a very large trade when we put up a block of a million shares of SPY that traded around $100 at that time, or roughly $100 million notional.

One afternoon, during a reasonably quiet trading session, I received a call from one of the salespeople on the equities desk. He asked for a market in 5 million shares of the NASDAQ-100 ETF (at the time people simply called them Qs). This ETF contains a basket that is similar to the NASDAQ-100 Index. As I was discussing price with the salesman and about to give him my two-way market, he interrupted me with "Make that 10 million shares." Seconds later, as I was calculating my price, he said, "Actually, make it 19 million shares. I'm a seller, what's your bid?" I gave him a bid price. He said, "Sold!" and hung up the phone. I had just bought over $500 million in QQQs from a large asset manager! The risk of the position was now mine, and I needed to get myself hedged quickly.

That's how large blocks typically happened, and they still happen that way today. In a matter of seconds, massive amounts of capital and risk change hands from the client base to the liquidity provider community, and back again. This ability to move risk in such size and speed is what drove growth in the products and also growth in the trading ecosystem surrounding the products.

Today, after years of evolution and growth in the ETF market, large trades like that have grown more commonplace and can be even bigger. This has required the trading community to grow in size and to improve its ability to manage large-scale risk quickly and efficiently. The trading community is no longer comprised of just institutional trading desks at big banks but contains trading desks at all sizes of institutions, even boutique market makers and liquidity providers dedicated to ETF trading only. The proliferation of faster electronic trading, colocation, and more types of liquidity providers has added tremendous depth to most listed ETFs and has attracted more users to the space. But it remains necessary for the newer large users of ETFs to understand their options when moving big size and which of those options to use in various scenarios.

I'll go through the main methods of executing ETF orders, and then I'll detail each of those processes. After that, I'll give a variety of examples of how to use your Bloomberg to identify certain types of trades that have taken place, which can give you insight on what is going on in a particular ETF and a better idea of market sentiment.

Types of Trade Executions

There are several types of executions that a customer can pursue when looking to add or unwind a large exposure in an ETF:

- Using an electronic trading system themselves to trade the ETF using limits or market orders.
- Calling a block liquidity provider and asking for a risk market.
- Calling a liquidity aggregator and asking for a market.
- Using an algorithm on either the basket or the ETF.
- An NAV-based execution.

As I discuss each type, it will become apparent to you that each method can be appropriate for certain situations. They will differ regarding when execution occurs and who takes on varying degrees of risk. A block liquidity provider who makes a risk market is taking on the full risk of hedging a position, and there is a fee embedded in the price, called the risk premium. On the other hand, utilizing the underlying to derive an ETF price in agency-style trading puts the risk of time and price on the customer. And you can therefore theoretically trade closer to NAV. These types of decisions affect both the cost of trading and the timing of execution.

Then there are the decisions as to whether to deal with a capital committing desk, which can be providing liquidity against your order flow using its own

KEY POINT:

NAV-based executions involve having a broker execute the underlying basket on the client's behalf and giving the ETF execution at the price implied by that basket execution. If you buy the exact basket of an ETF in its creation unit form, you are essentially trading at the NAV of the ETF plus transaction costs. This can involve an AP doing a creation or redemption on your behalf but is not limited to that process.

capital, versus one of the agency liquidity providers that specialize in either aggregation or algorithmic trading.

Block Market Making

On any given day, millions of shares of ETFs trade in block form through the liquidity-providing community. You can see running streams of blocks by using the MBTR functionality on your Bloomberg, as shown in Exhibit 6.2. In the screen, you can see the time of trade, the ticker of the ETF, the amount of shares in the block and the price, and the exchange on which it was printed. You are able to customize this screen to monitor a certain portfolio of ETFs that you care about, with minimum size or price constraints. The screen in Exhibit 6.2 is constraining blocks to at least 500,000 shares and looking at all available exchange-traded products.

Most of the large broker-dealers provide access to block markets in ETFs for clients. You can call a traditional broker-dealer trading desk of the remaining big bank-brokerages. Or you can also contact the mid-tier brokerages that are growing their businesses to compete with the old-school behemoths. There are differences, however, in whether they are capital-committing desks or agency desks, so always be sure to ask what trading capacity is offered by your liquidity provider.

What you will find, however, is that most of the big banks, and even most ETF liquidity providers now, have certain products in which they are good and others in which they are not as good. By "good," I mean that their market will be as tight as the competition versus being somewhat wider than what you would get elsewhere, due not to the traders or their skills, but the infrastructure of their particular firms. The large banks, for example, are typically particularly good in domestic and international equity funds, where their use of sophisticated portfolio trading systems and global infrastructure provides them with the proper tools to manage such risk. The traditional bank structure, however, may also disadvantage them when the need arises to trade cross-asset ETFs comprised of currencies, bond, or commodity underlying components. Technology has typically not been shared by the different asset-class trading groups, nor have strong relationships developed. The growth of the ETF business and the equitizing of a wide variety of asset classes have happened at a faster rate than banks have been able to modify their internal relationships and trading systems. The wide variety of asset classes trading within an equity wrapper does not fit easily into the traditional silos of the bank trading business. For example, if the equity ETF desk cannot get treated at least on par with clients of the firm when calling the fixed-income desk for bond pricing to hedge risk of an ETF with such exposure, there is no way that they can then compete with external ETF desks that have either broken down the walls of these traditional silos or with newer ETF desks at firms that can get client pricing from any external firm.

STEP-BY-STEP

Creating a list of ETFs to monitor blocks:

1. EXTF.
2. Select 1, ETFs by Region.
3. Select 1, United States.
4. Under the Output tab, select Basket.
5. Input a name, and choose 1<Go> to create the basket.
6. MBTR—to get to the screening criteria page.
7. Under Source, choose Portfolio.
8. Under Name, choose the name of the new basket you created.
9. Input a volume minimum if desired to constrict your output.

KEY POINT:

When a broker is committing capital against your order, it means that they are using firm money and balance sheet to take the other side of your trade. In this way, they are able to offer you immediate execution without going outside to the formal exchanges. There have historically been concerns that this process causes confusion in terms of fiduciary duty and alignment; that is, with the firm now at risk, will they be able to provide best pricing? To remove any sense of impropriety, some firms run what are known as agency execution only, where they do not take any position against their client. In this way, they say that they are always directly aligned with getting the client the best price.

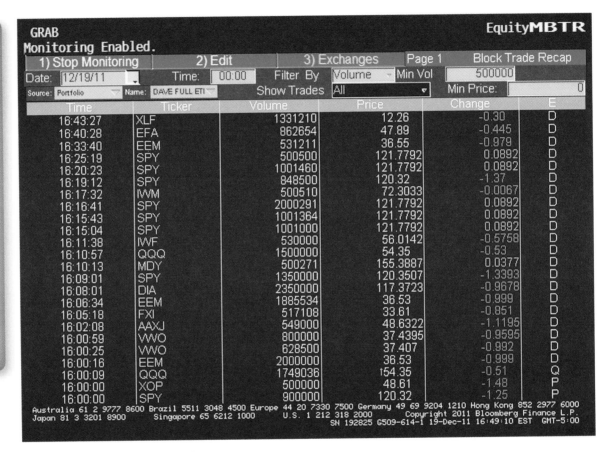

Exhibit 6.2 ETF Large Blocks
Reprinted with permission from Bloomberg. Copyright 2012 Bloomberg L.P. All rights reserved.

Another issue for the large broker-dealers is size of the desk. There are typically five to seven traders in the equity division on a big bank ETF desk, covering the more than 1,500 available products. This is a low ratio and makes it difficult to be good at the wide variety of products that don't trade frequently but still have large capacity. While this structure might make sense because a high percentage of the assets and volumes are in the top 10 percent of products, the real growth of the industry over the last few years from a client perspective is in that other 90 percent of products. These can be hard to cover for trading desks without a dedicated trader for each asset class or smaller groups of funds. In particular, a lot of the newer ETFs do not fit easily into the pricing and trading systems for standard equities. Those that contain currencies or bonds require additional tweaks to trading and risk systems that were primarily designed to handle equity ETFs and their baskets.

To fill the niche left open by structural deficiencies, specialized ETF desks have grown at broad market-making firms, and the traders on those desks can be treated as clients of the various big banks in specific products. If you're on a trading desk of an ETF market-making firm, you might be able to have a relationship on the fixed-income desk at one or several of the big banks to trade bonds so you can quickly and cheaply hedge your fixed-income ETF exposure. You will then be able to turn around and make a bigger and tighter market in the fixed-income ETFs than even the

ETF trader at that same bank against which you are competing.

These more specialized ETF market-making firms also tend to have more traders, each focusing on a specific sector of ETF or asset class. They are typically paid in relation to the profits and losses of their trading book, as opposed to their pay being a function of the overall ETF trading business or, even worse, the broader business unit in which the business might reside at a large bank. Another interesting attribute of these newer specialized ETF market-making firms is that they typically don't have their own in-house sales forces because they are proprietary trading firms, not set up to handle customer order flow directly.

To facilitate the growth in the offshoot of specialized ETF market-making firms, the ETF liquidity aggregator has developed to funnel client order flow to them. In a sense, they act as an outsourced sales force for proprietary trading firms, while at the same time acting as an outsourced trading desk for the client base. Let's take a look at what happens when you call a large bank or ETF liquidity-providing business for a market, and then we'll compare that to the newer-style business of the aggregators.

Say you are a client who wants to trade a large block in an ETF. You have decided that you want instantaneous execution, meaning that you can call up, ask for a risk market, and agree to a price, and you are filled immediately. In this case, you are transferring any risk to your trading counterpart. Your first thought

KEY POINT:

The establishment of an ETF desk typically starts with the building of a system that takes in a daily file of all ETFs and their underlying baskets. This system then generates a fair value for each product and has the ability to either trade the ETFs versus the baskets electronically or take in a position adjustment (for example, if a trading desk sells 1 million shares of an ETF to a client) and then hedge using the basket while monitoring overall risk exposure. If the product is not using listed underlying assets, then the system cannot work the hedge.

might be to call a large bank or a specific ETF market-making firm. When you do this, you will get the market that the specific firm you have called is willing to make. The benefits are clear: You have a relationship with this firm for research or whatever other services you require, and they are willing to utilize their firm's capital to provide you with an instantaneous execution. This can result in your trading very large blocks immediately, in a much bigger size than would have been apparent from looking at the screen market.

There are some potential downsides as well. In this scenario, you have become a captive client to the desk as far as pricing goes. Yes, you always have the ability to shop around and call several big banks for markets, but that takes time and tends to generate noise in the markets about your trade. Being a captive client means that you will be made a market that is the best that they can make within their specific situation. Let's see what might be affecting that situation. For example, a large customer might have called five seconds before you did, putting the desk in a big risk position. They might then be slightly more risk averse when making a market to you, causing them to be wider than they might have been at some other point. Or you may be calling about an ETF in which they don't trade a lot of shares or may be unfamiliar with. The market that they make could be wider than someone with more direct knowledge about the product.

It is important to also understand traders' motivation and their pay structure. Costs of trading are critical when traversing the ETF market. When you

are managing a portfolio of ETFs, your goal is to be trading at as close to fair value as is possible at all times. To do that, you must have an understanding of where things should be trading as compared to where you are getting quotes and what you are paying for risk markets.

When you call a desk and ask for risk market, you are paying a risk premium on that market. There is a risk that between the time the trader says that they will sell to you or buy from you some amount of ETF shares, their hedge has moved away from the price you traded at. To protect themselves against that slippage, they will widen their spread to a point that is competitive enough but also gives them enough cushion against loss. The risk premium is designed to protect them from slippage and hopefully even provide profits. This is typically how they get paid, via commissions and trading profits. You pay this risk premium in exchange for their taking the market risk and possibly losing money. If you don't need an immediate execution and are still using risk markets to execute, then you are possibly paying the risk premium for no reason.

Let's compare this to the way that a liquidity aggregator would handle the trade.

Liquidity Aggregators

As I mentioned earlier, the evolution of how traders provide liquidity in ETFs, and the growth in the number of ETF market-making firms, has also led to an evolution in the way customers can access that liquidity. Using a liquidity aggregator will sound the same from a process standpoint as using a broker-dealer trading desk because it still involves the customer calling up and asking for a market in a particular ETF. However, the source of the execution is very different.

Let's look at the process of executing large blocks in ETFs before the liquidity aggregators migrated to their current market positions, and then we'll see where they are today. Their role has a profound effect on the client base and is a result of client demands for best execution measurement and transparency.

In the recent past, a customer called a broker-dealer for a market in a large block of ETF shares. Since the ETF desk was making a market based on various assumptions about hedging, they would build in a risk premium as we have discussed. Basically the various levels of spreads would have looked like this:

- The basket is the first level of liquidity, and that would represent the base for the spread of a risk market.

- The ETF market-making firms would be making markets right around the basket, or their eNAV, and would present a second layer of liquidity. They build in an additional spread to cover the infrastructure costs and aim for a profit for their business.

- Last, an ETF desk could use an interdealer broker (IDB), who would talk to the other ETF desks and see where they would make markets in the ETF. Typically, their markets would be based around the basket, plus a spread to incorporate a profit to cover the bigger infrastructure typically present in a large bank.

This spread and trading infrastructure would look like Exhibit 6.3 in graphical form.

More recently, as demand has risen from a newer trading clientele for access to large block liquidity, the IDB has evolved into a liquidity aggregator. They have also shifted to occupy a position between clients and all other market participants to provide a competitive mechanism for pricing. The difference is where the spread resides. In the older form of execution, the broker-dealer trading desk was able to keep any difference in spread between where they traded against the customer and where they could potentially trade their hedge or unwind versus the various other market participants. In the newer world of liquidity aggregation, the client is able to directly reap the benefits of getting pricing from a variety of market participants. The liquidity aggregator is not adding an additional spread and is thus enabling the customer to achieve a market based on a wide variety of liquidity providers' competing markets. This results in potentially tighter prices to the client and sometimes, by combining multiple large liquidity providers, bigger sizes than possible before. The liquidity aggregator is acting as an informal market for block trading of all ETF liquidity providers.

A new version of the execution landscape looks like Exhibit 6.4.

This new landscape, where the liquidity aggregator faces the client directly, is also enabling multiple liquidity providers to participate on blocks in a way not typical when dealing with a broker-dealer. This is spreading out the risk from one participant to

show your direction to give them an indication of how they'll be trading. This takes some risk out of the equation and sometimes enables the market maker to be tighter than if they were required to quote a two-sided market,

DEFINITION:
Slippage

Slippage is when you make a market based on certain market parameters, but before you're able to get your hedge on, the prices change. If you plan to pay $9.95 for the components and then sell the resulting ETF at $10, but you end up paying $9.98, the slippage would be 3 cents.

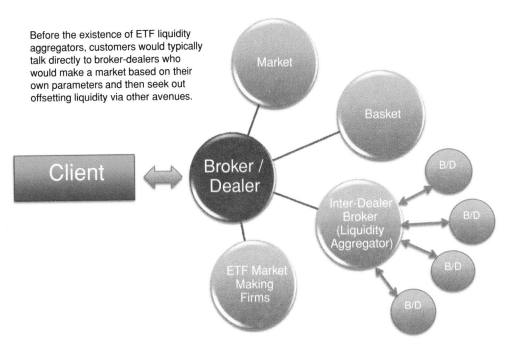

Before the existence of ETF liquidity aggregators, customers would typically talk directly to broker-dealers who would make a market based on their own parameters and then seek out offsetting liquidity via other avenues.

Exhibit 6.3 Trade Flow before Liquidity Aggregators

multiple on larger prints. From a negative perspective, this creates the need for more participants to be involved, all trying to access underlying liquidity at the same time. This can add noise to the markets. But that should be offset by assuming that multiple liquidity providers will use a variety of hedging strategies, so as

a group, they are able to provide far greater liquidity than would be possible from one desk.

This is a compelling model for trading large blocks and trying to get a good assessment of the market. It does have limits, primarily when trying to trade the underlying basket directly. If customers

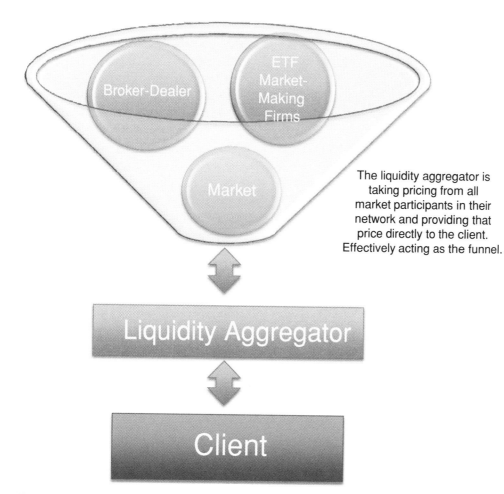

The liquidity aggregator is taking pricing from all market participants in their network and providing that price directly to the client. Effectively acting as the funnel.

Exhibit 6.4 Trade Flow with Liquidity Aggregators

want to have the basket traded on their behalf or to have a creation or redemption done for their account, they would have to speak with the portfolio trading desks of the various broker dealers who have direct access in the global markets for trading underlying equities, bonds, or currencies. Also, since the liquidity aggregators in the marketplace are agency-style traders, they are typically not able to complete leftover pieces of orders if they cannot get the entire required size. They are satisfying a strong demand from the client base for competitive pricing in a transparent manner. They have become an important part of the infrastructure for the liquidity provider community.

Trading the Underlying Basket

Another way to execute ETF trades in block size would be to have a broker execute trades in the underlying stocks and then give you the implied price in the ETF. In theory, if you are executing in the underlying stocks, there should be no difference in cost versus the ETF, except for the risk premium. What you are getting is a price based on the actual trading prices of the underlying stocks—essentially true fair value at the time of execution. If you instructed the broker to buy the whole basket at the closing price, you would be buying the ETF at NAV, assuming they were able to get those executions, and assuming cash in the fund is zero. Otherwise, to go from a basket purchase to an ETF price would require an adjustment for the cash in the fund.

When trading the underlying for an implied ETF price, you are not paying the risk premium that would be included when someone is making a market to provide an immediate execution. This is because you are assuming the risk of the market movements until the execution is complete.

For example, if the client gives the broker-dealer an order to go into the Indian market and buy the basket underlying the ETF at the close, the client is exposed to basket price moves between the time the order is given and when the local market opens and the trades can be executed. Say the client decides at 1 P.M. EST to do this trade, and the Indian markets close at 3 A.M. EST the next day, 14 hours later. The client will be exposed to the risk of 14 hours of potential market movement, but no risk premium will be charged. Many times I speak with clients who are managing a portfolio that is not time sensitive over a 24-hour period. They are running a model that gives signals to trade but is not sensitive to whether they trade today or tomorrow. Yet they are still going out to the markets and paying for risk capital and for market assumptions when they don't necessarily need to. Sometimes this is an unfortunate by-product of the legacy trade booking systems that many clients are using. To place an order for a desk to go out overnight and trade for you, and give you the execution in ETF terms the following day, you would have to have a way to book the trade today, without getting an execution until the following day. This is very difficult for the advisor client base and has forced them into using risk markets instead of being able to trade agency in the underlying. Hedge funds and other institutions have been able to do this for years because they have a night desk, or at least can reach out to the night traders at the brokerage firms and give the orders. This enables them to place the orders on the actual trade date. But it is very difficult for the advisory businesses to get around the legacy systems that restrict various trading activities.

Utilizing Algorithms

The growth in electronic trading, the speed at which people can trade, and the growth of the ETF market have all collided to drive demand for algorithmic trading in the products. In the ETF market, you have the benefit of being able to use algorithms on either the ETF itself or the underlying basket.

ETF trading volume is important to understand when you are trying to utilize algorithms for execution. If you are going to be trading a low-volume ETF using a volume weighted average price (VWAP) algorithm, for example, you need to be concerned about becoming the price driver by chasing volume. If the size in which you are trying to trade is a small fraction of the ADV of the ETF, then you can trade the product using an algorithm without having an impact on pricing.

There are also algorithms now that take advantage of the differing trading attributes of ETFs as compared to stocks. They slow down executions to try to allow liquidity providers to reload, they leave size on the bid or offer to avoid adjustment by the rest of the market, or they do various other things to try to take advantage of the fact that the ETFs trade within a community that is utilizing a wide variety of trading techniques to provide liquidity in the products. In Chapter 4, I discuss the calculation of implied daily tradable shares, a concept very important in algorithmic trading because it provides insight into how many ETF shares you may be able to execute in basket form. For an algorithm to be effective at basket trading, it needs to take the liquidity of the underlying basket into consideration and not just the ETF itself. Several firms are now starting to roll out to clients algorithmic systems that assess ETF liquidity in baskets and futures when available.

Trade Advertisement

There are ways to monitor the markets in terms of who is trading what blocks and who is trading large amounts of ETF volume. These reports can be important for understanding which firm has been active in a particular ETF. I have generated a ranking screen for all ETFs on a year-to-date basis through the end of October 2012. In Exhibit 6.5, you can see the top 22 names on that list. In the exhibit, you can see that Knight Trading had the second highest advertised volume of ETFs traded, garnering nearly 14 percent of market share. This is a substantial achievement for a firm that got into the business of facilitating ETF flow for clients in roughly early 2009. What's important to

remember is that this is an accounting of all the volume at each particular firm as self-reported. It does not distinguish between trading volume that was sent electronically versus volume that was traded in block form. There is no distinction between high-touch order flow and low-touch order flow. When the large banks report trading volumes it is often difficult to distinguish between advisor generated and institutional trades.

You can also create this report for a single ETF by changing the securities space along the left side of the screen.

Another way to look at brokerage trading activity is via the indications of interest (IOIA) and trade advertisement reporting function. Often when brokerage desks trade large blocks, they advertise them so that people who have an interest in that particular ETF will know to call them. Or a trader who is trying to do something in a particular ETF can put out an indication of interest (IOI) that gives people an idea of what they would like to do. If you wanted to see the daily trading activity in VWO for the day, you could type the line that you see in Exhibit 6.6 into your Bloomberg terminal.

Many of the major broker-dealers now have ETF market-making businesses facilitating flow for clients. There are variations between capital commitment and agency, or those with specialties like fixed income or international equities. It is important to speak with your relationship manager to get an understanding of the ETF trading desk, what type of business they specialize in, and what they do with order flow in funds

KEY POINT:

Another problem for advisors and their custodian firms is the inability to speak directly to the in-house market-making desks at the large banks. Typically, advisor order flow is routed to the execution desks dedicated to the wealth management business within a firm. Because of rules around discretionary trading and the use of firm capital, the execution desk cannot speak directly to the firm ETF market makers. This is a legacy of old-school client protection rules developed before the growth of the ETF business. Nowadays the liquidity process for ETFs relies heavily on the injection and transfer of liquidity between the basket and the fund. This also causes problems because big firms send a lot of order flow to competitors for execution and then want reciprocal trades in exchange. This can run contrary to the concepts of best execution standards for clients.

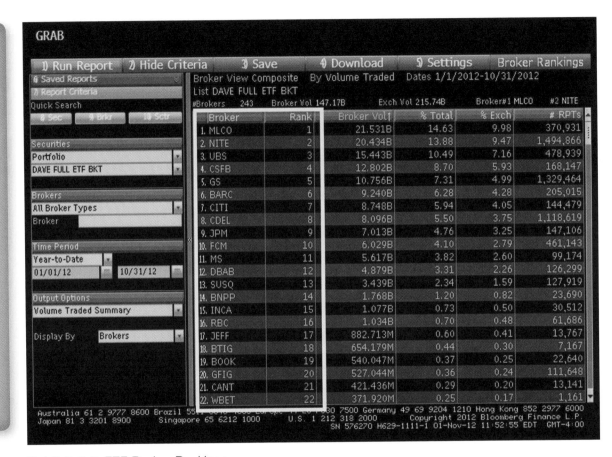

Exhibit 6.5 ETF Broker Rankings

Exhibit 6.6 Indications of Interest Keystroke

with harder-to-trade underlying baskets. Many of the firms are willing to facilitate your order flow but then will look to lay off the risk in the market, which might lead to investors not getting as tight a price as if they went to a desk that specialized in that particular fund type. Then there are broad ETF-specific firms with hundreds of traders dedicated to trading the entire spectrum of products. Many of these firms are trading very high percentages of ETF volume but are not advertising their flow because they are not trying to attract customer business in that manner.

Summary

Trading ETFs efficiently is one of the keys to utilizing the products. Investment advisors and portfolio managers who have mastered these techniques have been able to take their businesses to higher levels, producing better returns and building more diverse portfolios, than those who have not taken the time to learn these techniques. One of the keys is to have conversations with various trading counterparts before you are in the stressful moments of trading. Ensuring that your chosen liquidity providers have an understanding of your business and your goals enables you to have a mutually beneficial relationship. Throughout the book, I express the importance of trading as a component of the ETF structure. Users of the products take on the responsibility of managing their own execution in exchange for a measure of independence from the other holders of the fund. This is a key feature of the products and is really a place where users of the products can separate themselves from the pack.

Notes

1. Gary Stone and Ron Taur, "ETFs: Use the Right Tool," *Automated Trader,* Q3 2010.

> **KEY POINT:**
>
> High-touch order flow is orders that are actually handled by a trader on a desk, either by making a market or working an order in some other way. Low-touch order flow is sent electronically from the clients, and it goes directly through the firm's systems, possibly interacting with dark pools before routing out to exchanges. There is no trader manually interacting with low-touch order flow.

> **STEP-BY-STEP**
>
> Generating broker ranking reports—multibroker
>
> 1. Type RANK <GO>.
> 2. Select a time period.
> 3. Select a portfolio, or ETF list.
> 4. Hit 1 <GO> to run the report.

> **STEP-BY-STEP**
>
> Generating broker ranking reports—single broker
>
> 1. Type VWO <EQUITY> RANK <GO>.
> 2. Select a time period.
> 3. Hit 1 <GO> to run the report.

Test Yourself

1. If you ask a liquidity provider for a market in an ETF, that market is good for what time frame?
   a. One hour
   b. Several seconds to a minute
   c. The rest of the day
   d. Until you decide to trade on it several days later

2. True or false—An ETF trading desk that is willing to commit capital means that when you are buying, they are buying along with you, following your positions.

3. True or false—One way to try to minimize impact when trading a low-volume ETF is to have an execution house trade the underlying basket on your behalf.

Answers: 1. b   2. False   3. True

CHAPTER 7

Examining ETF Trading Strategies

One of the most frequent questions that I encounter in my discussions with clients is "How can I trade a large block in an ETF that has a small average daily volume?" This is going to be a high-touch order, and the ETF liquidity provider ecosystem is well adapted for facilitating this type of order flow. It's not something that can be done electronically. The environment of market regulation and high-speed systematic trading makes it somewhat impractical to show large size on the screen and expect not to be gamed by other market participants. Therefore, on-screen liquidity of an ETF is not a good indication of the size that can be traded without impact. A liquidity provider can show extremely large size in almost any ETF via a simple phone conversation.

Trading a Large Block in a Low-Volume ETF

In Exhibit 7.1, you can see the trading history page for an ETF.

In the yellow circle, you can see that the average daily volume for this ETF is 23,391 shares per day. In the red circle, you can see that on 7/6/11 the fund traded 803,561 shares. Digging deeper, you can see in Exhibit 7.2 that a block of 775,000 shares traded just after the open on that day at 9:43:54 A.M. It's also interesting that the fund only traded a total of six times that day.

So it seems that this is the case of a customer doing a trade in this fund either to enter or exit a position in

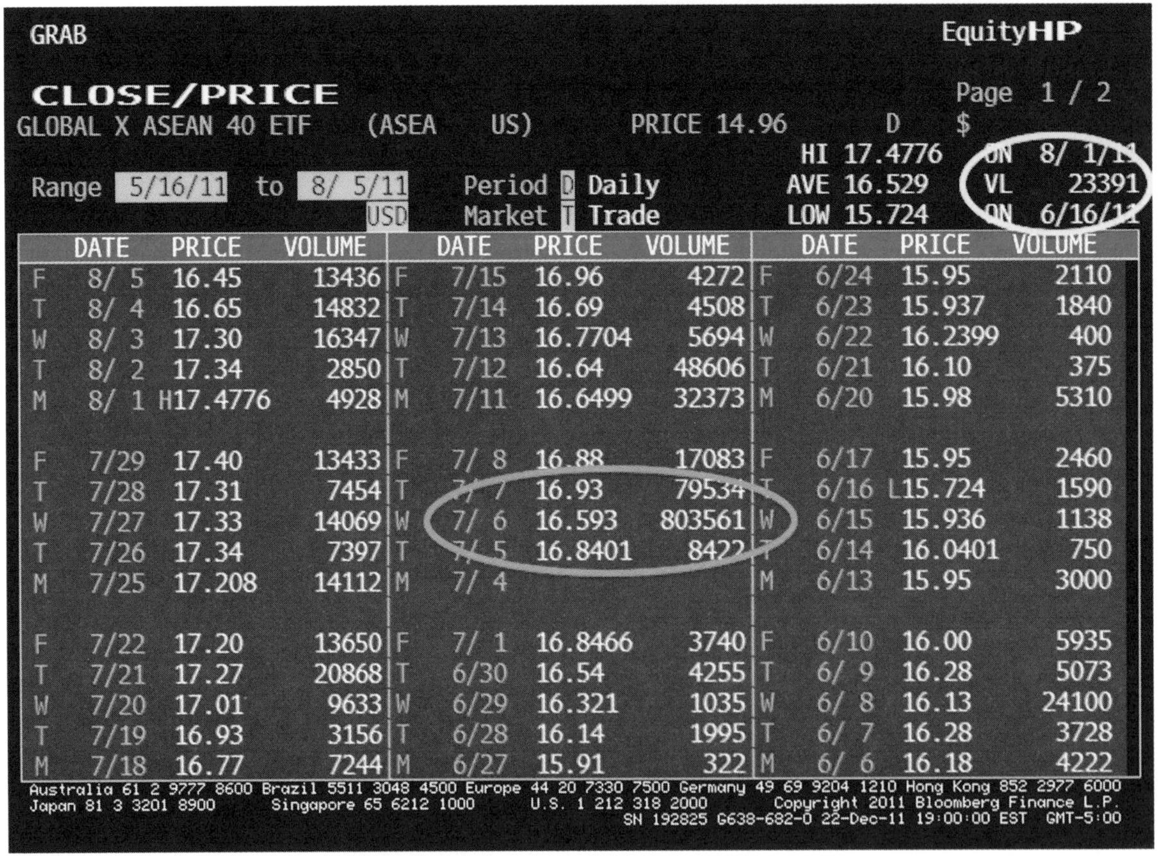

GRAB EquityHP

CLOSE/PRICE Page 1 / 2

GLOBAL X ASEAN 40 ETF (ASEA US) PRICE 14.96 D $

HI 17.4776 ON 8/ 1/11

Range 5/16/11 to 8/ 5/11 USD Period D Daily Market T Trade

AVE 16.529 VL 23391

LOW 15.724 ON 6/16/11

	DATE	PRICE	VOLUME		DATE	PRICE	VOLUME		DATE	PRICE	VOLUME
F	8/ 5	16.45	13436	F	7/15	16.96	4272	F	6/24	15.95	2110
T	8/ 4	16.65	14832	T	7/14	16.69	4508	T	6/23	15.937	1840
W	8/ 3	17.30	16347	W	7/13	16.7704	5694	W	6/22	16.2399	400
T	8/ 2	17.34	2850	T	7/12	16.64	48606	T	6/21	16.10	375
M	8/ 1	H17.4776	4928	M	7/11	16.6499	32373	M	6/20	15.98	5310
F	7/29	17.40	13433	F	7/ 8	16.88	17083	F	6/17	15.95	2460
T	7/28	17.31	7454	T	7/ 7	16.93	79534	T	6/16	L15.724	1590
W	7/27	17.33	14069	W	7/ 6	16.593	803561	W	6/15	15.936	1138
T	7/26	17.34	7397	T	7/ 5	16.8401	8422	T	6/14	16.0401	750
M	7/25	17.208	14112	M	7/ 4			M	6/13	15.95	3000
F	7/22	17.20	13650	F	7/ 1	16.8466	3740	F	6/10	16.00	5935
T	7/21	17.27	20868	T	6/30	16.54	4255	T	6/ 9	16.28	5073
W	7/20	17.01	9633	W	6/29	16.321	1035	W	6/ 8	16.13	24100
T	7/19	16.93	3156	T	6/28	16.14	1995	T	6/ 7	16.28	3728
M	7/18	16.77	7244	M	6/27	15.91	322	M	6/ 6	16.18	4222

Australia 61 2 9777 8600 Brazil 5511 3048 4500 Europe 44 20 7330 7500 Germany 49 69 9204 1210 Hong Kong 852 2977 6000
Japan 81 3 3201 8900 Singapore 65 6212 1000 U.S. 1 212 318 2000 Copyright 2011 Bloomberg Finance L.P.
SN 192825 G638-682-0 22-Dec-11 19:00:00 EST GMT-5:00

Exhibit 7.1 Checking for High-Volume Days (HP)

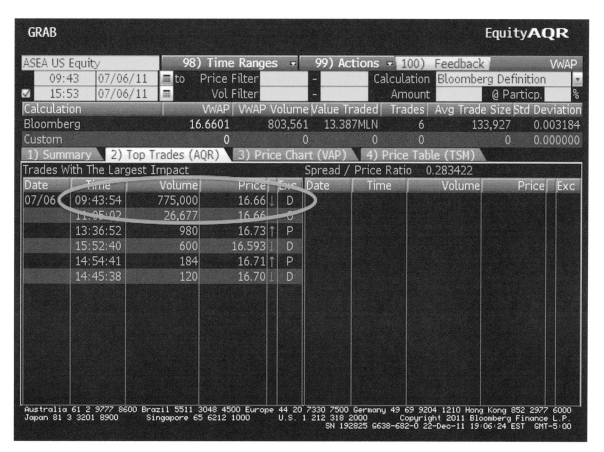

Exhibit 7.2 Checking for Large Blocks (AQR)

the fund. Since the fund does not trade a lot of volume, it would not make sense for the customer to use an algorithm to try to trade at the VWAP or some other strategy because its size would completely swamp the calculation and the order would probably not get completed anyway. Sometimes, as in the case of an advisor trading through one of the wealth platforms, it is possible to call the execution desk and get a trader who is inexperienced in the ways of ETF trading who advises that certain sizes cannot get executed based on the ADV. This is simply not the correct way to make the assessment. A history of prints to the contrary bears witness to the fact that there is still a lot of misinformation in the marketplace and that the education process needs to continue.

Another concern would be to see what kind of effect this trade might have had on the market. In Exhibit 7.3, you can see the Trade/Quote Recap (QRM) for that time period.

Since there isn't much intraday trading in this particular ETF, it's not uncommon for the spread to be wider because there are costs to trading the product in small size for a liquidity provider. In this case, there was approximately a 1 percent spread. As I mentioned earlier in this book, this is not really a concern because any large block trade is going to take place at the eNAV (implied fair value). The bid and ask are somewhat irrelevant in this scenario and in many block trade situations. Unfortunately, sometimes business media new to these products will analyze funds based on spread because that is what is most easily seen in terms of

price on the screens. You can see that the trade took place right near the middle of the spread. We still don't know whether it was a buy or sell, but at least we can see from looking at the tape that the market had not moved for the four minutes before the trade, and it seems that the wide spread was situated around the fair value of the fund.

The last piece of the puzzle, then, is to take a look at shares outstanding. In Exhibit 7.4, you can see the shares outstanding for the fund over the same time period.

On the day following the trade, the shares outstanding increased by 800,000. The fund's creation unit size is 50,000 shares so an authorized participant put through a 16-unit creation. Bloomberg provides you with the creation unit size of each ETF on the ETF's DES3 page. It is clear now that the client was a buyer and bought a large block from a liquidity provider who then turned around and created new shares with the issuer by buying and delivering the underlying basket. Since an AP can only create or redeem in round lots with the issuer, more than the client block was created to facilitate settlement, and the market maker sold off the difference of 25,000, plus some they might have had in residual, which probably explains the 26,677 print that took place an hour after the big block. We can assume that the market maker will probably have no more ASEA shares on their books.

Last, it should be noted that the client bought a block of shares that represented three times the AUM of the fund. Essentially the client bought $12.9 million

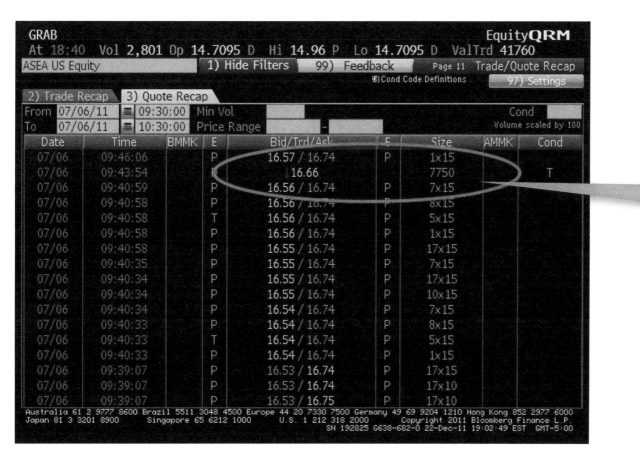

Exhibit 7.3 Checking the Spread (QRM)

GRAB   Index **HP**

CLOSE/PRICE   Page 1 / 2
ASEASO   Glbal X Ftse Asean 40 SO   PRICE 1400.000
                                                         HI 1200.0000 ON 7/28/11
Range 5/16/11 to 8/ 5/11   Period D Daily   AVE   574.1379
                         USD   Market M mid/trd   LOW   250.0000 ON 7/ 7/11

	DATE	PRICE	VOLUME		DATE	PRICE	VOLUME		DATE	PRICE	VOLUME
F	8/ 5	1150.000		F	7/15	1150.000		F	6/24	250.0000	
T	8/ 4	1150.000		T	7/14	1100.000		T	6/23	250.0000	
W	8/ 3	1150.000		W	7/13	1100.000		W	6/22	250.0000	
T	8/ 2	1150.000		T	7/12	1100.000		T	6/21	250.0000	
M	8/ 1	1150.000		M	7/11	1100.000		M	6/20	250.0000	
F	7/29	1150.000		F	7/ 8	1050.000		F	6/17	250.0000	
T	7/28	H1200.000		T	7/ 7	L250.0000		T	6/16	250.0000	
W	7/27	1200.000		W	7/ 6	250.0000		W	6/15	250.0000	
T	7/26	1200.000		T	7/ 5	250.0000		T	6/14	250.0000	
M	7/25	1200.000		M	7/ 4			M	6/13	250.0000	
F	7/22	1150.000		F	7/ 1	250.0000		F	6/10	250.0000	
T	7/21	1150.000		T	6/30	250.0000		T	6/ 9	250.0000	
W	7/20	1150.000		W	6/29	250.0000		W	6/ 8	250.0000	
T	7/19	1150.000		T	6/28	250.0000		T	6/ 7	250.0000	
M	7/18	1150.000		M	6/27	250.0000		M	6/ 6	250.0000	

Here is the creation of 775,000 shares, the following day.

Australia 61 2 9777 8600 Brazil 5511 3048 4500 Europe 44 20 7330 7500 Germany 49 69 9204 1210 Hong Kong 852 2977 6000
Japan 81 3 3201 8900   Singapore 65 6212 1000   U.S. 1 212 318 2000   Copyright 2011 Bloomberg Finance L.P.
                                       SN 192825 G638-682-0 22-Dec-11 19:05:35 EST GMT-5:00

Exhibit 7.4 Looking for Shares Outstanding Changes (SO HP)
Reprinted with permission from Bloomberg. Copyright 2012 Bloomberg L.P. All rights reserved.

of a fund that only had about $4.1 million in assets at the time of the purchase. Then, through the process of creation, the client assets came into the fund so that at the end the fund had total assets of approximately $17 million. The client then represented only about 75 percent of the AUM, when it seemed that going into the trade, they would be about three times the size of the fund. You can see the AUM by going to the DES page of any ETF.

To make a market in that size, a market maker typically has a correlating hedge to use in the product. So when selling an Indian ETF, they might be buying another ETF that holds Indian equities. They might hold a basket of ETFs that, in various weights, correlates well to the movements of the Indian basket. They might even be using a basket of the Indian ADRs that trade in the U.S. markets as hedges. The market maker is trying to calculate an eNAV of this basket while the Indian names are closed and trade a proxy vehicle as a hedge until the Indian market opens and they can then unwind their hedge. To that fair value calculation, they add a buffer to account for the risk involved if their hedge does not track well or if some other market event causes their hedge to provide a different return than the ETF. I refer to this additional buffer as a risk premium that the client is paying for to get the instantaneous execution on the large block. This risk premium is embedded in the price that the market maker shows to the client for trading and is where competition becomes important, because different trading firms and different traders have various levels

of risk tolerance and fair value assessments. This is why two traders can make very different prices in the same ETF at the same time, especially on ETFs where the underlying is not immediately accessible. This can be used as a valuable tool by investors.

If you would like to understand the price your market maker is quoting, you can ask for their estimated fair value, as well as how much they are charging for the risk premium. But keep in mind that these are just the assessments of one particular trader. Sometimes, however, a trader may not want to break down the variables in their pricing because their risk models and trading assumptions are proprietary information that is key to their profitability. Regardless of how or why a liquidity provider makes a price, the benefit to the client is the option for instantaneous execution on a size that is seemingly too big for the screen markets. An ETF trading in U.S. markets with holdings in India, for example, is trading at prices that are the result of all the various market participants making estimates of where the underlying basket will be trading when the underlying market next opens. It is a price discovery vehicle. Its price is showing the consensus of where people think it should be, but that can often be far from the reality of where that underlying basket actually trades hours later. It is important to decide whether you need to pay the risk premium for the immediate execution or to take on the market risk during the time lag until complete execution. This is yet another reason to understand what you are trading, to have an estimated fair value yourself so you can

> **KEY POINT:**
>
> As can be seen from this scenario, when you buy a large block in an ETF, you are typically not taking another client out of their ETF position. In other words, you are not buying shares that exist in the market. You are most likely buying from a liquidity provider who will be having new shares created to represent your additional investment assets. This is the beauty of continuous issuance and its work as a release valve on the pressures of supply and demand.

benchmark your price, and to know what is included in the price you are paying. This works to the benefit of smaller investors as well because spreads on a wide variety of popular ETFs tend toward a penny (the smallest quoted increment) in small size. This can be tighter than it would cost to actually trade the basket, as we saw earlier in this book.

Negotiating Your ETF Trading Prices

It is surprising to me how many investors in significantly sized blocks of ETFs agree to trade at whatever price is offered to them. In a sense, that is the equivalent of walking into a car dealer, without doing any price research, and paying whatever the salesman says you have to pay for the car without any haggling. The block trading market in ETFs, where liquidity providers make markets in large size to the advisor community, is a negotiable marketplace.

Let's clarify a few terms before I go into a further explanation of what I mean. When you are trading in very small size in ETFs, either 100 shares or 1,000 shares, or even sometimes 5,000 shares, your order flow typically interacts with other order flows electronically. If you see an offer for 1,000 shares at $10.10 and you have 1,000 shares to buy, you have the option to take the offer or bid lower for your size. You can certainly bid $10.05 for your 1,000 shares. It will be a function of the market and the other sellers that can see your bid as to whether you get filled. Or you can

just take the 1,000 shares offered at $10.10 and move on to whatever else you have to do that day.

If you are trading in larger size, what is typically referred to as a block, which usually means more than 5,000 or 10,000 shares, often you will be trading against an ETF liquidity provider, usually via the phone. In this case, if you have a block of ETF shares to execute, in many ETFs you would be well served to call up a liquidity provider to get a market in the fund, so that you can trade the whole block at once. If you're an advisor and you work on a platform, most of the time your execution desk will have contacts at a variety of ETF liquidity providers, and they will be able to call them on your behalf to get bids and offers for your block trade. This means that if you have 25,000 shares to buy in a particular ETF, you can call your execution desk and ask them to get you a market in that particular fund. What you are asking is for the execution desk to reach out to a liquidity provider and come back to you with a bid and an offer in your size (25,000 shares). It is at this point that investors typically don't realize they have a third choice between the most obvious two responses.

The most obvious two choices you have when your execution desk comes back to you with a market in the ETF are:

1. To trade at that price.
2. To not trade at the price shown.

Typically, when a customer chooses the second choice, it's because the price appears to be too high versus the quoted market. You do have a third option, however. The third option that you have is to negotiate against the offer. This requires some knowledge about what might be the fair value of the fund you are trading. It also involves the risk that if you try to negotiate against a shown offer, it may possibly be rescinded. Here's an example: You have 25,000 shares to buy in a fund. You call up your execution platform desk, or you call a liquidity provider directly (either works), and you ask for a market in 25,000 shares. Say the market you are quoted is 50.05 bid and offered at 50.15. You can say, "Okay, I buy those," and you will be buying the 25,000 shares at 50.15, or you can say, "No thank you" and hang up the phone. Your third option is to say, "I'll pay you 50.10 for 25,000 shares." At this point, the liquidity provider who is making the market gets the choice. They can say, "Sold" and sell to you at the lower level, they can offer at some better level in between the two (maybe at 50.12), or (and this is the potential risk) they are perfectly justified in moving their offer higher now, perhaps being willing to sell only at 50.17. This is the risk of negotiating and really happens only in an extreme case. More typically, if the liquidity provider doesn't want to trade at a better price, they will just reiterate their first offer.

I had a client situation that demonstrates how this process can possibly save you a lot of money in your ETF executions. The client was a buyer of several hundred thousand shares of an ETF. They called their platform execution desk and asked for a market. The desk reached out to a liquidity provider, and the client was shown an offer in the fund that was 8 cents above the offer that was being quoted on the screen (those were for small size). At that moment, the difference between the quoted offer and the offer for the larger size seemed too large for the client, who said, "No thank you" and then called my office. We leave the pricing of funds up to the professionals who are actually going to be offsetting the risk and respect their judgment tremendously. We do perform sanity checks, however, and help clients understand the rationale behind pricing they are seeing. In this case, we advised the client that if they thought the offer was too far away, they could, and maybe should, show a counterbid to see if the liquidity provider might be interested in trading at a better price. The client called them back and showed them a slightly lower bid for the shares. The level was acceptable, and the trade was executed at only 4 cents above the quoted offer. This all happened in the span of two minutes, so the market had not moved. The client saved a significant amount of money on that particular execution and, even more important, felt comfortable with the price paid. And the client developed a skill to use going forward. In addition, the liquidity provider got to make the sale, which is their goal in the end. All sides of the transaction were happy.

Negotiation is not going to help you all the time, and sometimes it won't be needed at all. But it's powerful to know that the business of pricing large blocks and the prices at which those trades take place are negotiable.

Executing Daily Rebalances in Low-Volume ETFs

Another issue that arises in the ETF marketplace now is that big investors are able to get large trades executed in low-volume ETFs but are having difficulty managing their daily cash and position changes when executing smaller size in the same funds.

Let me explain the situation further before offering a solution. In our example, the client is an asset manager, either a registered investment advisor (RIA) or a pension or endowment, running a portfolio of ETF positions. They have decided that this particular ETF with the Indian underlying provides the right exposure for their objectives. For our example, we'll use a hypothetical fund. The fund trades only 9,800 shares per day on average. The ETF has about $75 million in assets. The client is intending to make an initial investment of $50 million dollars at an ETF price of approximately $60, meaning they will be buying 833,000 shares at first. They also figure that on a daily basis they have somewhere around $1 to 2 million worth of rebalance business to handle. So every day they will want to be trading somewhere in the range of 15,000 to 30,000 shares, which is approximately 1.5 to 3 times the ADV. They are concerned because they see a wide spread in the fund of roughly 20 cents and don't want to be at the mercy of the market makers on a daily basis when trying to get their orders executed.

Standardized liquidity has not been achieved across all ETFs, but a sophisticated investor will not let a wide spread and low volume deter them from using a product. The goal for this client is to trade at a consistent spread around fair value daily. Remember from earlier in the book that many market makers have slightly different calculated eNAVs because of differing risk assessments, financing fees, and other assumptions. Some market participants pay different amounts to trade and at different speeds, which also plays into the calculations. This is why it is incumbent on the client to develop an understanding of how fair value is calculated and to develop a relationship with a broker to understand their process for determining their trading price around fair value.

I have seen large blocks of ETFs hit the tape at prices far beyond fair value, prices much worse than other competing liquidity providers would have been willing to trade. Some clients are calling three or more different liquidity providers in ETFs and asking each for their best market in the ETF. This can work against clients by introducing market noise. Clients are quoting numerous trading desks far in advance of the execution and tipping off the entire street about their trading intentions. They are giving the liquidity providers time to adjust their positions and the markets before the trade gets to the tape. This can all be working against them. These clients might also be using the ETF market spread as the basis for determining good pricing, which, as I stated, is not always a good barometer, especially since the spread can be moving around based on the pending trade.

The solution to this is to make an arrangement with a broker to trade at a fixed distance from calculated fair value every day. How does this work? Both parties must agree to the fair value calculation that is being used. The liquidity provider will be able to buy or sell the ETF and put on a hedge to lock in the trade. The distance that execution takes place from the fair value is meant to accommodate revenue to the liquidity provider if the commission is not explicitly paid, slippage on tracking, and cost of managing the positions over time, since they will potentially be held for several days or longer before creation or redemption can be processed. This type of process removes any variability from the marketplace on executing these daily orders because the client trading in the U.S. market is trading at a price considered to be fair value, regardless of the spread. Instead of continually asking for a bid or offer in an ETF, you are able to discuss fair value of the fund and trade based around that price.

There are several stipulations that would be needed for an agreement like this to work properly:

1. Both parties must agree to a model price, also known as fair value or eNAV. This is something that has not been pursued aggressively enough over the last 10 years. If you are managing several hundred million dollars or more in ETFs, then you should be calculating fair values as a part of your business to understand where the street is pricing the funds. If you have your own models, you will undoubtedly come to a different price from your counterparty, but you can then have an educated conversation about the nuances of each. There is no liquidity provider that is trading an ETF without a calculated eNAV, and therefore to be on the same playing field, you should be as well.

2. This must be a long-term agreement. This is not an arrangement where multiple liquidity providers around the street will agree to trade with you at a fixed distance from fair value and you retain the potential to play between the various fair values you get. Part of the intrinsic agreement involved here is that the counterparty knows that you trade with them daily, but nobody else on the street knows this is happening. This enables the counterparty to position their portfolio properly and manage the position. This works for you as well, because you are still trading at fair value plus or minus the agreed-upon spread, with the added convenience of making only one phone call for the best price. The liquidity provider is managing a long-term position because you are trading in less than a creation unit, so they are unable to simply flatten the position every night.

3. This type of arrangement comes from a partnership. Your liquidity provider counterparty must understand that their role is to help you achieve your goals as a client. In return, you must provide loyalty, trust, and an understanding of the business goals of an ETF liquidity provider. If you are always setting liquidity providers up in blind competition for your business each time you do

> ### KEY POINT:
> Clients can arrange with ETF liquidity providers to trade at fixed levels around some agreed-upon ETF fair value calculation. This enables both parties to achieve goals of limiting risk, eliminating market noise, and facilitating transactions.

a trade, then no client-provider relationship will be developed, and therefore there is minimal good will. Good will and the potential for repeat business usually yield better pricing.

4. The trickiest part of this arrangement is that at times you may potentially be trading at prices that are beyond the displayed screen prices. To understand this, envision the fund price on the screen showing 20.10 bid and offered at 20.30, while the fair value for the fund is 20.40, based on your agreed-upon calculation. You have an agreement in place where you trade 3 cents around fair value, so in this scenario, you could be buying at 20.43, and selling at 20.37. If you are a seller, you will feel great because you are essentially causing your liquidity provider to be paying 20.37, .07 above the offer, which is contrary to their nature. If you are a buyer, however, you will be paying 20.43, which is .13 above the offer. This is contrary to the nature of a client. In reality, since you're trading at a calculated fair value daily, this is more important than the prices being displayed on the screens. Regulations, however, require the liquidity provider to sweep the top of book to print your trade at the agreed-upon price if your price is outside the NBBO. This means if you are a buyer at 20.43, the liquidity provider has to buy all the quoted offers between 20.30 and 20.43 to print your trade. You and the trader need to agree who gets to keep the cheaper purchases; that is, either you get a price improvement or the liquidity provider gets some

of their hedge on at cheaper prices. This will only work if the depth of book is light and the sum of the quoted offers is less than your trade.

This solution for executing order flow removes the variability of managing a large execution with daily or frequent rebalances. I would have been happy to agree to this as a trader, and there were situations in the past where I did agree to trade at fixed distances from fair value. But it must be understood that this takes place in the context of a relationship between a client and their broker. If there is no understanding of each party's business, then this type of scenario cannot work.

Assessing the Impact of an ETF Trade

Since the market environment changes on a subsecond basis, it is always difficult to determine the market impact of a particular trade. As markets move throughout the day, these changes inevitably have an impact on liquidity and spreads.

One method that people use to assess potential market impact is the portfolio trading assessment algorithms. These are also sometimes known as pretrade analytics.

These are systems that take the past history of variables, such as volumes and volatility in stocks, ETFs, or derivatives, and attempt to determine what type of liquidity or impact might occur in the future. In many stock executions, these algorithms are very effective.

However, they are sometimes lacking in the ETF markets for a variety of reasons. For one, they do not include various market makers that have not participated in the past but are now active in providing ETF liquidity. If the algorithms are looking only at the volume of the ETF itself, the entire liquidity scenario is not being accurately explained. The liquidity of the underlying and proxy hedge vehicles that allows the market maker to provide liquidity in the ETF is what algorithms cannot predict. The algorithms thus typically underestimate potential liquidity and overestimate potential costs, rendering both clients and other market participants continually surprised at the liquidity that shows up in particular large prints. It is wiser to understand the liquidity picture of the underlying and any proxy hedges to get a better idea of price impact.

Exhibit 7.5 shows the transaction cost analysis screen (TCA) for an ETF I used as an example previously. As we saw earlier in this chapter, the fund traded a block of 775,000 shares right in the middle of the displayed spread on 7/6/11. In the yellow highlighted box, you can see the pretrade analysis for the same fund in the same amount of shares. Bloomberg calculations estimate that there would be a 19.8 percent impact to the price of the fund by trying to buy 775,000 shares, almost $3 of price move. Part of the problem with this algorithm is that it is trying to estimate without understanding that the underlying, the Asian basket, is closed or that there are other hedges that might correlate well to the fund. It seems to be looking at the volume of the ETF itself.

Liquidity in the ETF will be limited by the liquidity of the underlying assets, whatever they may be, and the ease with which market participants can trade those assets or trade correlating hedges. Beyond that, I think one of the best ways to assess potential market impact is to look at past trades of similar size and see how they impacted the markets.

I use a variety of Bloomberg screens for funds to walk through a low-tech liquidity analysis of big blocks in several ETFs. Those screens are HP—which shows the daily volume and price of an ETF, AQR—which shows for a specific date range the largest blocks and the price and time at which they traded, and QR, quote recap, which shows the printed trades of an ETF and the printed IV for the ETVIV ticker. Last, I use QRM to see what the bid-ask spread was in the market when the block traded.

In the following examples, I show three ETFs with an analysis of a large block trade in each and what visual impact its trade had in the market.

Scenario 1: A Large Block in a Single Currency ETF

The first screen is the HP screen for a single currency ETF, in Exhibit 7.6. By looking on the top right, I can see that the ETF typically traded 274,496 average shares per day over the last year, or a notional amount of roughly $7 million dollars per day. If I scan each day, I can see that on 8/1/11, the fund traded 3,214,228 shares, significantly more than its ADV.

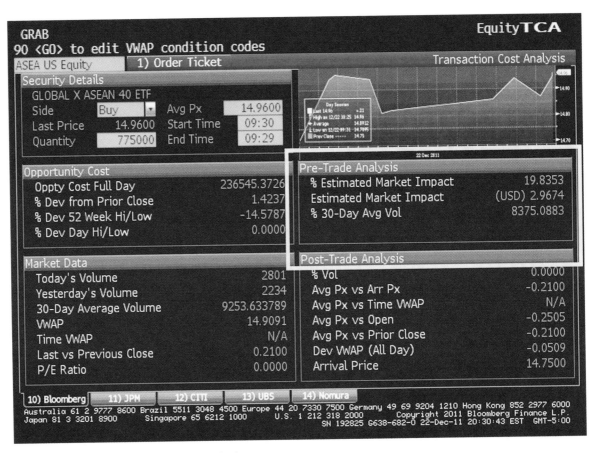

Exhibit 7.5 Transaction Cost Analysis

GRAB   EquityHP

CLOSE/PRICE
WISDOMTREE CHINA YUAN FU (CYB   US)   PRICE 25.30   Y $ Page 1 / 1

Range 6/27/11   to 8/26/11   Period D Daily   HI 25.2773   ON 8/16/11
                          USD   Market T Trade   AVE 24.9883   VL   362991
                                                        LOW 24.8174   ON 7/12/11

	DATE	PRICE	VOLUME		DATE	PRICE	VOLUME		DATE	PRICE	VOLUME
F	8/26	25.2186	129392	F	8/ 5	24.8859	314509	F	7/15	24.8859	330960
T	8/25	25.1892	86328	T	8/ 4	24.925	222394	T	7/14	24.8663	260251
W	8/24	25.2088	164130	W	8/ 3	24.9642	176780	W	7/13	24.8467	287151
T	8/23	25.2382	292027	T	8/ 2	24.9709	567241	T	7/12	L24.8174	311272
M	8/22	25.199	61462	M	8/ 1	24.9446	3214228	M	7/11	24.8467	359787
F	8/19	25.2284	351909	F	7/29	24.9642	203882	F	7/ 8	24.8859	221134
T	8/18	25.199	214073	T	7/28	24.9739	485570	T	7/ 7	24.8761	232205
W	8/17	25.2382	217386	W	7/27	24.9837	161963	W	7/ 6	24.8565	578560
T	8/16	H25.2773	808599	T	7/26	24.9348	101852	T	7/ 5	24.8957	222687
M	8/15	25.2577	231299	M	7/25	24.925	56151	M	7/ 4		
F	8/12	25.2773	469977	F	7/22	24.9054	222156	F	7/ 1	24.925	105097
T	8/11	25.1795	413426	T	7/21	24.8859	273385	T	6/30	24.8761	120748
W	8/10	25.0033	560686	W	7/20	24.8671	132393	W	6/29	24.8565	212975
T	8/ 9	24.9054	226225	T	7/19	24.8369	155713	T	6/28	24.8565	919206
M	8/ 8	24.9446	549441	M	7/18	24.8369	407599	M	6/27	24.8272	337413

Australia 61 2 9777 8600 Brazil 5511 3048 4500 Europe 44 20 7330 7500 Germany 49 69 9204 1210 Hong Kong 852 2977 6000
Japan 81 3 3201 8900   Singapore 65 6212 1000   U.S. 1 212 318 2000   Copyright 2012 Bloomberg Finance L.P.
                                        SN 192825 G509-406-0 04-Jan-12 19:55:09 EST GMT-5:00

Exhibit 7.6 Isolating High-Volume Days (HP)
Reprinted with permission from Bloomberg. Copyright 2012 Bloomberg L.P. All rights reserved.

Next, I want to understand what the composition of that volume was on the day. In Exhibit 7.7, I show the AQR screen for that trading day. You can see a list of the trades for the day sorted by volume. On this particular day, there was one large block of 1,624,555 shares that traded at 9:48:55 A.M. Later in the day at 14:51:24, it also traded a block of 833,491 shares. Then, in Exhibit 7.8, we will look at the bid and ask spread at the time of the trade.

The QRM screen function on Bloomberg enables investors to see the bid, ask, trade price, and size on a running basis throughout each trading day. This makes it reasonably simple to decipher what might be happening in large trades when they occur. You can see in Exhibit 7.8 that at 9:48:55 A.M., the time we learned about from the AQR screen, that the block of 1,624,555 (truncated to 1,625k) did indeed trade at a price of 25.50. At the time of 9:48:51 (4 seconds before the trade printed to the tape) the market was showing a bid and ask spread of 25.54 bid for and 25.55 offered (the asking price). This shows that there was a 1-penny spread in the ETF, but if you look at the size, you can see 50 × 30, which indicates there were only 5,000 shares bid for and 3,000 shares offered. This displayed market would make it seem that trying to trade a block of more than a million shares would be an impossible task or would have a tremendous impact on the price. But at 9:48:55, you can see the block print of 1.6 million shares at 25.50, 4 cents below the published bid. Using the simple calculation of .04 / 25.50 shows that the price of the trade was .0015 percent (15bps) below the bid at the time of trading.

The size of the block was for ~$41 million, significantly more than the typical daily notional traded in the fund, with significantly less impact than an algorithm would have predicted, given the volume of the ETF.

It is important to understand that you cannot extract how much impact a trade multiple times that size would have on a linear basis. It really depends on how much liquidity is in the hedge and at what levels and on how good your liquidity provider is at positioning a particular ETF at that point in time. There is a valid argument that the block could have been three times the size it was, or even greater, and could have traded at the same price. Again, a lot can depend on the depth of liquidity in the hedge and the underlying.

Scenario 2: A Large Block in a Bond ETF

Let's take a look at another example, an emerging market bond ETF, and see what else can be learned from information gathering. In Exhibit 7.9, we see the HP screen for another ETF. This fund has traded an average daily volume of 272,106 shares, approximately $14 million daily. By scanning across the volume numbers, you can see that on 9/27/11 the fund traded 4,352,425 shares.

Digging deeper into the AQR screen for that day, Exhibit 7.10, you can see that the fund traded a block of 3,949,735 shares at 10:35:20 A.M., at a price of $48.72. This was the largest block trade of the day, roughly 28 times the size of the next largest trade, which was a smaller block of 136,369 shares.

GRAB   Equity**AQR**

CYB US Equity		98) Time Ranges ▾	99) Actions ▾	100) Feedback	VWAP
09:30	08/01/11 ▣ to	Price Filter	-	Calculation Bloomberg Definition ▾	
✓ 16:00	08/01/11 ▣	Vol Filter	-	Amount	@ Particp. %

Calculation	VWAP	VWAP Volume	Value Traded	Trades	Avg Trade Size	Std Deviation
Bloomberg	24.9445	3,214,228	80.177MLN	939	3,423	0.024928
Custom	0	0	0	0	0	0.000000

1) Summary **2) Top Trades (AQR)** **3) Price Chart (VAP)** **4) Price Table (TSM)**

Trades With The Largest Impact   Spread / Price Ratio 0.011858   Page 1/2 ◁ ▷

Date	Time	Volume	Price	Exc	Date	Time	Volume	Price	Exc
08/01	09:48:55	1,624,555	24.9544 ↓	D	08/01	15:57:36	8,000	24.9544	T
	14:51:24	833,491	24.9054	D		15:59:44	7,800	24.9446	P
	15:59:44	25,800	24.9446	P		15:56:38	7,800	24.9544	K
	15:19:58	19,200	24.9544	P		15:54:30	7,700	24.9544	P
	15:54:30	11,800	24.9544	T		12:59:01	7,500	24.9837	T
	15:57:36	10,000	24.9544	P		15:57:38	7,400	24.9544	K
	15:53:52	9,800	24.9544	P		15:54:30	7,300	24.9544	P
	15:53:48	9,800	24.9544	P		15:44:42	7,300	24.9544	J
	15:53:46	9,800	24.9544	P		15:44:42	7,300	24.9544	J
	15:53:50	9,700	24.9544	P		15:56:38	7,000	24.9544	T
	15:38:42	9,300	24.9544	P		15:57:38	6,800	24.9544	T
	15:38:40	9,300	24.9544	P		13:00:13	6,067	24.9837	K
	15:57:38	9,200	24.9544	P		15:56:43	6,000	24.9544	K
	15:38:38	8,175	24.9544	P		15:59:44	5,000	24.9446	P

Australia 61 2 9777 8600 Brazil 5511 3048 4500 Europe 44 20 7330 7500 Germany 49 69 9204 1210 Hong Kong 852 2977 6000
Japan 81 3 3201 8900   Singapore 65 6212 1000   U.S. 1 212 318 2000   Copyright 2012 Bloomberg Finance L.P.
SN 225124 H621-303-0 04-Jan-12 20:01:32 EST GMT-5:00

Exhibit 7.7 Checking for Large Blocks (AQR)

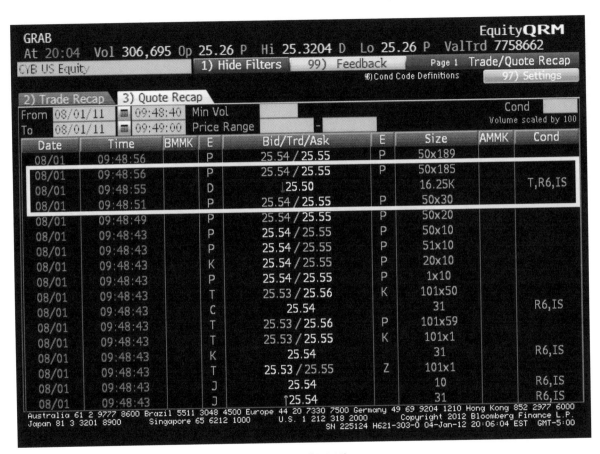

Exhibit 7.8 Checking Distance from the Market (QRM)
Reprinted with permission from Bloomberg. Copyright 2012 Bloomberg L.P. All rights reserved.

GRAB   EquityHP

CLOSE/PRICE
WISDOMTREE EMRG MKTS DEB (ELD   US)   PRICE 49.10   P $ Page 1 / 1

Range 8/29/11 to 10/28/11   Period D Daily   HI 53.7866   ON 9/ 1/11
                        USD   Market T Trade   AVE 50.4713   VL   411164
                                                   LOW 47.1531   ON 9/22/11

	DATE	PRICE	VOLUME		DATE	PRICE	VOLUME		DATE	PRICE	VOLUME
F	10/28	51.4689	204129	F	10/ 7	49.0169	673458	F	9/16	51.299	165215
T	10/27	51.4589	318961	T	10/ 6	48.9334	276317	T	9/15	51.6387	374308
W	10/26	50.1701	217961	W	10/ 5	48.352	262693	W	9/14	51.3989	297205
T	10/25	49.9204	166919	T	10/ 4	47.5228	458103	T	9/13	51.8884	175006
M	10/24	50.0811	150242	M	10/ 3	47.6526	164908	M	9/12	52.1838	267689
F	10/21	49.7406	163384	F	9/30	48.0622	319654	F	9/ 9	52.9274	389880
T	10/20	49.5288	225773	T	9/29	48.332	169273	T	9/ 8	53.357	407844
W	10/19	50.0303	154512	W	9/28	48.1122	478090	W	9/ 7	53.5967	610675
T	10/18	50.1002	114868	T	9/27	48.8914	4352425	T	9/ 6	53.377	306507
M	10/17	50.0503	76431	M	9/26	47.9424	730666		9/ 5		
F	10/14	50.4399	122287	F	9/23	48.3919	248349	F	9/ 2	53.6966	191714
T	10/13	50.0702	188188	T	9/22	L47.1531	761644	T	9/ 1	H53.7866	289890
W	10/12	50.2501	261585	W	9/21	48.9813	874319	W	8/31	53.7866	370922
T	10/11	49.7506	139808	T	9/20	50.0802	460181	T	8/30	53.7566	293952
M	10/10	49.8305	163555	M	9/19	50.1002	780744	M	8/29	53.6267	270998

Australia 61 2 9777 8600 Brazil 5511 3048 4500 Europe 44 20 7330 7500 Germany 49 69 9204 1210 Hong Kong 852 2977 6000
Japan 81 3 3201 8900   Singapore 65 6212 1000   U.S. 1 212 318 2000   Copyright 2012 Bloomberg Finance L.P.
                                            SN 225124 H621-303-0 04-Jan-12 20:10:41 EST GMT-5:00

Exhibit 7.9 Checking for High-Volume Days (HP)

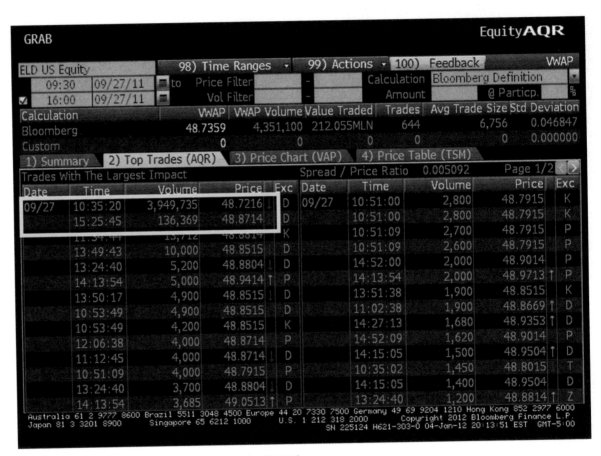

Exhibit 7.10 Checking for Large Blocks (AQR)

Looking at the QRM screen for the block trade, in Exhibit 7.11, you can see the print of the trade (truncated to 3,950k) at 10:35:20 at a price of $48.77. You can see the previous eight seconds of quotes and trades on this screen. At 10:35:19, you can see that the bid-ask spread was somewhat wide at 48.80–49.09, with very small size showing. The iteration of this quote changed six times in one second with the largest size at 1 × 9, which represents 100 shares bid for and 900 shares offered. You can see that the fund traded two lots of 100 shares, one lot at 48.82 and one lot at 48.81 just prior to the print. At about 10:35:12, eight seconds before the large print, the market was 48.81 bid for 100 shares. The various exchanges are also represented on this screen. In this case, the T represents NASDAQ Intermarket, and the P represents NYSE Arca exchanges.

We see a print of approximately $192 million notional taking place 3 cents below the published bid. This is .00061 percent, or 6bps, below the bid. Thus the impact of a trade that is almost 14 times the average daily volume of the fund is only six basis points.

There is another way to assess market impact, but it includes a variety of assumptions of which the customer must be aware. In the following screen shot, Exhibit 7.12, I display the QR screen for the published indicative value for the same fund at the time of the trade. One thing to be aware of is that the indicative value is published on a 15-second time lag. Another is that the indicative value is based on the closing price of the underlying basket. In the case of this fund, which holds bonds from emerging markets, most of those underlying bonds are not trading at 10:35 A.M. EST. This means the indicative value is a representation of the last traded value of the underlying, with a real-time spot-rate currency adjustment to present a USD value. It's not actually representing where the fund should be trading when the underlying are closed. This distinction must be made to understand how to use the ticking IV of a fund. If the underlying were domestic stocks, the only lag would be 15 seconds, and using it would be a somewhat practical way to assess whether the trade was in line with fund value. In this case, the IV is about 30 basis points above the trade price. It would be incorrect to refer to this trade having taken place at a discount because of the timing difference between the bond close and when the fund is trading.

Next we will analyze a trade in a currency basket ETF to see what a large-size print may look like on the tape.

Scenario 3: A Large Block in a Currency Basket ETF

Let's again start with a look at the HP screen of the fund to find a suitable day with large volume. In Exhibit 7.13, we can see an average daily volume of 271,053 shares, equaling out to a notional of approximately $6 million daily. While there are several days with significantly higher volume than the average, on 9/12/11 the fund traded more than 4 million shares, making that day a suitable candidate for our analysis.

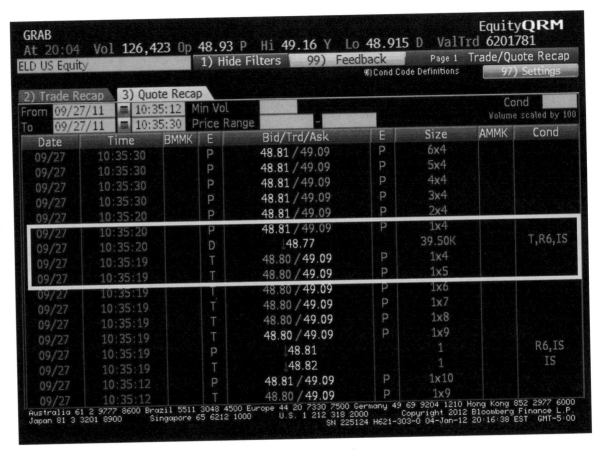

Exhibit 7.11 Checking Distance from the Market (QRM)
Reprinted with permission from Bloomberg. Copyright 2012 Bloomberg L.P. All rights reserved.

GRAB
DELAY 20:00 Vol 0 Op 49.0886   Hi 49.1623   Lo 49.0281   Prev 49.2113   Index **QR**

Trade Recap

Time `10:36`   Min Vol   Page 1
Date `9/27`   Price Range [   ] To [   ] High   49.0228 Low   48.2681   USD
ELDIV   WTree Emerg Loc Debt IV   PRICE 49.1465

Time	Price	Time	Price	Time	Price	Time	Price	Time	Price
10:36↑	48.9513	10:32↓	48.9585	10:27↓	48.9591	10:23↑	48.9463	10:18↑	48.9404
10:36↓	48.9498	10:32↓	48.9597	10:27↓	48.9621	10:23↓	48.9401	10:18↓	48.9342
10:36↑	48.9523	10:31↑	48.9677	10:27↓	48.9644	10:22↓	48.9430	10:18↑	48.9378
10:36↑	48.9488	10:31↓	48.9675	10:27↑	48.9704	10:22↓	48.9465	10:18↑	48.9367
10:35↑	48.9480	10:31↑	48.9708	10:26↑	48.9647	10:22↓	48.9476	10:18↑	48.9361
10:35↑	48.9449	10:31↓	48.9678	10:26↓	48.9566	10:22↑	48.9510	10:17↓	48.9396
10:35↓	48.9435	10:30↑	48.9704	10:26↓	48.9609	10:21↑	48.9382	10:17↑	48.9458
10:35↓	48.9456	10:30↓	48.9691	10:26↑	48.9597	10:21↑	48.9365	10:17↓	48.9440
10:34↓	48.9519	10:30↓	48.9639	10:25↑	48.9539	10:21↑	48.9360	10:16↓	48.9450
10:34↑	48.9572	10:30↓	48.9655	10:25↓	48.9466	10:21↓	48.9357	10:16↓	48.9452
10:34↑	48.9564	10:29↑	48.9658	10:25↓	48.9487	10:20↑	48.9401	10:16↓	48.9458
10:34↑	48.9549	10:29↓	48.9644	10:25↑	48.9492	10:20↓	48.9376	10:16↑	48.9514
10:33↑	48.9562	10:29↑	48.9713	10:24↓	48.9470	10:20↑	48.9427	10:15↓	48.9482
10:33↑	48.9512	10:29↑	48.9667	10:24↓	48.9474	10:20↑	48.9415	10:15↓	48.9542
10:33↓	48.9504	10:28↑	48.9649	10:24↑	48.9504	10:19↑	48.9393	10:15↓	48.9573
10:33↓	48.9526	10:28↑	48.9598	10:24↑	48.9484	10:19↑	48.9392	10:15↑	48.9474
10:32	48.9539	10:28↓	48.9593	10:23↓	48.9481	10:19↑	48.9363	10:14↑	48.9426
10:32↓	48.9539	10:28↑	48.9637	10:23↑	48.9514	10:19↓	48.9361	10:14↓	48.9419

Australia 61 2 9777 8600 Brazil 5511 3048 4500 Europe 44 20 7330 7500 Germany 49 69 9204 1210 Hong Kong 852 2977 6000
Japan 81 3 3201 8900   Singapore 65 6212 1000   U.S. 1 212 318 2000   Copyright 2012 Bloomberg Finance L.P.
SN 225124 H621-303-0 04-Jan-12 20:20:24 EST GMT-5:00

Exhibit 7.12 Checking Indicative Value (IV QR)
Reprinted with permission from Bloomberg. Copyright 2012 Bloomberg L.P. All rights reserved.

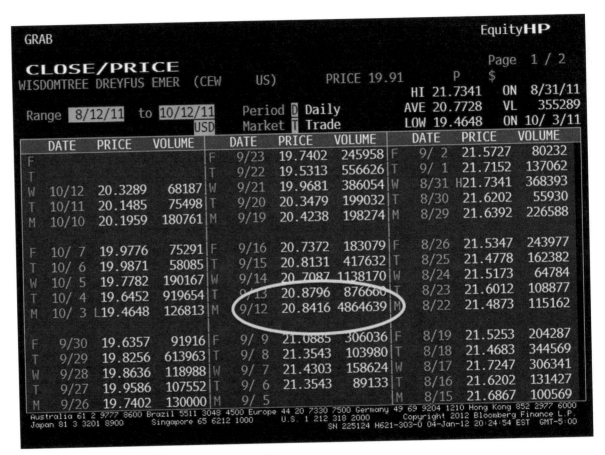

Exhibit 7.13 Checking for High-Volume Days

Turning to the AQR screen for that day, Exhibit 7.14, we see that at 9:52:42 A.M. the fund traded a block of 4 million shares. The notional on the block was $88 million, 14 times the typical notional traded in the fund. There were two other blocks that day of roughly 160,000 shares at the same price.

In the following QRM screen, Exhibit 7.15, we can see what was going on in the market at the time of the trade and immediately beforehand. The fund was showing a 2-cent-wide spread of 22.04 bid for and offered at 22.06. But again the size shown on both sides of the market was very small. At 9:52:40, there were between 400 and 5,000 shares offered at 22.60. At the same time, there was a bid for roughly 500 shares.

In this case, the print takes place right in the middle of the published market at 22.05. This would appear to be zero slippage for a block trade that is 800 times the displayed offer and an even greater multiple of the bid size.

If you look further into the market, the second QRM screen, exhibit 7.16, shows you two more minutes of time. It shows no unusual activity and no significant price move. About a minute before the trade, the market was approximately three pennies higher, with a 22.07 bid and offered at 22.08, both still for small size.

Last, in the final screen, exhibit 7.17, we can see the QR screen for the indicative value of the fund. While this is an emerging markets currency ETF, the indicative value should be representing what the currency market is valuing its underlying holdings at throughout the day. The currency markets typically trade 24 hours a day, although liquidity ebbs and flows in particular currencies as their main trading markets open and close. In this case, the indicative value of the fund was approximately 22.12 at the time of the trade. This is about 7 cents above the trade price, about 31 basis points.

A Tale of Two ETF Trades

My final example in this chapter focuses on an ETF in which two trades took place that clearly demonstrate the difference between investors who have mastered the execution process and those who have not. In Exhibit 7.18, you can see the HP screen for the ETF. In the red circle, you can see the average daily volume of the fund at 235,834. In the purple circle, you can see that on 9/27/11, 4,675,041 shares traded, about 20 times the ADV. You can also see in the yellow circle that on 11/10/11, 120,161 shares traded, which is about half the ADV. This is a fund where the underlying basket of bonds does not trade during the U.S. trading day.

In Exhibit 7.19, you can see the quote recap from the fund on the day of the large trading volume. At 11:07 A.M., there was a large block trade of slightly more than 4 million shares, as highlighted in the yellow box. You can also see the price at which the trade took place, $49.91. Since we haven't yet looked at pricing of the fund, let's take a closer look at the market in the fund about that time.

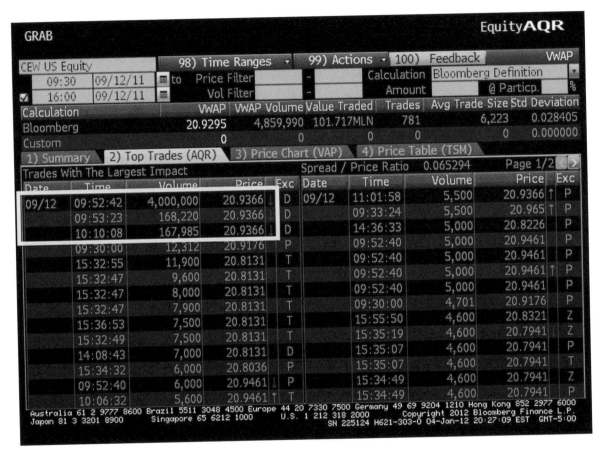

Exhibit 7.14 Checking for Large Blocks (AQR)
Reprinted with permission from Bloomberg. Copyright 2012 Bloomberg L.P. All rights reserved.

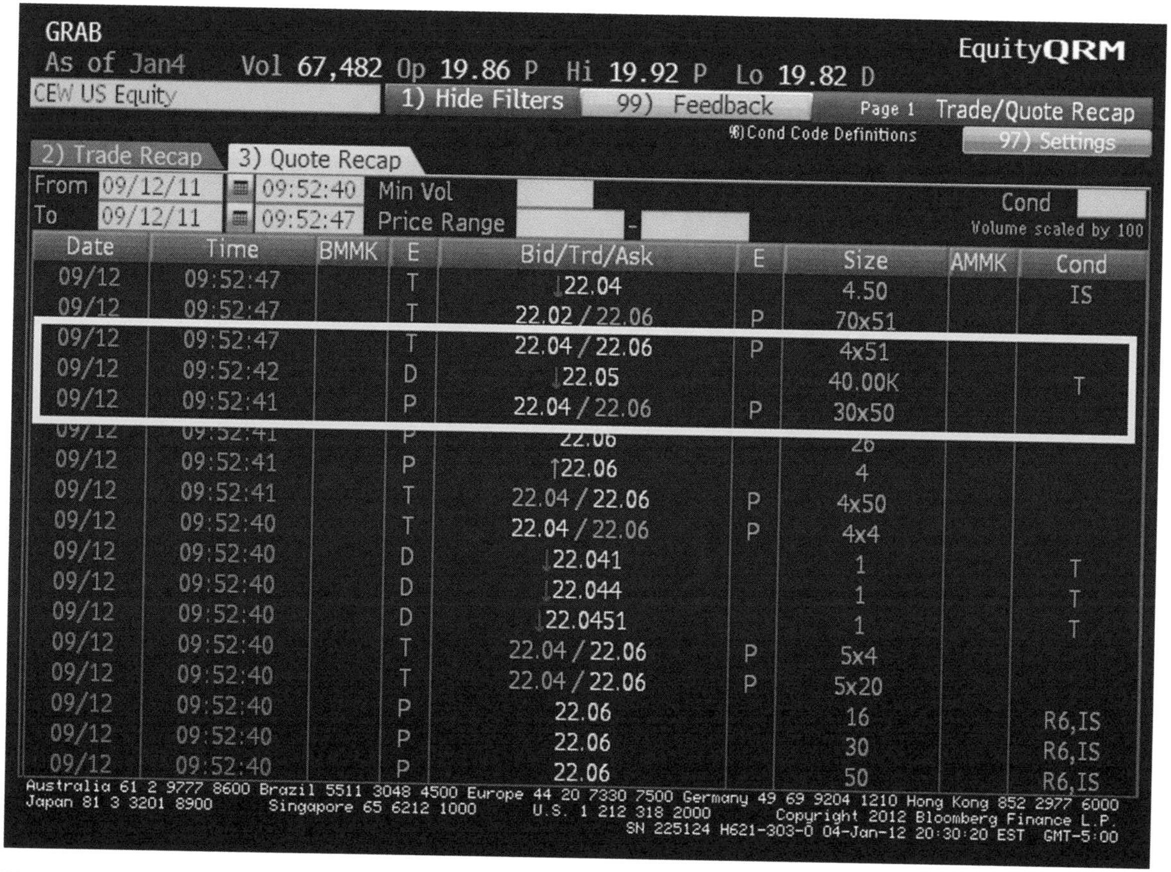

Exhibit 7.15 Checking Distance from the Market (QRM)
Reprinted with permission from Bloomberg. Copyright 2012 Bloomberg L.P. All rights reserved.

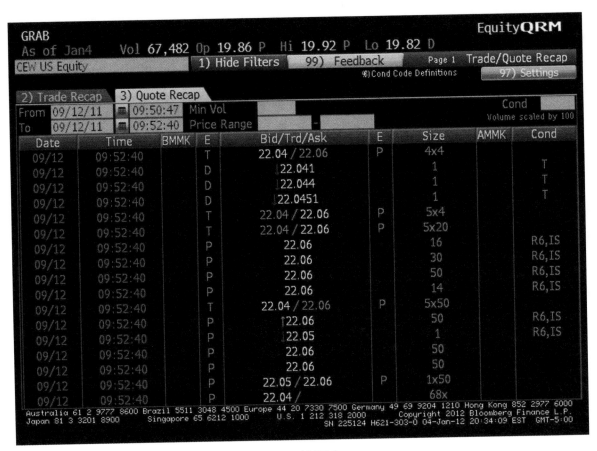

Exhibit 7.16 Checking Changes in the Market (QRM)

GRAB
Index **QR**

At DELAYED   Op 19.9191 Hi 19.9493 Lo 19.8863

Trade Recap

Page 1

| Time | 09:53 | Min Vol | | | | USD |
| Date | 9/12 | Price Range | | To | | High | 22.2987 | Low | 21.9880 |

CEWIV   WTREE Dreyfus Em Cur IV   PRICE 19.9395

Time	Price	Time	Price	Time	Price	Time	Price	Time	Price
09:53↑	22.1387	09:49↑	22.1251	09:44↑	22.1244	09:40↓	22.1222	09:35↓	22.1254
09:53↑	22.1349	09:49↓	22.1243	09:44↓	22.1220	09:40↓	22.1245	09:35↓	22.1259
09:53↑	22.1342	09:48↓	22.1247	09:44↓	22.1227	09:39↑	22.1249	09:35↓	22.1270
09:53↓	22.1317	09:48↓	22.1256	09:44↑	22.1237	09:39↓	22.1244	09:35↓	22.1272
09:52↑	22.1322	09:48↓	22.1269	09:43↑	22.1226	09:39↑	22.1247	09:34↑	22.1274
09:52↓	22.1311	09:48↓	22.1275	09:43↓	22.1218	09:39↑	22.1234	09:34↑	22.1260
09:52↑	22.1313	09:47↓	22.1269	09:43↑	22.1226	09:38↑	22.1227	09:34↑	22.1258
09:52↑	22.1309	09:47↑	22.1282	09:42	22.1215	09:38↑	22.1221	09:34↑	22.1251
09:51↑	22.1285	09:47↑	22.1279	09:42↓	22.1215	09:38↓	22.1233	09:33↑	22.1252
09:51↑	22.1292	09:47↓	22.1272	09:42↓	22.1222	09:38↓	22.1252	09:33↓	22.1249
09:51↓	22.1268	09:46↓	22.1277	09:42↑	22.1236	09:37↓	22.1265	09:33↓	22.1255
09:51↓	22.1269	09:46↑	22.1287	09:42↑	22.1228	09:37↑	22.1282	09:33↑	22.1264
09:50↑	22.1275	09:46↑	22.1264	09:41↑	22.1220	09:37↑	22.1273	09:32↓	22.1247
09:50↓	22.1273	09:46↑	22.1250	09:41↑	22.1214	09:37↑	22.1258	09:32↓	22.1254
09:50↑	22.1276	09:45↑	22.1252	09:41↑	22.1236	09:36↑	22.1250	09:32↑	22.1261
09:50↓	22.1228	09:45↓	22.1237	09:41↓	22.1223	09:36↓	22.1242	09:32↓	22.1253
09:49↑	22.1258	09:45↑	22.1242	09:40↓	22.1225	09:36↑	22.1258	09:31↓	22.1265
09:49↑	22.1252	09:45↓	22.1239	09:40↑	22.1230	09:36↓	22.1242	09:31↓	22.1286

Australia 61 2 9777 8600 Brazil 5511 3048 4500 Europe 44 20 7330 7500 Germany 49 69 9204 1210 Hong Kong 852 2977 6000
Japan 81 3 3201 8900   Singapore 65 6212 1000   U.S. 1 212 318 2000   Copyright 2012 Bloomberg Finance L.P.
SN 225124 H621-303-0 04-Jan-12 20:37:32 EST GMT-5:00

Exhibit 7.17 Checking Indicative Value (IV QR)

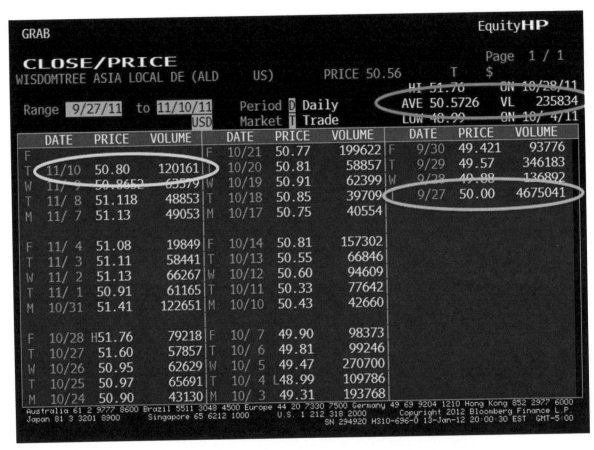

Exhibit 7.18 ETF Historical Price and Volume

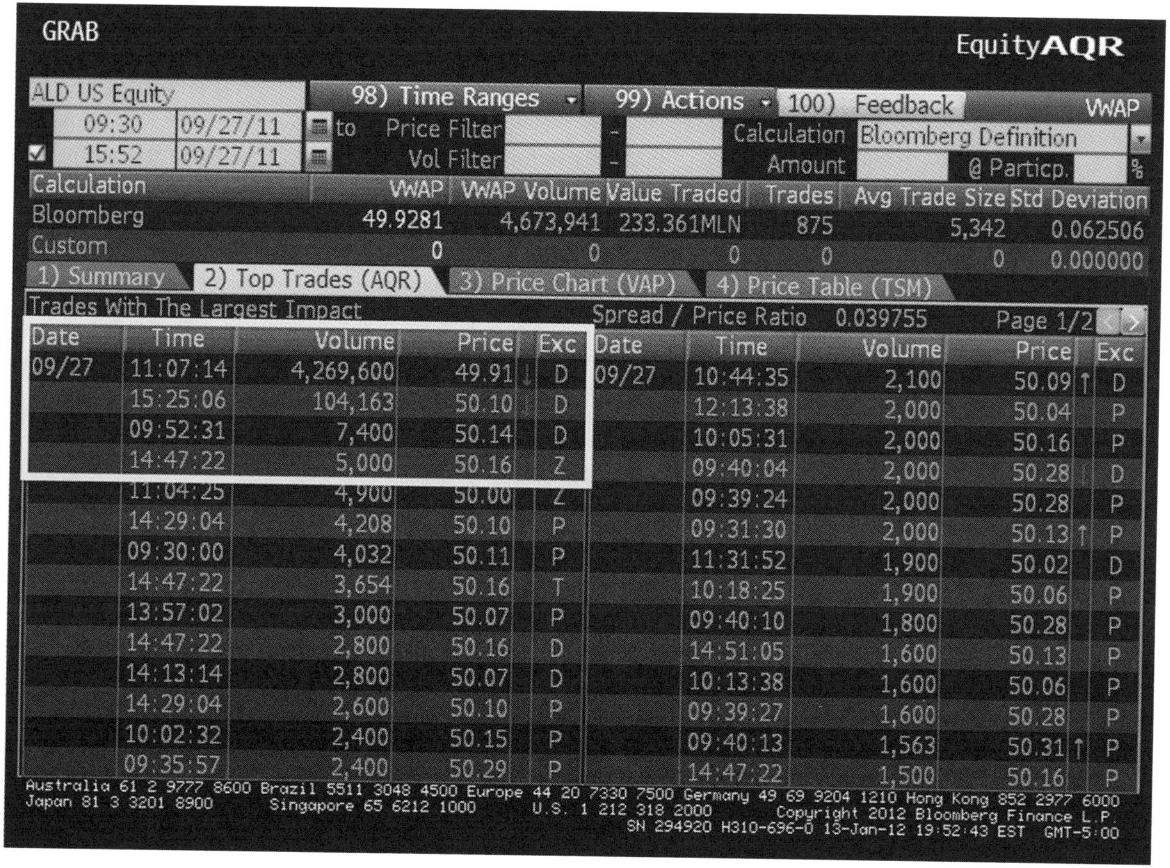

Exhibit 7.19 ETF Quote Recap

Reprinted with permission from Bloomberg. Copyright 2012 Bloomberg L.P. All rights reserved.

In Exhibit 7.20, we can see a screenshot that shows the bid and offer and sizes of each in the fund over a two-minute period just before that trade. It shows that the market was about 4 or 5 cents wide but that the size being displayed was a paltry 400 to 500 shares in total. And then we can see the print at 11:07:14 of 4,270,000 shares (displayed on the tape as 42.70K) at $49.91.

In this case, a savvy investor was able to trade more than $200 million of bonds that trade in markets that are closed during our trading hours at a price only 8 basis points below the displayed bid on the screen. That appears to be an excellent trade. And it seems as if the client was able to call up a liquidity provider, negotiate a price for the block of shares, and make the sale without being disruptive to the marketplace.

Now let's look at the other trading day I highlighted and see an example of where things can go awry. In Exhibit 7.21, we can see the quote recap screen for the same fund, but this time on a different day, 11/10/11.

There is nothing extraordinary about the big blocks on the day except for the pricing. The largest block of the day, 29,945 shares, and the third largest block of the day, 5,700 shares, both traded at a price of $53.15. This seems a little odd because most of the other prints on this screen for that day were in the $50.80 to $51.00 range. You can see the time of the prints as 13:33 P.M., in the afternoon. In Exhibit 7.22, we can see the quote recap screen for that time period. It starts at the bottom with the prints at $53.15, but then 13 minutes later, the market is showing a 6-cent-wide

spread at a much lower level, $50.74 to $50.80. We need one more screen to try to get an understanding of what happened in this ETF on that trading day.

In Exhibit 7.23, we can see the daily price graph for the fund on 11/10/11. You can see via the white line along the bottom that the fund was trading at about $50.80 all day long, except for early in the morning, at about 10:00 A.M., when we see a large uptick, highlighted by my red arrow. What happened is this: The client called up their broker, who was very inexperienced in trading ETFs. They asked for a market in the fund, and the broker, using a low average daily volume number, quoted the market $4 higher than where the fund was trading at the time. The client agreed, and the block was printed in two pieces at a price above $55.00. I was alerted several hours later when I got to my office because of price alerts that I have set up on my system. The broker had advertised the trade, and I was able to call them up and ask why they had traded such a small amount of shares so far away from the market. Eventually, they agreed to amend the trade down to a price of $53.15, which we saw in Exhibit 7.21 as the price of the blocks. In this case, to buy a mere 35,000 shares, the client had paid more than $2 over the quoted market. To buy less than $2 million of the stock, they had pushed the price almost 4.5 percent. This can happen if you have not taken the time to pay attention to how you are executing in ETFs, who you are using for your execution, and how they are handling your order flow.

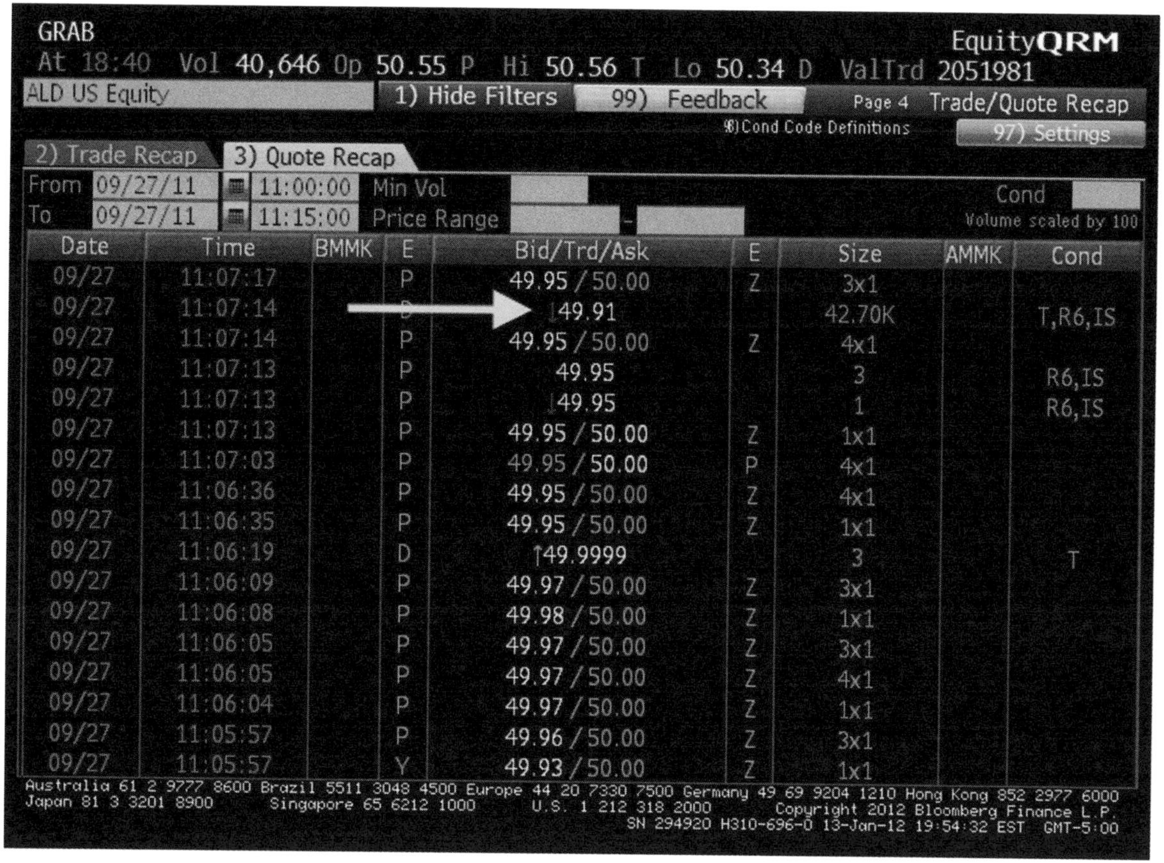

Exhibit 7.20 ETF Quote Montage

Reprinted with permission from Bloomberg. Copyright 2012 Bloomberg L.P. All rights reserved.

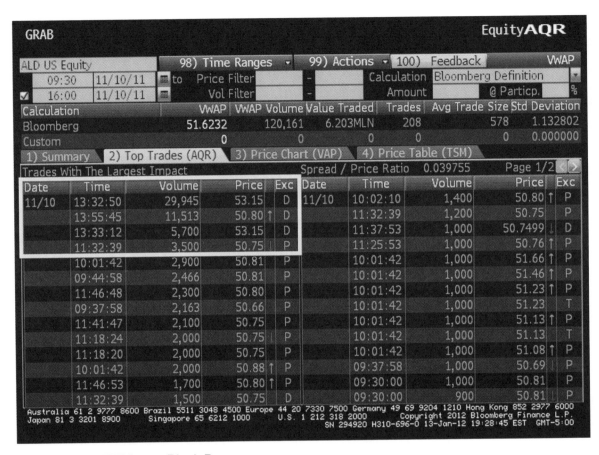

Exhibit 7.21 ETF Large Block Recap

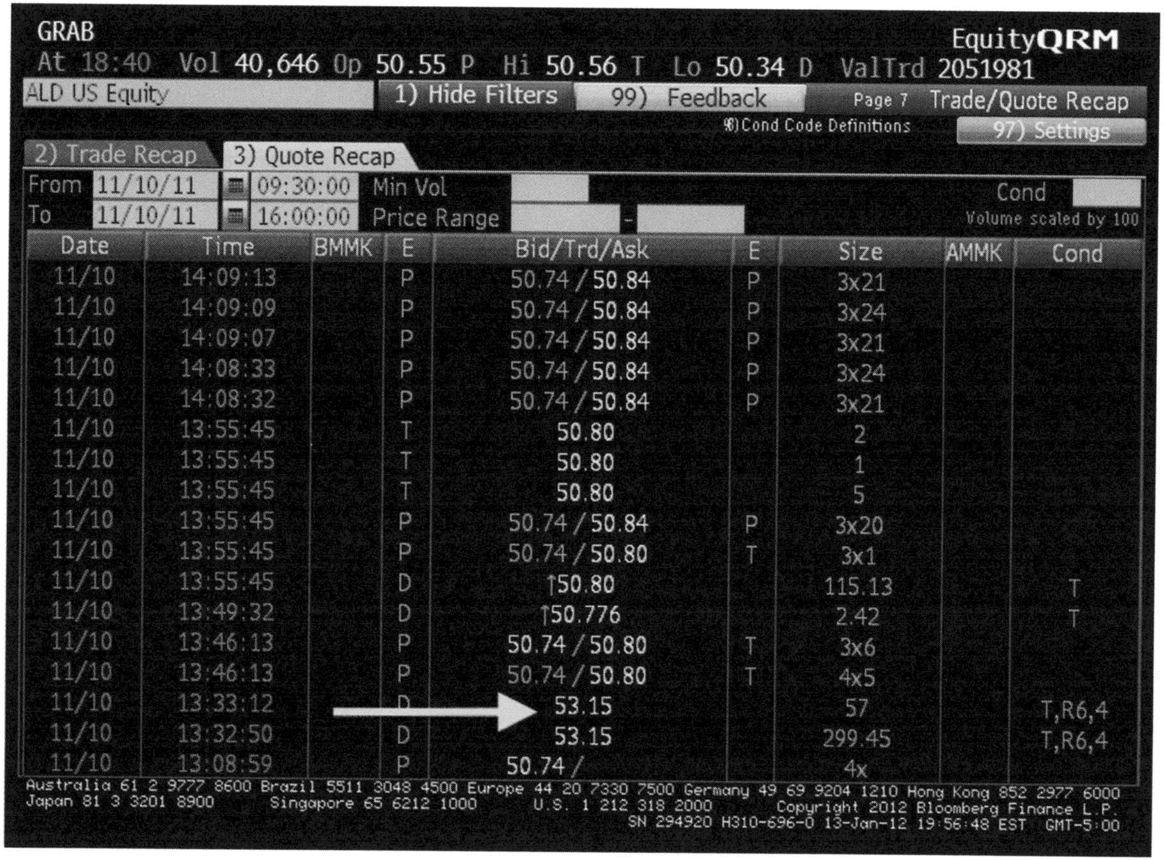

Exhibit 7.22 ETF Streaming Bid/Ask/Trades
Reprinted with permission from Bloomberg. Copyright 2012 Bloomberg L.P. All rights reserved.

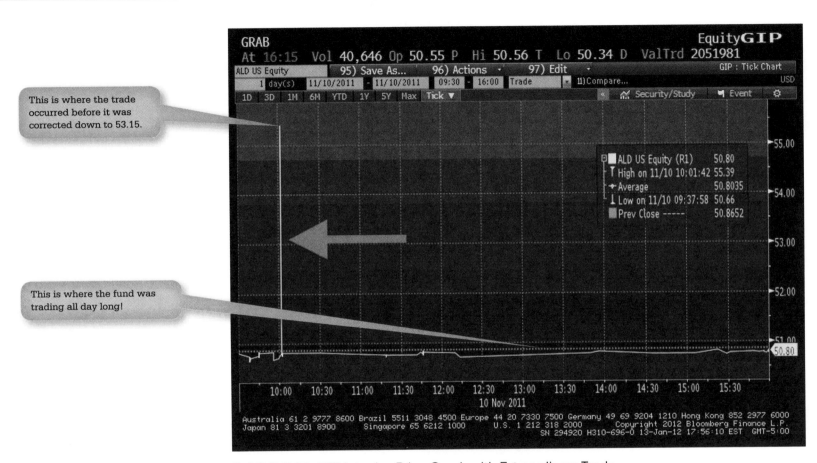

This is where the trade occurred before it was corrected down to 53.15.

This is where the fund was trading all day long!

Exhibit 7.23 ETF Intraday Price Graph with Extraordinary Trade

Reprinted with permission from Bloomberg. Copyright 2012 Bloomberg L.P. All rights reserved.

The Keys to Trading ETFs

1. Understand the fair value of the product you intend to trade.

2. Try not to trade during the first fifteen minutes and last fifteen minutes of trading.

3. Try to focus trading of ETFs with various underlying assets at times when those assets are trading and overlapping with U.S. trading hours.

4. Utilize the full arsenal of trade types when available.

5. Place limits within reasonable range of fair value, where they can realistically expect to be executed.

6. Utilize ETF Liquidity Providers for blocks of more than 5,000 shares or 25% of ADV..

7. Get a feeling for how much of an impact in the market your trade might create as compared to other trades of similar, or larger size, in the past.

8. Understand when you need to utilize risk capital from traders versus when you can have them trade the basket on your behalf.

9. Develop a relationship with your execution platform or liquidity provider. An open trusting relationship helps them to understand your goals and helps you to achieve them by navigating a complicated ETF trading landscape.

10. Do not undervalue the true cost of not paying attention to the execution of your ETF positions. Executing efficiently in the ETF markets is critical for the performance of your portfolios and can be easily achieved with a small amount of work.

Video:
Keys to Trading ETFs

www.wiley.com/go/abnervg

Summary

In summary, it is difficult to determine exactly what the right price is for a large block trade, what type of spread, or how far from the current market you might need to trade. You can, however, make several inferences from the information presented here and have an educated opinion as to where you want to trade. The pricing of large blocks in ETFs, where the block is significantly larger than the average daily volume, will involve dialogue with the liquidity community that can access alternate liquidity for you. Using past trading history of the products you are trading enables educated interactions in which both parties can achieve their goals. But it should be noted that the block history of an ETF might also provide different results than an algorithmic analysis of the underlying.

We also see from these examples that the time of the trade is important. Trading earlier in the day, when a market maker has more opportunity to get a good hedge on, is sometimes preferable to trading within a few minutes of the closing bell, when hedging becomes more difficult. Time of day also has an impact on pricing when the underlying components are in foreign markets because they may be still open during our morning but will have closed by our afternoon, as are those in Europe. It would be natural to assume that more liquidity would be available in an ETF when the underlying can be traded as a hedge. Two different variables that should be built into pricing expectations are where the price should be in relation to the market and in relation to the indicative value.

Last, there are market conditions to consider. If there is extreme market volatility, spreads will naturally be driven wider and the risk tolerance of the liquidity community driven lower. They will be looking for more spread in the trade to account for the greater risk of not being able to hedge as efficiently.

There are also a variety of methods that can be pursued to get blocks executed. These range from using risk capital to having someone trade the basket on your behalf and implying an ETF price for execution.

Bottom line, it is wise for you to understand what you are trading, what the underlying is, and where you think it is valued. You can use Bloomberg as a key resource to start gathering information on how your ETF trades and make educated trading decisions. But if you are ever in doubt, ask questions and have a dialogue with your liquidity provider so you both are on the same page. Education and relationships with the trading community can only serve to benefit you, the investor, in the long run.

Test Yourself

1. True or false—When a market maker shows you a market, it is nonnegotiable.
2. True or false—If you are looking at a small ETF with a very liquid domestic stock basket, pretrade analytics systems that look only at the volume history of that ETF are going to give you a good indication of the possible trading impact of a large block trade in that fund.
3. True or false—If the underlying basket is closed, it is impossible to trade a large block in that particular ETF.

Answers: 1. False   2. False   3. False

CHAPTER 8

Product Labeling and Structural Impact

Product structure is one of those topics in the ETF industry that can become inside baseball extremely fast. This bewilders investors and creates a general feeling of risk and concern that there might be unintended ramifications to the products. In general, the bulk of assets in ETFs are in plain vanilla structures that are registered under the Investment Company Act of 1940. This provides a variety of protections for investors. But as with any investment, research and education about your purchase are necessary to ensure the investment goals you desire.

As with most things, the news regarding an industry tends to focus on the outliers, and it is no different in the ETF industry. A significant percentage of the news stories written about ETFs focus on certain product structures, namely, leveraged, inverse, and derivatives-based ETFs that contain only a small portion of the assets in the industry. A variety of issues or concerns regarding ETFs have arisen with the growth of the industry. I would categorize these as:

- Concerns about transparency and reporting standards
- Counterparty concerns:
    a. Derivative use
    b. Stock lending
- The impact of methods of achieving leverage
- Managerial conflicts of interest
- Increased trading volatility
- Possible systemic risk of the products

All of these concerns stem from the structure of the products and the nuances between the different types of structures that are available. The chatter that has arisen about some of these products has attracted the attention of regulators to the industry, and in general, the ETF structure has fared well in that light. The issuers have already started a move toward greater transparency in all products because of the higher standards demanded by investors and regulators. Over the next few years, the asset management industry in general will be undergoing tremendous changes in the regulatory environment, and the ETF market will be both positively and negatively affected by some of these regulations. The largest issuer of ETFs has recently put forward a concept statement about the labeling system for the products in an effort to create more clarity throughout the ETF landscape. I'll discuss ETF labeling in this chapter. In addition, I'll provide some further details on differences in the structure of products and the potential effect that those differences can have on your portfolio.

ETF Structures and Product Types

Securities Laws for Investment Companies

ETFs are investment companies, they are so-called 40 Act funds, and the issuers and distribution network are governed under the same regulatory framework as mutual funds. There are also variations of the ETF structure that are still investment companies but are governed by the slightly different rules of the Securities Act of 1933. The entire product universe is now sometimes also referred to as exchange-traded products (ETPs). In many cases, the terms ETF and ETP are used interchangeably, and this is where confusion can arise.

According to the Investment Company Institute, four principal securities laws govern investment companies. These are the clearest and most concise descriptions of them that I've found:

The Investment Company Act of 1940— "Regulates the structure and operations of investment companies through a combination of disclosure requirements and restrictions on day-to-day operations. Among other things, the Investment Company Act addresses investment company capital structures, custody of assets, investment activities (particularly with respect to transactions with affiliates and other transactions involving potential conflicts of interest), and the duties of fund boards."[1] Most ETFs are registered under this act that provides for various protections for investors.

The Investment Advisers Act of 1940— "Regulates investment advisors. Requires all advisors to registered investment companies and other large advisors to register with the SEC. The Advisers Act contains provisions requiring fund advisers to meet recordkeeping, custodial, reporting, and other regulatory responsibilities."[2]

The Securities Exchange Act of 1934—"Regulates the trading, purchase, and sale of securities, including investment company shares. The 1934 Act also regulates broker-dealers, including investment company principal underwriters and others that sell investment company shares, and require them to register with the SEC."[3]

The Securities Act of 1933—"Regulates public offerings of securities, including investment company shares. The 1933 Act also requires that all investors receive a current prospectus describing the fund."[4] This is typically used by ETNs, Grantor Trusts, ETCs and limited partnerships.

A variety of products have been created for investors under these regulations. In Exhibit 8.1, you can see a breakdown of the different types of ETPs and where they fit within the product spectrum. While it's commonly acknowledged that ETP should be the umbrella term for the product set, many people also interchangeably use ETF when referencing the products. Even the title of this book and my first book, *The ETF Handbook*, could, and maybe should, be using ETP because of their broad references to the variety of the products, but ETF is the marketable and most recognized term. Ask yourself, would you have picked up this book if it had been called *The Visual Guide to ETPs?*

The Senate held a hearing on market microstructure with the subtitle "An Examination of ETFs." They chose the term, but in reality, they were mostly focused on exchange-traded products.

	Product	Regulatory	Recourse	Structure	Examples		Taxation
ETP	ETF	1940 Act SEC N1-A	Portfolio of securities	Unit Investment Trust	SPDRs, Diamonds, QQQQ, BLDRs		Ordinary income
				Registered Investment Co (RIC)	**Physical replication**	FXI, GXC, EPI, PIN, GDX, SIL	Ordinary income
					Derivatives based	PEK, WDTI	Ordinary income
	ETV / ETC	1933 Act SEC and CFTC S-1	Custodian credit	Grantor Trust	GLD, IAU, CurrencyShares		Ordinary income or 28% max long-term rate for collectibles
				Commodity Pool / Limited Partnership	USO, UNG, DBC, GSG		60% long-term rate; 40% short-term rate; blend for derivatives
	ETN	1933 Act SEC S-1	Counterparty credit	Unsecured note	iPath, Elements, and GCE		Ordinary income

Exhibit 8.1 The ETP Umbrella

This is a perfect example of the identification problem facing the industry. The push to clarify the labeling system in the ETP arena has been around for many years. Recently, the product set has grown, and issuers have moved down the curve of structure design away from the plain vanilla type of ETFs, increasing the need for product structure clarification. A managing director at BlackRock, in his comments to the committee, emphasized that the lack of a clear labeling system is enabling market critics to blame the entire product set because of the structure or performance of a small subset of the industry. It is important for investors to understand the structural differences between the different types of ETPs and the risks and return impact associated with those differences. This knowledge will help the investor weed through some of the acrimonious headlines on so-called ETFs and save investors undue concern regarding risk.

Evolution of the Label

In 1993, the listing of the State Street SPDR S&P 500 (SPY) marked the beginning of the current era of the ETF product in the United States. Exchange-traded funds, as a term, was used unofficially to cover listed index products and included other products such as closed-end funds, which, contrary to the current implications of ETF, do not disclose their underlying holdings daily and have a fixed amount of outstanding shares. It was not until more of these newer products became popular in the mid to late 1990s that the label ETF came to refer specifically to the products that trade on exchanges and also provide daily transparency and open-ended issuance.

The NYSE Euronext, the exchange on which the highest percentage of products have listed, uses a classification system delineating an ETP umbrella that includes several subtypes of products that differ in legal classification and risks. I have paraphrased the general labeling concepts from the exchange as follows:[5]

- An exchange-traded fund (ETF) is an investment vehicle that combines key features of traditional mutual funds and individual stocks. ETFs are open-ended securities registered under the Investment Company Act of 1940.

- Exchange-traded vehicles (ETVs) are open-ended trusts or partnership units registered under the Securities Act of 1933. This category often includes commodity and currency trusts. They are treated differently from a regulatory standpoint than standard ETFs and can have different tax implications.

- Exchange-traded notes (ETNs) are senior unsecured and unsubordinated debt obligations of the issuer. They are designed to track the total return of an underlying index or other benchmark, minus investor fees. ETNs are different than ETFs because they are subject to the creditworthiness of the issuer, adding another principal risk to the main market risk associated with the underlying holdings.

Although this is a step in the right direction, there should be a more detailed agreed-upon industry labeling standard to clarify all the nuances. BlackRock, via the release of a concept paper on regulation and product labeling,[6] recommends that investors would be better served with a universal standard that would eliminate the somewhat interchangeable terms for the fund classifications. They propose utilizing the ETP, ETF, and ETN labels; they separate out commodities funds from ETVs, calling them ETCs; and they propose utilizing the term exchange-traded instrument (ETI) instead of exchange-traded vehicle (ETV).

We do need a universal labeling system to make it easier for the investing public to understand what instruments they are investing in and what advantages and risks each carries. I think this would be best served in a detailed label system similar to the food label. The labeling system should include defining variables such as whether the fund is active or passive. Is it leveraged? Is it swap based? Does it utilize derivatives? What other risks are associated with positioning it within a portfolio?

The Bloomberg DES page begins to collect all those various pieces of data per product. In the yellow highlighted section of Exhibit 8.2, you can see the appropriations section that provides various details about the underlying basket and the structure. Although it still makes use of a fund type of classification, it goes deeper for clients to gain a better understanding of the specific details of the funds. It is unwieldy, with too many outliers, to attempt to sum up the

ramifications of more than a thousand products in only five categories.

It is now incumbent upon investors to understand all the information on the type of product they are planning to invest in and the portfolio ramifications. The key product components stemming from differences in structure involve purity of exposure, tax treatment, and shareholder protection from issuer insolvency. For a given exposure, the differences in structure create differences in trading and performance. For instance, because ETNs have implicit counterparty exposure to the issuer, credit ratings of the issuer impact the price of its ETN. This was most evident at the height of the financial crisis when ETNs of big banks traded at discounts to NAV because of concerns about bank credit. Investors must understand the nuances of structure of the product they trade to quickly assess the impact of outside risks on the performance of their investment.

Impact of Structure

Let's go through some examples of structural differences and examine impact on the actual fund.

Example: Derivative Based versus Physical Replication in Registered Investment Company (RIC) ETFs

China has historically been one of the more difficult markets to access for foreign investors. Securities

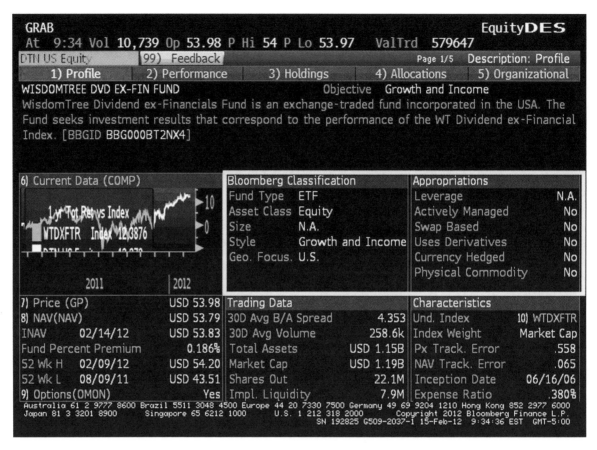

Exhibit 8.2 The DES Screen Shows the Type of Fund and a Group of Appropriations Regarding the Underlying Holdings

Reprinted with permission from Bloomberg. Copyright 2012 Bloomberg L.P. All rights reserved.

listed on the Chinese stock exchanges are primarily categorized into A-shares or B-shares. A-shares are only open to investment by Chinese citizens. B-shares are open to foreign investors but have traditionally consisted of less desirable and limited offerings. Hong Kong–listed Chinese securities fall primarily into the H-share class. Those shares are open to all investors, but listings comprise only the largest and most global-facing companies in China. At times, H-shares can trade away fro+m the value of the locally listed companies they are representing. Therefore, an investment in an H-share is not pure exposure to the local A-share company but is as close as you will get without specific Chinese government approval to invest directly in the Chinese market.

A qualified foreign institutional investor (QFII) program was initiated in recent years to allow foreigners to receive quotas for A-share investments. The application process and lead time are complicated and lengthy, allocation for foreign investors is limited, and approval for more quota is not always granted. ETFs listed in the United States that provide pure A-share exposure are extremely hard to produce because of the quota allotments. Instead, most ETFs with China exposure invest through US-listed ADRs or H-shares.

Recently, a China ETF was launched in the United States. It tracks, currently using swaps, an index of 300 A-share stocks listed on the Shanghai and/or Shenzhen exchanges. In Exhibit 8.3, you can see a chart showing the performance of the fund and the index. You can see that the performances of the ETF and of the index are quite different. This is not because of poor portfolio management. The premium demanded to purchase anything giving exposure to the locally listed Chinese market and the costs to achieve that exposure are going to be reflected as a cost to the fund, impacting performance.

The fund has traded at a premium because the swaps used to achieve the exposure are bought at premiums. The issuer had not yet been granted QFII status, leading to allocation of A-share quota. Instead, the fund invested in swaps that are linked to the return of the China A-shares market. The counterparty to the swaps has QFII status and maintains the ability to invest directly in A-shares. So the fund is using the incremental available A-share quota of other institutions to provide local exposure, but then the fund has counterparty risk to those issuing the swaps. As such, the ETF has a structural risk profile more like an ETN than a physically replicated ETF, due to the counterparty risk in the underlying swap.

When the fund launched in October 2010, it began trading at a double-digit percentage premium over its net asset value. You can see in Exhibit 8.4 that the premium of the fund from October 2010 to December 2011 averaged approximately 10 percent. This reflected the cost to gaining exposure through the swap. The premium, however, is not consistent and fluctuates with the demand for A-share access.

The returns realized by investors in the fund may depend not only on the performance of the Chinese A-shares market but also on the movement of this

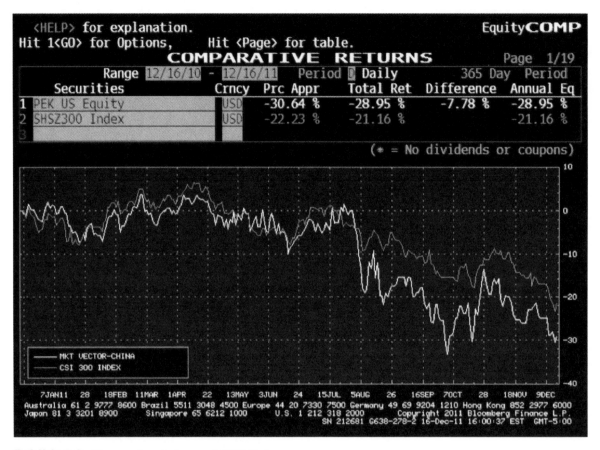

Exhibit 8.3 Comparing Index and ETF Returns
Reprinted with permission from Bloomberg. Copyright 2012 Bloomberg L.P. All rights reserved.

Exhibit 8.4 Premium Chart of a China ETF

Reprinted with permission from Bloomberg. Copyright 2012 Bloomberg L.P. All rights reserved.

premium. An investor who buys in when the China ETF is trading at an 8 percent premium and sells when the premium has reached 10 percent will, all else being equal, pick up some additional return unrelated to the change in price of the underlying stocks. Conversely, if the premium decreases or narrows completely, returns could be adversely impacted.

In Exhibit 8.5, you can see the premium and discount chart of another China ETF. This fund is providing exposure to a basket of stocks that are listed in Hong Kong as H-shares. They are freely tradable by investors without QFII quota, and therefore the fund typically trades around the NAV. The fund displays a very different premium and discount perspective.

Why can't any premium be arbitraged away? In general, for the creation process to work, authorized participants must exchange a basket of the securities underlying the ETF in exchange for newly created shares. When shares of an ETF are trading for more than the fund's fair value, traders buy the basket of individual securities and then sell the ETF at a premium, netting an arbitrage profit in the process. Due to limitations in certain markets, the QFIIs that have access are able to charge a premium for the difficult-to-access exposure. The premiums are not arbitrary but defined by the actual costs in the marketplace. When the underlying securities are trading with an embedded high cost of access, the ETF premium must reach a certain threshold before the liquidity providers are incentivized to create additional shares on an arbitrage basis. Just because there is a premium doesn't

mean there is an arbitrage opportunity. It all depends on the accessibility of the underlying. And the presence of a premium does not always indicate any problem in the fund. In this case, it is simply reflecting the extra cost of attaining a difficult-to-achieve exposure.

Example: ETN versus ETF Structure

India is another example of one of the most populous regions in the world that harbors a market that is sometimes difficult to access. Until recent years, one of the few ways to access the Indian market on the open exchange was through an ETN product. Shares of an ETN represent debt—unsubordinated, unsecured debt—so investors are exposed to the issuer's credit. In the fall of 2007, the note halted creations for a time when India decided to temporarily limit foreign investor inflows into its markets. This caused the shares to trade at a sharp premium above its net asset value. In 2008, the Indian government instituted controls on derivative products tied to the country's market that then impacted the issuer's ability to create more shares of its ETN. That contributed to the note trading as much as 24 percent above its net asset value before returning back toward flat when the restrictions were lifted. When a fund has to limit creations or redemptions, the shares trading in the secondary market can become unmoored from the underlying asset value. Because of this, premiums and discounts cannot be as effectively narrowed as they would be by the continuous issuance ability of other ETPs. You can see a premium discount chart of this ETN in Exhibit 8.6.

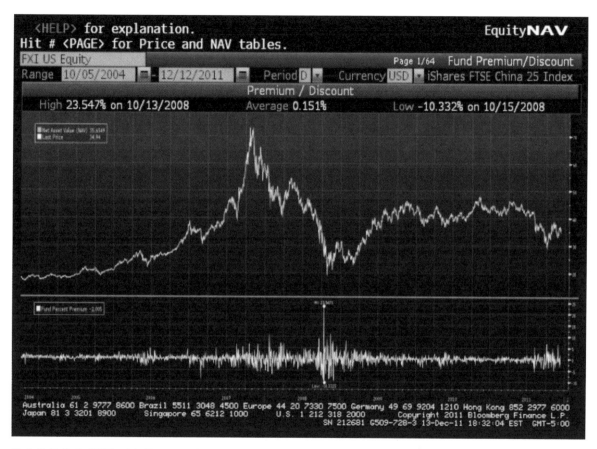

Exhibit 8.5 ETF with Easy to Access Underlying Holdings

Reprinted with permission from Bloomberg. Copyright 2012 Bloomberg L.P. All rights reserved.

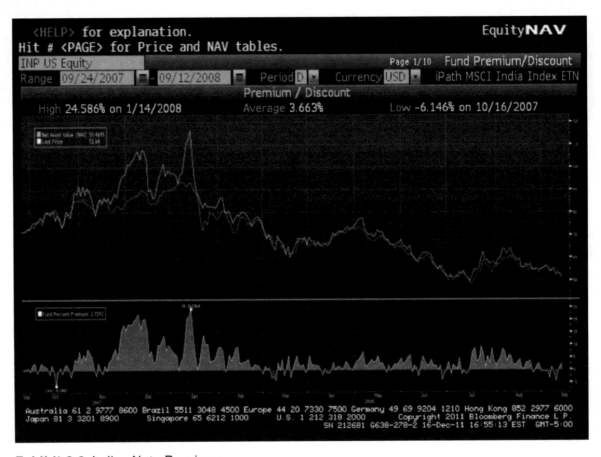

Exhibit 8.6 Indian Note Premiums

It is highly volatile, with the premium moving sharply with demand. As investors are entering the product, the premium rises. If the asset class goes out of favor, then redemptions can take place, taking some of the pressure off the fund and causing it to trade back toward parity.

Another risk to consider is the issuer risk that comes with all ETNs. In 2007, the Indian ETN was the only open-ended exchange-traded product covering India. It attracted good volumes despite the counterparty risk of the ETN structure. You can see, on the very right of Exhibit 8.6, that in September 2008, when Lehman Brothers declared bankruptcy and the fate of some of the other big banks was questioned by market participants, the note traded at discounts of up to 5 percent. This reflected the issuer risk and not necessarily the outlook on the Indian underlying basket. This is a good example of the additional risk of ETNs. Several new Indian products have since been offered in the ETF structure. As a result of having Indian FII status, they are able to invest in Indian companies that are eligible to be purchased by foreign investors. As an Indian FII, and by investing all of its assets in a wholly owned subsidiary in Mauritius, the funds have favorable local Indian tax withholding. In Exhibit 8.7, you can see a discount premium chart of an Indian ETF. You can clearly see that it is more constant than the predecessor ETN. It is oscillating around zero, reflecting the daily ability to create and redeem shares in the fund.

Example: ETF That Experiences Underlying Market Closure

Prior to the unrest and subsequent overthrow of the Mubarak government, Egypt had been considered a popular frontier market. However, the Egyptian market closed for trading at the beginning of 2011, from January 27 through March 23, because of the political revolution that was occurring in that country. During the nearly eight-week closure, the Egypt ETF continued to trade in the United States, despite the fact that creations and redemptions were halted with the inability to access the underlying basket because the market was closed. Through weeks of turmoil and unrest, the ETF traded over a wide range representing more than a 20 percent move in the markets. Shorting became very expensive, as it was limited to the percentage of shares outstanding in the stock loan program. No more shares could be issued to facilitate share loan requirements when an investor sold short. The fund was still free to trade, however, and it acted as a very valuable price discovery tool during the period. The fund became one of the few tools that investors could use to express their views during this volatile market situation. In Exhibit 8.8, you can see the market dislocation and the premium that the fund moved to as a result of the inability to create new shares over that time period. The solid functioning of the product is also exhibited by the fact that the fund snaps back to trading at standard small premiums and discounts again as the market reopened and began trading more normally.

KEY POINT:

See Exhibit 8.7. The discount and premium appear to be relatively constant, but why is there any discount or premium in the Indian ETF at all? This chart reflects the closing price at 4 P.M. on the ETF's primary exchange, in the United States. In ETFs with a basket of underlying holdings that trade in a different market (India) than the fund, there will always be a difference between the NAV and the fund closing price. In a normally functioning product, the discount or premium will snap back to zero at the open of the underlying market, and you see the high variability on a daily basis and a more even dispersion. This is quite different from a long-term discount or premium as presented in a CEF or product with other structural nuances.

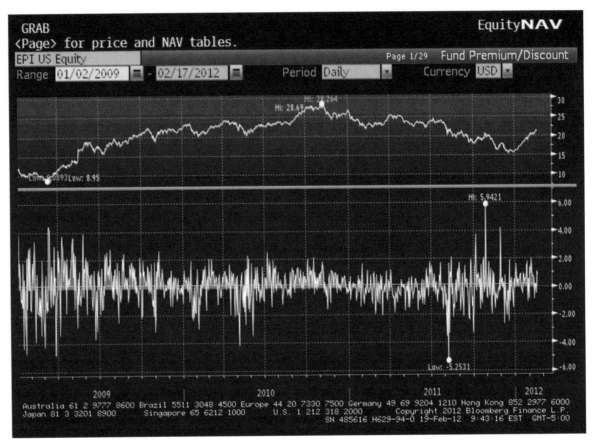

Exhibit 8.7 Indian ETF Premium/Discount Oscillator
Reprinted with permission from Bloomberg. Copyright 2012 Bloomberg L.P. All rights reserved.

GRAB
<Page> for price and NAV tables.   Equity**NAV**

EGPT US Equity   Page 1/19   Fund Premium/Discount
Range 02/18/2010 ▣ - 02/17/2012 ▣   Period Daily ▼   Currency USD ▼

Hi: 22.0142 Hi: 22.16

EGPT US Equity
■ Net Asset Value (NAV) 13.2132
■ Last Price   13.04

22.00
20.00
18.00
16.00
14.00
12.00
10.00

Low: 9.24 Low: 9.3839

Hi: 2.9158

EGPT US Equity
■ Fund Percent Premium   -1.3107
■ Fund Percent Premium Average   1.5772

30
20
10
0

Low: .5655

Mar   Jun   Sep   Dec   Mar   Jun   Sep   Dec
        2010   2011   2012
Australia 61 2 9777 8600 Brazil 5511 3048 4500 Europe 44 20 7330 7500 Germany 49 69 9204 1210 Hong Kong 852 2977 6000
Japan 81 3 3201 8900   Singapore 65 6212 1000   U.S. 1 212 318 2000   Copyright 2012 Bloomberg Finance L.P.
                                                SN 485616 H629-94-0 19-Feb-12 9:59:19 EST GMT-5:00

Exhibit 8.8 Halted Underlying Holdings Chart
Reprinted with permission from Bloomberg. Copyright 2012 Bloomberg L.P. All rights reserved.

KEY POINT:

Allowing a fund to continue to trade even though creations and redemptions are halted enables natural market forces to move it to a level of expected fair value. This has enabled the generation of a wide variety of price discovery tools for previously hard-to-value assets. It's incumbent upon investors to understand the potential ramifications of market events and how they may affect the pricing of the funds in which they have positions.

KEY POINT:

A strong demand for fund shares can actually come from two views of market exposure. If there is an overall demand to get long exposure, then there can be strong demand in terms of buying pressure on the fund. Or if there is a strong demand to short the fund for purposes of hedging other exposures or taking a negative view, this can also drive demand to create shares in a fund to facilitate the required stock loan borrows. It is not always so easy to determine from simply watching creations and changes in shares outstanding what will happen in price terms in a fund.

> **DEFINITION:**
> **Near month**
>
> The near month is the closest expiration date.

> **DEFINITION:**
> **Contango**
>
> Contango is when the futures contract price is higher than the spot price.

> **DEFINITION:**
> **Backwardation**
>
> Backwardation is when the spot price is higher than the futures contract price.

> **DEFINITION:**
> **Far month**
>
> The far month is typically the expiration date of the longer maturity.

Example: Commodity Structures

On the topic of commodity structures and means of getting exposure, it is important to mention the effect of the futures market on the limited partnerships based on natural gas prices and uses of the near month futures contract to achieve that exposure. A natural gas fund is a good example of the reasons that an ETV, particularly one on futures, can trade at a premium or a discount.

In July 2009, a natural gas fund suspended the creation of any new shares because they ran out of a pre-approved number of shares the fund had registered with the SEC. This was the result of strong demand for fund shares, which naturally led to demand for futures contracts underlying the fund.

It took a little over two months to get a request granted by the SEC for an increased allotment of more shares. During that time period of halted creations, the fund traded at a premium up to 19 percent. This premium quickly dissipated when creations resumed because it was a result of structure and not the underlying performance. See it graphically illustrated in Exhibit 8.9 and highlighted by the yellow circle.

Next I want to discuss a phenomenon in the futures market that seriously affected the investment goals of the fund. Actually, all ETPs using commodity futures are subject to this. Because futures have an expiration date, they must be continually rolled to maintain exposure.

In this case, the fund endeavored to use near month futures to replicate the moves in natural gas prices. But futures don't always trade around the spot price of the commodity they represent and can sometimes go into a state of contango or backwardation. Contango is the situation where the price to deliver a commodity in the future is higher than the spot price or shorter-term futures contract. If an ETP wants to hold near term futures and those futures are in contango, there can be a cost to investors. In simplest terms, futures expire regularly, and when they get close to expiration, the ETP has to roll from the near month to the far month.

They sell the near month, let's say at the spot price of natural gas, in this case, and buy the far month, which is typically more expensive. Since the fund has a defined amount of investment, or cash value, when it rolls, it buys fewer far month contracts than it originally held because of their higher price. The price deterioration happens when the spot price doesn't rise to the level the far contract predicts, and the value of the far contract decreases as it becomes the near contract. In Exhibit 8.10, you can see how drastically the fund underperformed the actual price of natural gas because of the compounding losses of the continuous future rolling when the futures were in a state of pricing contango during the time period.

Backwardation is the reverse of contango and can have a positive return effect on ETPs holding those futures. It is the case when the far month is cheaper than the near month or spot price, and when the fund

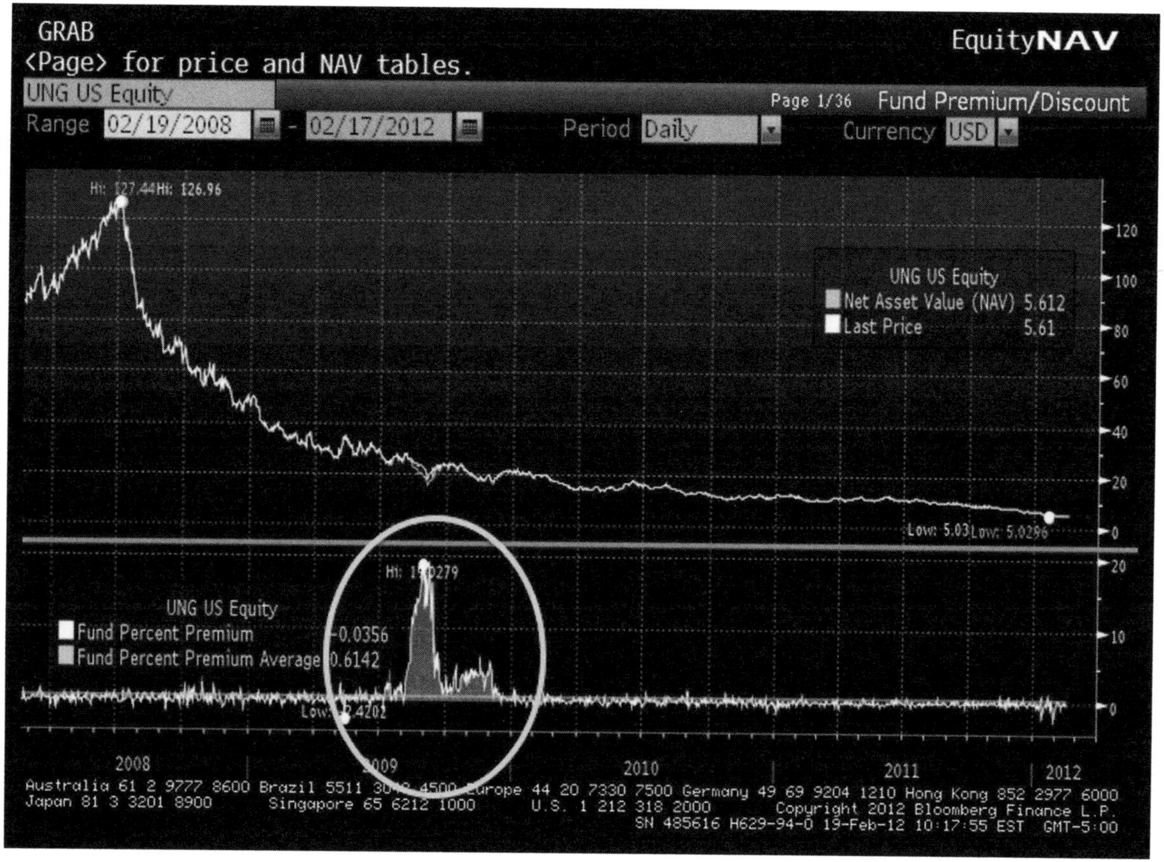
GRAB
<Page> for price and NAV tables.
EquityNAV
UNG US Equity
Page 1/36
Fund Premium/Discount
Range 02/19/2008 - 02/17/2012
Period Daily
Currency USD
UNG US Equity
Net Asset Value (NAV) 5.612
Last Price 5.61
Low: 5.03
Low: 5.0296
120
100
80
60
40
20
0
UNG US Equity
Fund Percent Premium -0.0356
Fund Percent Premium Average 0.6142
20
10
0
2008
2010
2011
2012
Japan 81 3 3201 8900
U.S. 1 212 318 2000
Copyright 2012 Bloomberg Finance L.P.
SN 485616 H629-94-0 19-Feb-12 10:17:55 EST GMT-5:00

Exhibit 8.9 Halted Creations Chart

Reprinted with permission from Bloomberg. Copyright 2012 Bloomberg L.P. All rights reserved.

KEY POINT:

Futures contracts have an expiration date. To maintain exposure over a period that is longer than the typical three-month expiry period of a futures contract, the exposure must be rolled from one period to the next period. The process for doing that is selling the contracts that are about to expire and buying new contracts that will expire further out in time. There is a cost to trading and rolling futures contracts.

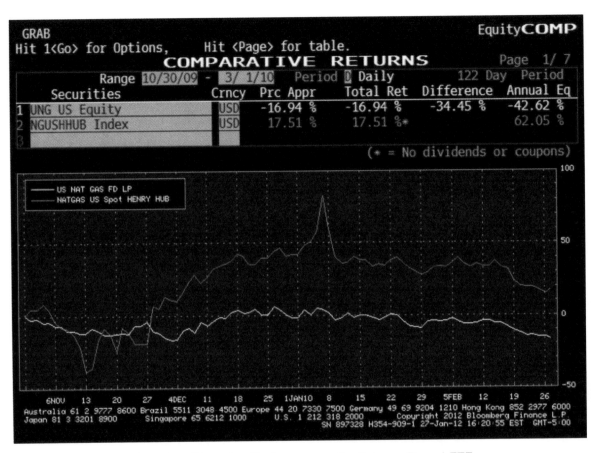

Exhibit 8.10 Chart Showing Diverging Performance of a Futures-Based ETF

Reprinted with permission from Bloomberg. Copyright 2012 Bloomberg L.P. All rights reserved.

rolls those futures, they acquire more contracts than previously held.

This is an interesting issue, and there are now ETPs structured to take advantage of this situation. There is a natural gas futures contango ETN designed to take advantage of an upward-sloping futures curve and profit from the state of contango. It is effectively providing short exposure to the front month and long exposure to the mid-term futures contract. Taking a look at Exhibit 8.11, you can see the difference in performance of one structure versus another. This is an illustration of why an investor needs to know how the ETP is structured and how the issuer plans on accessing exposure to the benchmark. Both ETPs are providing exposure to natural gas. One goes long the front month future, and one goes short the front month while going long the further-out contract. The difference is clear, and investors in either one of these should understand the nuances of the futures market and how that could affect their investment in different market scenarios. The bottom line is that as an investor, you should always be a risk manager as well, assessing the products you are getting exposure to and understanding how to predict their performance with market changes and other potential structural issues.

There are two parts to the investment process:

1. Determining your desired exposure
2. Determining the proper structure to achieve that exposure

As you can see, the varying structures can lead to vastly different returns on similar exposures. So it is important to understand the effects of the structure in which you are building a position. Another important consideration is the tax consequences.

A Discussion of Taxation Issues

Capital gains are taxed differently based on the type of asset you are investing in and the type of structure that is built around the asset. The taxation of a fund, and thereby its performance and return, can depend on a variety of factors:

- Fund creation and redemption activity
- Structure of the fund and attribution of the performance
- Index turnover
- Cash management
- Tracking error
- Expense ratios

Presented here are some concepts to be aware of when considering the tax ramifications of your position. Please seek an accountant for specific tax guidance regarding your fund holdings. These are examples of potential treatment of the various structures and can by no means be used as a representation for tax-planning purposes.

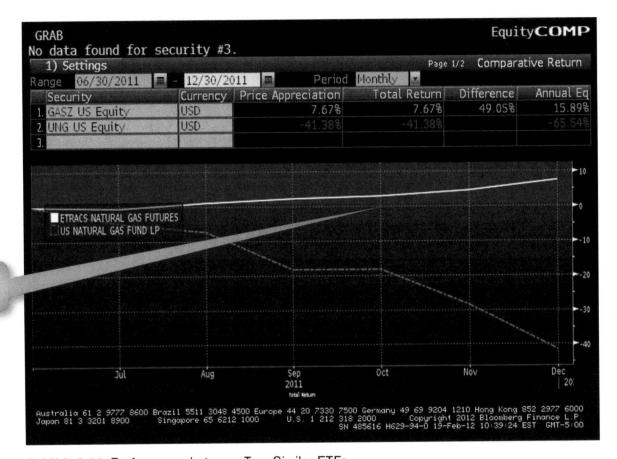

Note the spread in performance between the two funds.

Exhibit 8.11 Performance between Two Similar ETFs

Currencies

Two types of ETPs provide exposure to currencies as an asset class. There are products structured as grantor trusts, where tax liabilities typically flow through to shareholders. Any gains and interest income from the funds should be taxed as ordinary income, regardless of how long you hold the fund. You could hold the fund for five years, and when you sell, any gains would be taxed as ordinary income, not long-term capital gains.

Currency ETFs have different treatment for tax purposes. Because these funds access the currency space through money-market-like securities and are structured as ETFs rather than grantor trusts, they are taxed like traditional bond funds. If you hold the funds for a year or longer, the gains will typically be taxed as long-term capital gains.

Physical Metals

Precious metals and bullion are typically considered collectibles by the Internal Revenue Service (IRS). ETPs that hold gold or silver bullion, for example, are therefore usually taxable as collectibles. Long-term capital gains tax rates on collectibles may be as high as 28 percent.

Futures Products

ETPs that track futures contracts are typically subjected to marked-to-market rules that tax unrealized gains at the end of the year. Gains are taxed at a blend of 60 percent of the long-term capital gains rate and 40 percent of the short-term capital gains rate. At the current long-term tax rate of 15 percent and a typical 35 percent short-term tax rate, the blended tax treatment results in a nearly 23 percent tax liability.

ETFs as Extended Share Classes of Index Mutual Funds

Most ETFs from BlackRock, State Street, and many other fund companies are stand-alone funds. In contrast, many, if not all, Vanguard ETFs are a share class of a larger mutual fund, which gives investors several different ways to buy the portfolio. This multishare class has been the subject of discussion concerning whether the funds are more or less tax-efficient.

The stand-alone fund companies claim that their methodology is more tax-efficient because of the in-kind creation and redemption process that does not pool all investors' trading costs together within the fund. The alternative claims that their multishare fund structure is just as much, if not more, tax-efficient because it gives the fund manager additional flexibility. Only time will tell if one structure versus another adds or detracts meaningfully in terms of tax efficiency.

Booking and ETF Platform Execution Issues

Booking issues sometimes arise because of the global reach of ETFs and because of administrative systems that may not be equipped to handle lags in execution price. Some clients are excluded from accessing the liquidity of the underlying and trading on an agency basis to reduce impact because of timing differences. For example, in most India funds, the traders and market makers need to know on T-1 (the day before the actual trade date) that a client wants to trade locally. This is strictly because of timing logistics. The basket orders need to be sent out by the Indian local close, which is some time before trading in New York begins. In some instances, the issuer needs to be notified the prior day as well, and thus such orders need to be placed before close of business on T-1. Because of administrative processes and currency trading requirements, the final price is not always determined until T+1 or T+2. Therefore, if you want to access liquidity in certain emerging markets, you might give the order verbally on Monday but not get your final price until Wednesday. Some types of retail-based clients cannot tolerate such lags and are therefore asking wealth management execution platform desks to get immediate liquidity in ETFs. This can lead to a situation where the execution desk cannot access the liquidity of the underlying, or may be unfamiliar with the ETF, and either trades it like a stock, creating unnecessary impact, or trades on a risk market with a liquidity provider, paying an unnecessary risk premium. Meanwhile the client would have been willing to take the performance risk over that time period to lessen market impact and execution costs. The amount of ETFs traded by these advisory businesses has grown rapidly over recent years and is continuing

along that path. By various accounts, ETF trading can reach almost 40 percent of all stock traded on a daily basis (it usually hovers around 30 percent), which can be extrapolated to mean that wealth platform execution desks of the advisory businesses are getting closer and closer to trading a similar percentage of their business in ETFs.

The problems with not developing advanced execution methodologies can lead to an execution shortfall on the advisory desks trading these products and an administrative shortfall on the part of the customer. Some advisory execution systems are so antiquated that there are fees for trading away from the in-house desk even if that in-house desk doesn't have related flow or ETF liquidity-providing capabilities. Sometimes the flow is funneled to one specific broker-dealer only, which creates monopolistic qualities to the order flow. This is not best execution oriented and, in some cases, may not even satisfy the fiduciary responsibilities associated with client order flow.

Going forward, I would hope that the clients and liquidity providers continue to work together to find solutions for the simple logistical problems. I also hope that ETF-specific execution practices are adopted by trading desks and clients alike to avoid any unnecessary costs. The most immediate solution I can hope for is for customers to understand the structure of an ETF and seek assistance from a dedicated ETF trading desk on how to best execute their trade, given size, administrative constraints, and objectives.

ETF Trade Settlement—Fails to Deliver

Trade fails were a topic in the ETF news several years ago. Here are some details about how fails occur and what they mean in the ETF market.

When two entities engage in a transaction—that is, party A is buying what party B is selling—party A pays a mutually agreed price for party B's security. There is a risk, however, that party B will fail to deliver the security in the mutually agreed-upon time frame, thus creating settlement failure. The settlement, however, may occur a day or two later, still at the original agreed-upon price. This should be contrasted to a "trade failure," in which, regardless of extra time allotted, the trade will never settle. In both cases, whether settlement failure or trade failure, an investor's cash is not at risk of being lost. In the United States and many other countries, the money will have been residing at a clearinghouse or financial institution while the transaction is settling. The clearinghouse acts as an intermediary to mitigate the counterparty risk involved in trading. In the case of a settlement failure with securities that are eventually delivered, the investor is not in any different position than if the settlement failure had not occurred. In a trade failure, cash is returned to the investor and the loss is limited to the opportunity cost of having had that cash deployed. Below is the SEC's definition of trade settlement as defined in Rule 15c6-1 under the Securities Exchange Act of 1934:

Generally, investors complete or settle their security transactions within three settlement days. This settlement cycle is known as T+3 (or "trade date plus three days"). T+3 means that when a trade occurs, the participants to the trade deliver and pay for the security at a clearing agency three settlement days after the trade is executed so the brokerage firm can exchange those funds for the securities on that third settlement day. The three-day settlement period applies to most security transactions, including stocks, bonds, municipal securities, mutual funds traded through a brokerage firm, and limited partnerships that trade on an exchange. Government securities and stock options settle on the next settlement day following the trade (or T+1). In addition, Rule 15c6-1 prohibits broker-dealers from effecting or entering into a contract for the purchase or sale of a security that provides for payment of funds and delivery of securities later than the third business day after the date of the contract unless otherwise expressly agreed to by the parties at the time of the transaction.[7] However, failure to deliver securities on T+3 does not violate Rule 15c6-1.[8]

Settlement of Equities versus ETFs

ETF settlement failures take place at a higher rate than do single-stock equity failures. Throughout 2010, the average daily fails for U.S.-listed ETFs totaled approximately $1 billion per day in value.[9] During the last week in April 2011, the dollar volume of U.S.-listed

ETFs traded equaled approximately $305 billion notional or $61 billion per day.[10] Assuming fail rates remained constant from 2010 throughout the first quarter of 2011, we can see that approximately 1.6 percent of ETF trades are failing on a daily basis. Looking at this differently, we can also see that 98.4 percent of all ETF trades are clearing and settling properly. While it is always imperative to strive to correct any issues in the financial markets, we are far from crisis levels of settlement failures in the ETF markets.

ETFs and single-stock equities are treated similarly for the purposes of listing and secondary trading. However, different characteristics help explain why ETF trades fail at a somewhat greater rate. I'll go through the reasoning behind this increased rate of settlement failures and conclude with some recommendations on remedies. In the process, I'll also clarify the lack of risk to investors.

Why Do Settlement Failures Occur?

There are three main factors that contribute to settlement failures in ETFs:

1. **Settlement Date Differences:** In general, ETF trades take place between a client and a professional trader or market maker, as opposed to the client-to-client norm in single-stock equities. Very rarely is there a natural cross in ETFs, meaning that large-size blocks between two clients are traded against each other. The market simply works too fast for that to happen. Because of this, there can be a mismatch between settlement dates for market makers and standard clients. Trades are supposed to settle on T+3. If you are a short-seller, you are supposed to be bought in on T+4 if your trade has not settled. A long seller will get an extra day and be bought in on T+5 if he or she has not settled the trade. Market makers, however, have an extra day's leeway on being bought in when short-selling ETFs. Since market makers are considered to be short exempt, they are considered long sellers and are typically not bought in until T+5, or even sometimes T+6. This causes settlement issues because the timing used by market makers to arrange their short coverage for settlement will vary from that of standard investors. According to one stock loan desk, this market maker short exemption is the cause for most ETF fails.

2. **Stock Loan Latency:** The larger ETFs act like momentum products, which means if there is a market-moving story in a theme of an ETF, most investors are going to be trading in the same direction very quickly. Most clients and market makers borrow blanket amounts of certain ETFs they traffic in every morning just in case they need to short. The stock loan desks give these "locates" of shares to borrow with the notion that not all of them will be used, which is usually the case. However, in the momentum theory, if a market-moving event creates a windfall into a particular ETF and all those locates are used,

it may not be feasible to cover all those borrows by T+3, especially since the stock loan desk won't sort out the shortage until T+1, at which point they may ask for assistance from a trading desk to create more shares to cover their loans. The creation usually takes T+3 from that date to settle, so the original sell is already looking at T+4 until shares would come in to facilitate the settlement.

3. **Creation and Redemption Latency:** This latency can be caused by many reasons. One scenario is the one described previously, where the market (either market makers or investors) has an increase in short sales that cannot be covered for settlement until T+4. Another scenario occurs when some ETFs have complex creations due to time difference in underlying settlements, various market holidays for underlying settlements, and the general manual intervention needed to tend to all these nuances and details when dealing across the globe and in different asset classes. These can result in slight delays in settlement of creations that then cause delays in the settlement of those short sales reliant on the creation. If an ETF has failed for five consecutive days and the size of the trade(s) is greater than .5 percent of the fund, the ETF goes on the Regulation SHO Threshold securities list, and the security becomes subject to mandatory close out requirements as detailed by the regulation. It doesn't come off this list until all the fails have been cleared. So if one trade

that qualified for this settles on T+6 and another fail has just hit its T+5 day, then the ETF will remain on the list without disclosing the details of how long each particular trade is failing. The fact that ETFs are on the list more is merely a result of the high velocity and large number of participants trading these products. It is not an indication of a structural defect. Also, the manual and sometimes complex nature of settling creation and redemption adds to the likelihood of ETFs being on the list as opposed to single stocks.

Can Anything Be Done about Trade Fails?

Certain measures can be taken to reduce the number of fails in ETFs.

■ Increase the financial ramifications and/or penalties of incorrect bookings or other events leading to settlement failures.

■ Remove the extended time frame allotted to market makers for short sale settlement. However, this would potentially further mitigate financial arbitrage incentives and take liquidity out of the market.

■ Increase the stringency and transparency of the stock loan marketplace.

■ Reduce the ETF creation unit size. Creation and redemption sizes should be as small as possible to help eliminate stub positions on market-making books and encourage creation of new shares with as little risk as possible. That is, if a creation unit size is 100,000 shares and a market maker sells 80,000 shares to a customer, they are unlikely to overcreate to facilitate settlement and instead wait until they either have a full creation unit or are able to buy it back in the market over their five-day allotment for settlement.

Summary

Although ETPs can come in various different forms and structures, it is critical to the security of your investment to understand the particular structure that you are looking to get into and the various risks and return dynamics that it might produce. While the industry is moving ahead to make this process easier and more transparent, perhaps with a universal labeling system, it is still incumbent on investors to be their own advocates. Some risks cannot be forecasted, like political revolutions, but it is always better to understand the ramifications to the product and know that you chose the correct vehicle for your desired exposure. You need to quantify the price at which you gain access and accept that going into the investment.

Notes

1. Investment Company Institute, *2011 Investment Company Fact Book*, Appendix A, 191. Investment Company Institute, Washington, DC.

2. Ibid.

3. Ibid.

4. Ibid.

5. "Exchange Traded Products Q&A with Laura Morrison," *U.S. Trading News,* April 11, 2011.

6. "ETFs: A Call for Greater Transparency and Consistent Regulation," *BlackRock/Ishares,* October 2011.

7. 17 CFR 240.15c6-1; Exchange Act Release No. 33023 (Oct. 7, 1993), 58 FR 52891 (Oct. 13, 1993).

8. Exchange Act Release No. 56212 (Aug. 7, 2007), 72 FR 45544, n. 2 (Aug. 14, 2007) ("2007 Regulation SHO Final Amendments").

9. Ewing Marion Kauffman Foundation, "Canaries in the Coal Mine report," Exhibit 3, March 2011.

10. *MorganStanley SmithBarney US ETF Weekly Update,* May 2, 2011.

Test Yourself

1. True or false—The underlying structure of the fund that you purchase can have a significant impact on the returns of the product.

2. True or false—An ETF whose underlying basket has stopped trading no longer offers value to investors.

3. True or false—ETFs have more fails than regular equities because the users of ETFs are lazy and typically don't have enough money to settle trades.

Answers: 1. True   2. False   3. False

CHAPTER 9

Where to Find ETF Information

Awide variety of places offer information on ETFs. All the major broker-dealers offer some form of research on ETFs. Typically, the advisor platforms provide product research in the form of portfolio positioning types of pieces and asset class discussions. The institutional trading desks provide more data and trade-related research covering market action or news. The exchanges all have detailed information about the products that are listed and trade on their respective platforms or the whole universe of ETPs. Most issuers have educational sections of their websites, and the bigger ones like SPDR University provide comprehensive product education.

Since the first ETF was launched, a cornucopia of independent companies have also competed to provide information about the ETF industry. You can type almost anything following ETF into a web search engine, from ETF.com to ETF trends to ETF zone, and you will get to a list of relevant product-related sites. This chapter begins with a brief description of just a

few of the online resources that individuals and advisors can use to learn more about the ETF industry and its products. The remainder of the chapter focuses on the different ETF resources that exist for larger institutional investors and other interested professional traders. The companies referenced within this chapter are not ranked; they are discussed in random order. This is by no means an exhaustive list of information or all the websites available for ETF data. I am simply highlighting some valuable information for readers.

ETF Screening and Fund Information

There are a number of resources that you can use to supplement the knowledge provided for you in the pages of this book. Three very comprehensive sites are IndexUniverse, Yahoo!, and ETFdatabase. IndexUniverse was launched in 1999 and has a section dedicated to teaching newcomers about the ETF industry.[1]

The website includes articles and webinars that have the goal of providing a basic level of knowledge regarding the ETF industry. If you join the website and are a certified financial planner (CFP), you can receive continuing education credit. Yahoo!, a well-known search engine, has a section dedicated to educating people on the inner workings of ETFs.[2] Similar to IndexUniverse, Yahoo! offers a selection of articles that aim to provide a foundation of ETF-related knowledge for users. Presented here are some details about a variety of non-issuer-related sites and some of the information they provide.

Bloomberg

Bloomberg is providing ETF data on two levels, through the web and through their terminals. They each have different levels of information. The Bloomberg website is primarily thought of as a portal of information and news; however, it also has a section dedicated to ETFs.[3] In this section of Bloomberg's website, a user can view the top ETFs by assets under management (AUM) within a number of different categories (commodities, energy, leveraged, financial services, etc.). Bloomberg is a unique source of information in that it provides data and information on ETFs domiciled both inside and outside the United States. The data within these pages are not real time; however, a user who clicks on any of the individual ETFs is taken to a new page that includes real-time market statistics for that specific ETF. Bloomberg also provides its users with a free ETF Screener.[4] The ETF Screener allows users to search through the entire global universe of ETFs to find those that meet a select set of criteria. The following screenshot (Exhibit 9.1) shows what would happen if a user searched for all global ETFs with between $1 and 5 billion in AUM, an expense ratio below 0.50, and a year-to-date rate of return of above 25 percent. The user is then able to select an individual ETF to find more detailed statistical and fundamental information on that given ETF.

ETFdb

The mission statement of ETF Database (ETFdb)[5] is:

To provide daily coverage of the ETF industry that goes beyond the headlines

To educate the financial community on the benefits, drawbacks, complexities, and other issues associated with ETF investing

To provide financial advisors and individual investors resources to make intelligent, informed ETF investments

The team fulfills their mission statement by providing a seemingly endless array of ETF-related information. The data and information on the ETFdb website are dedicated to U.S.-domiciled ETFs. ETFdb offers a comprehensive ETF screener[6] that allows users to filter through the universe of U.S.-listed ETFs. This screener first requires users to select an asset class before they can further search through the ETFs. Depending on the asset class selected, the screener allows users to filter according to different parameters, as can be seen in Exhibit 9.2.

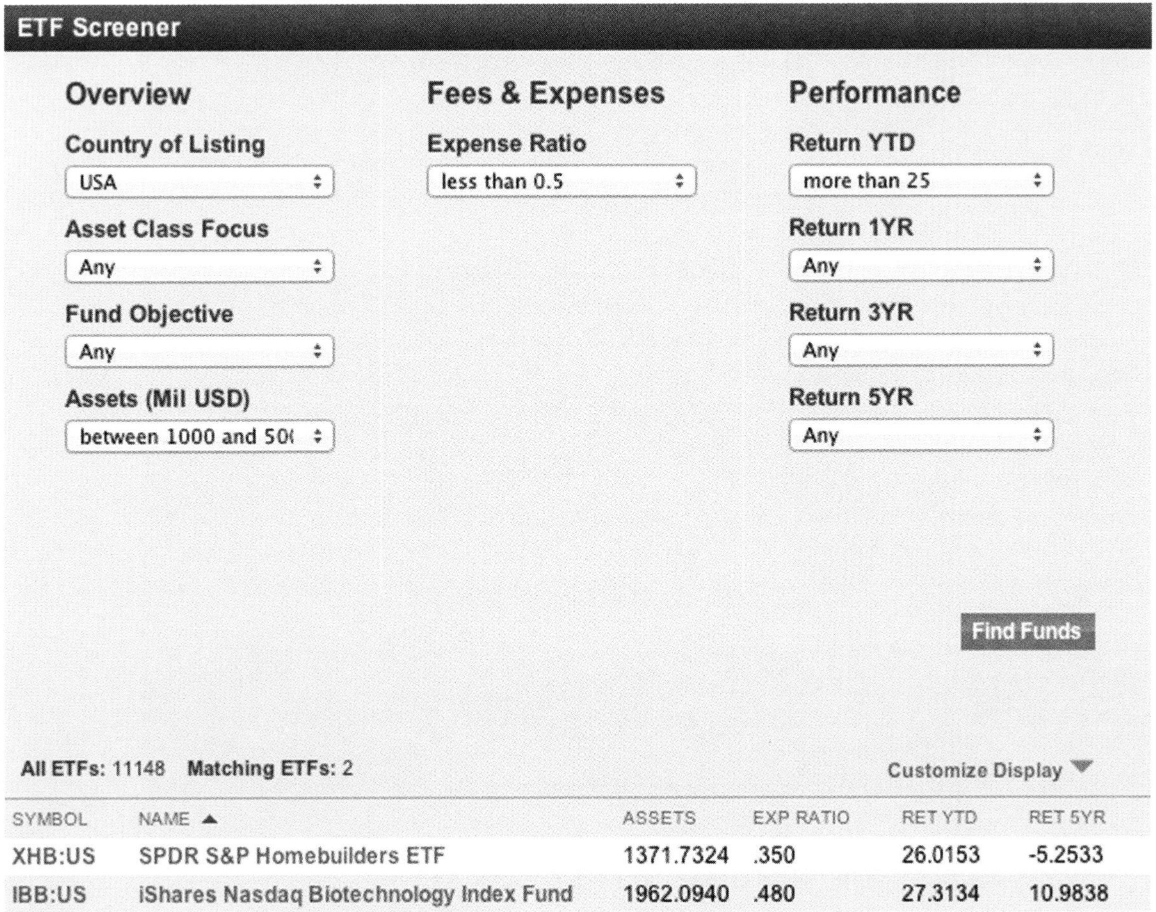

ETF Screener

Overview

Country of Listing

| USA | ⬍ |

Asset Class Focus

| Any | ⬍ |

Fund Objective

| Any | ⬍ |

Assets (Mil USD)

| between 1000 and 50(| ⬍ |

Fees & Expenses

Expense Ratio

| less than 0.5 | ⬍ |

Performance

Return YTD

| more than 25 | ⬍ |

Return 1YR

| Any | ⬍ |

Return 3YR

| Any | ⬍ |

Return 5YR

| Any | ⬍ |

Find Funds

All ETFs: 11148   **Matching ETFs:** 2   Customize Display ▼

SYMBOL	NAME ▲	ASSETS	EXP RATIO	RET YTD	RET 5YR
XHB:US	SPDR S&P Homebuilders ETF	1371.7324	.350	26.0153	-5.2533
IBB:US	iShares Nasdaq Biotechnology Index Fund	1962.0940	.480	27.3134	10.9838

Exhibit 9.1 Bloomberg.com ETF Screener

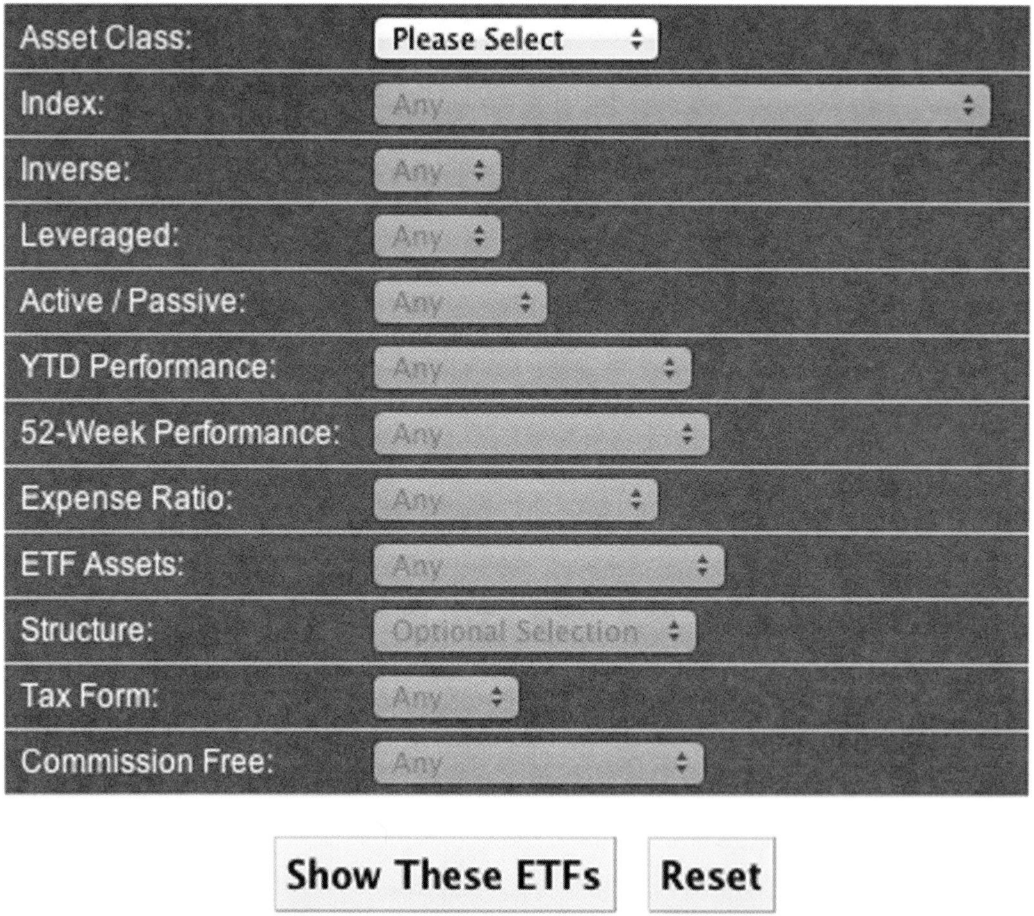

Asset Class:	Please Select ⬍
Index:	Any ⬍
Inverse:	Any ⬍
Leveraged:	Any ⬍
Active / Passive:	Any ⬍
YTD Performance:	Any ⬍
52-Week Performance:	Any ⬍
Expense Ratio:	Any ⬍
ETF Assets:	Any ⬍
Structure:	Optional Selection ⬍
Tax Form:	Any ⬍
Commission Free:	Any ⬍

Show These ETFs   **Reset**

Exhibit 9.2 ETFdb.com ETF Screener

Aside from the ETF Screener, ETFdb offers a number of additional tools to its users. The ETF Stock Exposure Tool allows users to search for a specific equity, and the tool returns all ETFs that hold that security, sorted by largest weighting percentage. In Exhibit 9.3, I wanted to know which ETFs hold the largest percentage of AMZN (Amazon).[7] While only the top 10 are shown in this screenshot, ETFdb provided the complete list of ETFs that hold AMZN.

Similar to the ETF Stock Exposure Tool, the ETF Country Exposure Tool[8] allows users to identify ETFs that have the largest weighting of securities domiciled in a given country. The Mutual Fund to ETF Converter[9] is a good tool for traditional mutual fund investors who might be interested in investing in ETFs instead. Users are prompted to enter the ticker for a mutual fund, and the tool provides a list of ETFs that are similar to the given mutual fund. The tool looks at the underlying index of the mutual fund and identifies ETFs that have the same underlying index. The ETF Head-to-Head Tool[10] allows users to compare two ETFs by looking at four different categories: overview, holdings, performance, and technicals.

Ticker	ETF	ETFdb Category	Expense Ratio	Weighting
PNQI	Nasdaq Internet Portfolio	Technology Equities	0.60%	9.88%
RTH	Market Vectors Retail ETF	Consumer Discretionary Equities	0.35%	9.24%
FDN	DJ Internet Index Fund	Technology Equities	0.60%	8.88%
WMW	Morningstar Wide Moat Focus ETN	All Cap Equities	0.75%	6.37%
MOAT	Market Vectors Wide Moat Research ETF	All Cap Equities	0.49%	6.22%
XLY	Consumer Discretionary Select Sector SPDR	Consumer Discretionary Equities	0.18%	5.80%
FCL	Focus Morningstar Consumer Cyclical Index ETF	Consumer Discretionary Equities	0.19%	5.01%
IYC	Dow Jones U.S. Consumer Index Fund	Consumer Discretionary Equities	0.48%	4.20%
VCR	Consumer Discretion ETF	Consumer Discretionary Equities	0.19%	3.97%
RWG	Large-Cap Growth Equity Strategy Fund	Large Cap Growth Equities	0.89%	3.63%
SKYY	ISE Cloud Computing Index Fund	Technology Equities	0.60%	3.56%

Exhibit 9.3 ETF Screens by Stock Holding

Aside from the ETFdb tools just described, the site offers a large selection of ETF-related articles and publishes new articles every day (weekends included). These articles are disseminated to users via both postings on the website and a daily e-mail blast. The home page of the website offers links leading to different centers, which are groups of pages dedicated to articles covering a given ETF topic (Financial Advisor & RIA, Alternatives, Emerging Markets, and Active ETFs). To ensure all interested parties can view ETFdb whether at home or on the go, the company also offers an iPhone and iPad application that has all of the same features found on the website.

The models of revenue generation for ETF websites typically rely on advertising dollars or offering some services for a fee via a paid subscription to the website. With regard to ETFdb, a significant percent of the information available on ETFdb is free, with a smaller piece as part of a paid subscription called ETFdb Pro.[11] The Pro section offers its users access to a number of additional ETF tools. ETFdb Portfolios[12] offers its users the ability to select from 34 different preconstructed ETF portfolios based on the requirements of that individual user. Portfolio examples include the cheapskate, high tech, and ex-us portfolios. ETF Scorecards[13] is a tool that provides qualitative and quantitative analysis of all U.S. ETFs, allowing users to compare ETFs across a multitude of dimensions. ETF Research Reports[14] are detailed reports issued monthly that provide additional detail into specific sectors of the ETF industry. ETFdb Category Reports[15] breaks down the universe of ETFs into 66 proprietary categories. It allows investors to more easily sort through the universe of ETFs.

Index Universe

Index Universe began covering ETFs in 2003. It is the self-proclaimed "leading independent authority on ETFs, indexes and index funds."[16] Index Universe is comprised of a primary website dedicated to the U.S. market and a newer sister website[17] dedicated to the European ETF market. Index Universe also offers its users a number of tools that can be used to further synthesize the ETF market. The Data Tool[18] is similar to an ETF screener in that it allows the user to filter the ETF universe for 33 different fields. This tool also

Name	Ticker	Exp Ratio	Asset Class	YTD	1-Mo	3-Mo	12-Mo	3-Yr	5-Yr	2011	2010	P/E Ratio
iShares Cohen & Steers Realty Majors	ICF	0.35000	Real Estate	13.69172	5.36387	3.35668	11.94791	34.00449	1.37284	10.15	29.14	37.74
iShares Dow Jones U.S. Real Estate	IYR	0.47000	Real Estate	14.50169	5.35191	3.52558	10.13648	30.32057	0.82940	5.46	26.59	27.06
SPDR Dow Jones REIT	RWR	0.25000	Real Estate	14.77936	5.50239	3.71497	13.02281	33.28564	1.94936	8.99	28.03	36.54
Vanguard REIT	VNQ	0.10000	Real Estate	14.60195	5.48464	3.61194	12.88520	33.11691	3.14550	8.56	28.42	41.27

Show 50 Results Per Page | Sort Results By: Name | Ascending | (Click on columns to sort)

Exhibit 9.4 Index Universe Data Tool

allows users to view as many as 33 data points for ETFs within a given asset class. Exhibit 9.4 shows a selection of data points for real estate ETFs with more than $1 billion in AUM.[19]

The ETF classification system[20] is a tool that furthers the power of the ETF Data Tool by allowing users to view many more descriptive and informative fields relating to all ETFs. This classification system can be used in conjunction with the ETF Analytics Tool[21] to view a range of similar ETFs.

The user then has the ability to select an individual ETF that will bring the user to a page of market data specific to that ETF. The source data for these tools comes from Markit, a financial services company that I discuss later in this chapter. The Fund Flows Tool[22] is an innovative tool in that it allows users to view the creation and redemption information for any ETF for any period in time (since 1993).

The remainder of the Index Universe website is primarily focused on articles, blogs, interviews, and comments related to the ETF industry. The articles posted on the website are broken down into asset classes to facilitate the user-friendliness of the website. Index Universe also offers a number of free webinars that speak to hot button issues and aim to increase the awareness of the website's users. Index Universe also has the longest-running free weekly e-mail within the ETF industry, providing information on new ETF launches, closures, and ETF articles.

Index Universe does not have a separate subscription-based section; instead, Index Universe has two additional ETF-related ventures. Index Universe typically holds several annual ETF-related conferences: Inside ETFs, Inside Commodities, Inside ETFs-Europe, and Inside Indexing (launched in March 2012). The goal of these conferences is to educate RIAs, individual ETF investors, and family offices about the entire ETF industry. These annual conferences typically have more than 2,000 participants from all aspects of the industry and have become industry staples. These conferences differ in pricing for RIAs, individual investors, service providers, ETF issuers, and other large institutions. In addition to the conferences, Index Universe also prints two ETF magazines: *The Journal of Indexes* and *ETFR,* which are both available online and in hard copy via an annual subscription.[23] These magazines provide more articles and greater detail about the index and ETF industries. They have also recently started a comprehensive ETF research site, called ETF Analytics, which will provide research and ratings on the ETF universe.

Morningstar

Morningstar, a major multinational firm, also has a free ETF section designed for small to midsize investors.[24] Much like its competitors, Morningstar also offers free ETF tools on its website. The ETF Screener is a dynamic tool allowing users to sort through all U.S.-domiciled ETFs based on more than 100 criteria. The ETF Screener can also be used to show ETF distribution charts, allowing a user to graphically view the strength of the ETF universe in one picture. For

Exhibit 9.5 Morningstar ETF Screener

example, the image in Exhibit 9.5 shows the expense ratios, the YTD return, and the 1-year return for a selection of ETFs.[25]

Morningstar also offers an ETF Performance table[26] that allows investors to sort through the ETF universe based on the ETF performance over a defined period of time. A user who selects an ETF receives a description of the ETF and a 20-minute-delayed quote. Morningstar recently began an ETF Launch Center[27] designed to provide its users with a list of all of the ETFs that have been recently launched. A user can then access additional information about any ETF, including the prospectus or any other documentation filed with the SEC. The remainder of Morningstar's free ETF website is dedicated to news articles and videos relating to the ETF industry. Unlike the other free websites, Morningstar has in-house RIAs and looks to increase their advisors' AUM; thus, many of the articles on their website are written for ETF investors looking to learn how to invest using ETFs, rather than to provide ETF information and statistics.

As many people know, Morningstar was originally a mutual fund rating company, and a lot of their ETF data is comprised of analytics, rankings, and ratings. On the Morningstar website, anything with a ⊞ next to it is available only for paying members of the website. Morningstar is a little different from ETFdb and IndexUniverse because their website contains thousands of pages of financial data unrelated to the ETF industry. By paying the annual subscription, users are allowed access to all of the other features available on the website. For ETF users, subscribing to Morningstar gives you the opportunity to use additional ETF tools. The ETF Analyst Favorites provide independent qualitative research for 300+ ETFs. The ETF Valuation Quickrank tool allows screening of the ETF universe using Morningstar specific data points. Also available is Morningstar's Cost Analyzer Tool.

XTF

XTF is a website primarily dedicated to providing rankings and ratings of ETFs using their proprietary rating system.[28] By signing up for a free membership, a user receives access to a selection of the data available on the website. Among other available information, XTF provides ratings, trends, market data, and holdings data for all U.S.-domiciled ETFs. XTF has a number of unique ETF tools on its website. The Fund Sponsors and Index Providers Tool helps identify all of the ETFs issued by a sponsor. The tool then allows a user to click on any ETF and view the market data and ratings information for that ETF. For example, the image in Exhibit 9.6 shows all five ETFs issued by ALPS Advisors, Inc.[29]

A user could then click on a ticker and see the information for the ETF in Exhibit 9.7.

Another unique feature of the XTF website is the Heatmap tool,[30] which breaks down the universe of ETFs into their underlying securities and groups the

Fund Sponsor	Index Provider
Name	**Market Cap**
All Fund Sponsors	$1,188.21B
AdvisorShares	$634.31M
ALPS Advisors, Inc.	**$3.83B**
Arrow Funds	$9.20M
Bank of New York	$9.43B
Barclays Bank PLC	$6.81B
BlackRock, Inc.	$485.18B
BNP Paribas	$16.10M
Charles Schwab Investment Management Inc	$6.77B
Citigroup	$6.20M
Columbia Management Investment Advisers LLC	$24.42M
Credit Suisse AG	$1.14B
Deutsche Bank AG	$12.56B
Direxion Shares	$6.04B
Emerging Global Advisors, LLC	$685.67M
ETF Securities	$3.67B

ALPS Advisors, Inc.   **5 ETFs**   **Market Cap: $3.83B**

ETF Symbol	ETF Description	XTF Rating Sort ▽	Exp. Ratio	Market Cap (US$)	Index Provider
AMLP	Alerian MLP ETF	5.9	0.85%	$3,607,938,176	Alerian Capital Management
GRI	Cohen & Steers Global Realty Majors ETF	2.4	0.55%	$67,878,000	Cohen & Steers, Inc.
CRBQ	Thomson Reuters/Jefferies CRB Global Commodity ETF	2.2	0.65%	$77,404,836	Reuters/Jeffries
SDOG	ALPS Sector Dividend Dogs ETF		0.40%	$2,562,051	S-Network Global Indexes
EQL	Alps Equal Sector Weight ETF		0.52%	$72,220,900	Bank Of America Merrill Lynch

Page 1 of 1 (5 items)   ◁ (p [1] ▷ size can be changed by **Premium** subscribers only)   Rows per page: [1(÷]

Exhibit 9.6 ETF Screener by Issuer

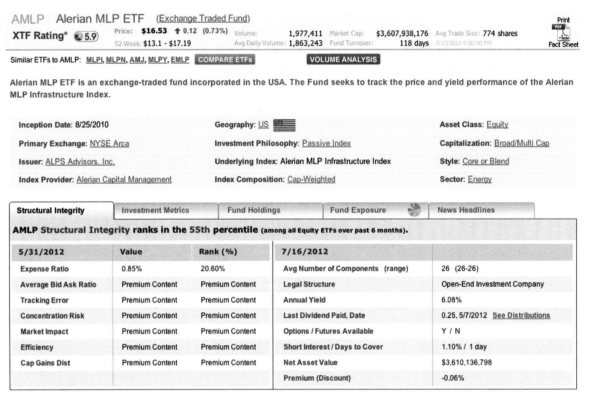

Exhibit 9.7 Single ETF Information

securities based on identifiers such as asset class, country, and industry. The research section on the XTF page includes the ETF Explorer,[31] XTF's version of an ETF screener, allowing its users to filter through ETFs and then view 18 data points for each ETF. The research section also allows users to compare up to six ETFs side-by-side, measure ETF performance and trading volume, and search for ETFs based on the securities they hold in their basket. There is no specific news section on the website; however, when a user looks at a specific ETF, they are able to view a news tab that pulls ETF-specific articles from Seeking Alpha.[32]

The subscription portion of XTF's website allows users to view a significant amount of more material than if they were using the site for free. While the free version allows access to most of the ETF tools, it does not include a full set of data. For example, the subscription version allows users to view the ETF analytics for 100 percent of all U.S. and Japanese listed ETFs, whereas the free version allows users to view ETF analytics for only the top 10 largest U.S.-listed ETFs. Similarly, ETF holdings are limited to the top 10 securities for free users, whereas subscription users can view all holdings. There are additional tools that are provided with a subscription.

ETF Data for Institutions and Professional Traders

Small and mid-level investors are not the only participants who need accurate, up-to-date ETF information. Large institutional investors and traders at major firms also require ETF-related information. The major difference between the two groups of investors is the type of information required. Institutional investors and traders require most of the same information as smaller investors; however, they typically require additional data, such as detailed basket data, forward-looking ETF dividend predictions, creation and redemption fees per ETF, excluded assets breakdowns, and many other fields that are unnecessary for the common ETF investor. Among the leading multinational financial

services companies that serve the industry by providing this information are DTC, Bloomberg, Markit, Morningstar, and Netik. The remainder of the chapter discusses the ETF-related services provided by some of these organizations.

DTCC—The Depository Trust & Clearing Corporation

They provide an extensive file daily containing ETF basket information as a service of the NSCC (National Securities Clearing Corporation). The NSCC is a subsidiary of DTCC that provides "clearing, settlement, risk management, central counterparty services and a guarantee of completion for certain transactions for virtually all broker-to-broker trades involving equities, corporate and municipal debt, American depository receipts, exchange traded funds and unit investment trusts."[33] The service handles creations and redemptions of ETFs and distribution of data.

Bloomberg

As I mentioned earlier, Bloomberg not only offers access to the global ETF markets but also provides its users with access to data, news, and information from the global financial marketplace. Bloomberg offers a number of services designed specifically for global institutional ETF investors and traders. To use the features offered by Bloomberg, one must purchase a terminal and a data license. Bloomberg provides basket data for all U.S. and global ETFs. A user can see the basket data by either viewing the basket of securities within a single creation unit or viewing the basket of securities within the funds portfolio. Since many traders use Excel to develop models to trade ETFs and to maintain their portfolios, Bloomberg offers its users the ability to pull most of their ETF data out of the terminal and into Excel spreadsheets. Bloomberg's solution provides its users historical information for each ETF that dates back to the launch of each ETF. Bloomberg also provides forward-looking ETF dividends for some of its U.S. ETFs.

Markit

Markit is a global financial services company that focuses a portion of its internal resources on providing vetted and accurate ETF-related data to traders and institutions across the globe. Markit provides its data to users via an XML feed. If requested by the end user, Markit can install the Markit Data Loader that seamlessly integrates Markit's data into a client's existing data systems, trading, and risk platforms. Markit provides header-level data (given NAV, calculated NAV, creation unit size, excluded assets value, total cash, estimated cash, and escrow) for all global ETFs and provides detailed basket information for all U.S. ETFs and all global equity ETFs. Markit breaks down a given ETF's excluded assets and escrow values (where applicable) for all equity ETFs. Markit also has the ability to calculate and distribute ETF data for custom ETFs, called "Bespoke ETFs," that have been constructed by their clients. In the future, Markit plans to expand its coverage to include basket data for all global ETFs.

One of Markit's unique services is what they call the Markit ETF Encyclopedia. Markit provides more than 250 pieces of descriptive data for all of the global ETFs, including but not limited to fields such as creation and redemption transaction fee, portfolio manager, primary exchange trading hours, and custodian. The purpose of the Encyclopedia is to provide users with all relevant information that would be needed to create and redeem baskets in any market in the world. Coupled with the Markit ETF Encyclopedia, the Markit ETF Dividends service provides up to four years of forecasted dividend dates, dividend amounts, and accrued dividends per share. Markit also analyzes intrayear accrued income ETF payments in order to calculate confidence levels for future income distributions.

Markit has two additional solutions for the European marketplace: Markit BOAT and Markit MSA. Markit BOAT is a solution that provides traders with information regarding the European OTC ETF market. This is important because unlike in the United States, most European trading is done via the OTC market. This tool helps users identify shifts in the market direction and trading patterns and to better understand market momentum. Markit MSA is a market share analysis tool that allows users to view aggregated trading volume rankings across multiple listings and highlights the most active brokers within an ETF and/or trading venue.

Morningstar

Morningstar provides ETF services to small and mid-level investors and also provides specific services tailored for the institutional marketplace. For the institutional marketplace, Morningstar provides data on all global and domestic ETFs. Morningstar is also unique in that it can deliver its data via multiple delivery platforms: API, XML, and software (Morningstar Direct and Advisor Workstation). A given institution can determine which delivery platform to use based on how that system best integrates with their existing systems. Similar to the data provided by Morningstar in other markets, the data the company provides to the institutional marketplace is primarily related to rankings and ratings and used to inspire investment ideas. Morningstar primarily targets large high-net-worth investment advisors who use the data provided by Morningstar to best identify investment targets for their clients.

Morningstar offers ETF analysis reports that contain more than 3,000 proprietary data points covering operational, portfolio, and performance (NAV and market price) characteristics of ETFs. As Morningstar's service is not primarily designed for traders, it does not cover data points such as estimated cash, total cash, excluded assets, and estimated ETF dividends. Aside from the ETF rankings and ratings services offered by Morningstar, a unique feature offered is the ability to provide ETF ownership information for the ETF industry. Through this feature, Morningstar identifies the companies, funds, and individuals who own ETFs. For example, Morningstar has data on all mutual funds that hold ETFs and the percentage of their assets that are invested in ETFs.

Netik

Netik[34] is a global financial services firm that focuses on providing ETF data to Delta One traders. Netik will either deliver its data as a flat file or provide its clients with a front-end system that will download the data directly from Netik's servers. Netik covers approximately 97.5 percent of U.S. ETFs and 50 percent of global ETFs. For all ETFs covered, Netik provides header data points including estimated cash, total cash, excluded assets total and breakdown, fractional share information, NAV, creation unit size, AUM, AUM in USD, and all relevant basket data points. In light of the most recent trading debacle at a global bank, Netik offers an interesting feature whereby they provide traders with the collateral baskets required for synthetic ETFs. Similar to Markit, Netik also offers the ability to calculate and provide daily data on Bespoke ETFs developed by their customers. Netik does not currently calculate ETF dividends; instead, they receive Bloomberg's ETF dividend feed and relay that information to their customers. In the near term, Netik will continue to expand its coverage to include additional global and domestic ETFs.

Summary

The companies identified in this chapter do not make up an exhaustive list of ETF information providers; these are just some companies that offer user-friendly platforms to access ETF data. There is no one company that is better than the rest; instead, each offers its own strengths, advantages, and weaknesses. I encourage you to try them all and build their usefulness into your business structure in the way that suits the business best.

Beyond the data providers and the broad websites are an abundance of research reports and data generated regarding the ETF market. BlackRock has been issuing the *ETF Landscape*[35] for many years. This report is a compilation of ETF market statistics, issuers, assets, and fund lists on a global basis. It does not provide market color or any commentary on specific products. Many people in the industry consider it the gold standard for ETF market statistics. There is the SPDRs University for online education. Typically, the big banks have two forms of ETF data coming out of ETF research departments, from the wealth management side and from the institutional side. These reports include model portfolios and deep dive analytics on product-specific information deemed valuable for the various target client bases. Last is the wealth of bloggers and writers covering the ETF industry. They write a tremendous number of articles covering the industry and its growth and are very attuned to every potential issue. A significant portion of what is written is well informed and valuable for the investor base. Their opinions and analysis are very important for continued growth and stability in the industry.

Notes

1. www.indexuniverse.com/etf-education-ce.html.
2. http://finance.yahoo.com/etf/education.
3. www.bloomberg.com/markets/etfs/.
4. www.bloomberg.com/apps/data?pid=etfscreener.
5. http://etfdb.com/.
6. http://etfdb.com/screener/.
7. http://etfdb.com/stock/AMZN/.
8. http://etfdb.com/tool/etf-country-exposure-tool/.
9. http://etfdb.com/tool/mutual-fund-to-etf/.
10. http://etfdb.com/tool/etf-comparison/.
11. http://etfdb.com/pro/.
12. http://etfdb.com/portfolios/.
13. http://etfdb.com/etf-scorecards/.
14. http://etfdb.com/etf-research-reports/.
15. http://etfdb.com/category-reports/.
16. www.indexuniverse.com/about-us.html.
17. www.indexuniverse.eu/index.php.
18. www.indexuniverse.com/data/data.html.
19. www.indexuniverse.com/data/data.html?task=showResults.
20. www.indexuniverse.com/ecs.
21. www.indexuniverse.com/analytics.

22. www.indexuniverse.com/data/etf-fund-flows-tool.html.

23. www.indexuniverse.com/subscribe.html.

24. www.morningstar.com/Cover/ETFs.aspx.

25. http://screen.morningstar.com/etfselector/etf_screen-er_version1.aspx.

26. http://news.morningstar.com/etf/Lists/ETFReturns.html.

27. www.morningstar.com/cover/list-new-etfs.aspx.

28. www.xtf.com/.

29. www.xtf.com/Research/ETFMarketplace/index2.aspx.

30. www.xtf.com/Research/HeatMap/.

31. www.xtf.com/Research/index.aspx.

32. http://seekingalpha.com/.

33. www.dtcc.com/products/index.ph?id=nscc.

34. www.deltaonedata.com/d1d/Site/me.get?web.home.

35. www2.blackrock.com/content/groups/international-site/documents/literature/etfl_industryhilight_q311_ca.pdf.

Appendix: Bloomberg Functionality Cheat Sheet

Throughout this book, several BLOOMBERG PROFESSIONAL® functions are used. For each Bloomberg function, type the mnemonic listed on the Bloomberg terminal, then press the <GO> key to execute. Each of the following functions can be run for a specific security by typing the ticker symbol of the security, followed by the YELLOW KEY corresponding to the asset class of the security, and then typing the mnemonic.

A standard command to pull up the description page on DTN would look as follows in Exhibit A.1.

The command in Exhibit A.1 brings up the screen seen in Exhibit A.2, the main description page for the WisdomTree Dividend Ex-Financials ETF.

To change to the variety of different functions available once you have pulled up a specific ETF, there is no need to retype the whole command. If you just type the code for the command that you want to see, it will bring up the appropriate screen. For instance, once you have typed in a security such as DTN + EQUITY + GO and are on the front page of the security information, and you want to see an intraday chart, just type

DTN + EQUITY + **DES** + GO

Exhibit A.1 Bloomberg Typing Code = DTN DES

This is where you can see the ticker of the fund being viewed.

This is where you can see the current Bloomberg function, DES.

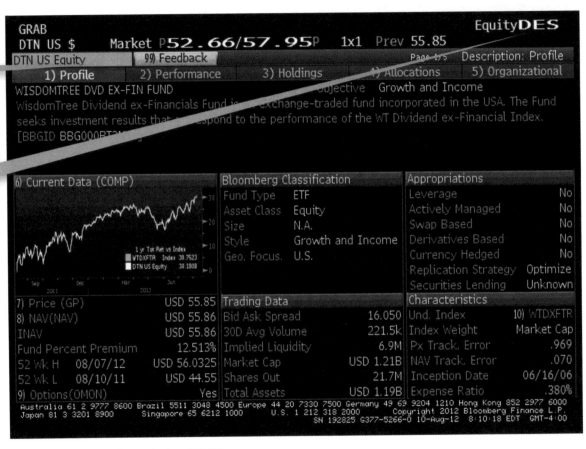

Exhibit A.2 ETF Description (DES)

$$\text{DTNIV} \; + \; \boxed{\text{INDEX}} \; + \; \text{DES} \; + \; \boxed{\text{GO}}$$

Exhibit A.3 Bloomberg Typing Code = DTNIV DES

in GIP + GO, and that functionality will be applied to the current security that you are working on.

Underlying ETF Data

There are a variety of standardized codes for ETFs that bring you to relevant pages for

- NAV (NV)
- Indicative value (IV)
- Shares outstanding (SO)
- Estimated cash (EU)
- Total cash (TC)

By appending the two-letter code to the end of any ETF ticker and using the INDEX button, you can get directly to those screens. A standard command to get to the description page of the DTN indicative value can be seen in Exhibit A.3.

If you want to see a graph of the shares outstanding of DTN over time, you would type the command seen in Exhibit A.4.

This command would bring up the screen in Exhibit A.5 that shows you a rapidly rising stream of increases in shares outstanding in the fund since late May 2011.

You can also compare data on multiple funds by using the standard Bloomberg codes and the underlying ticker data. For example, typing the keystrokes in Exhibit A.6 would bring you to a shares outstanding chart for DEM.

By adding two other funds to lines 2 and 3 as highlighted on the screen, you would be able to produce the following graph showing shares outstanding charts for three funds, as can be seen in Exhibit A.7. This is a four-year chart, but you can modify the data range. You can use this comparison function for any

$$\text{DTNSO} \; + \; \boxed{\text{INDEX}} \; + \; \text{GPO} \; + \; \boxed{\text{GO}}$$

Exhibit A.4 Bloomberg Typing Code = DTNSO GPO

Note the ticker has the SO appended to the end, and is being used with "Index."

Exhibit A.5 Shares Outstanding Historical Chart

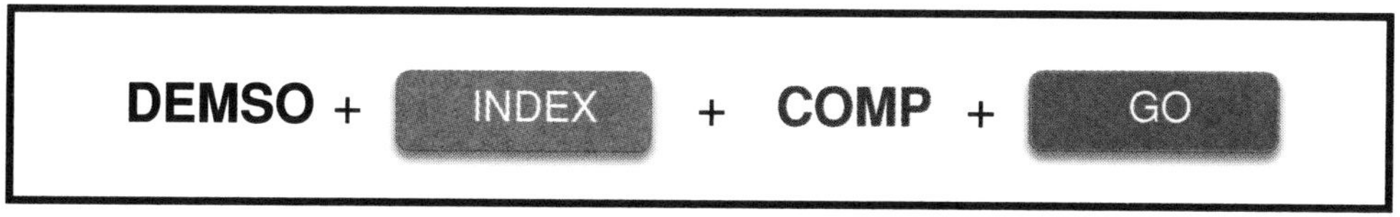

DEMSO + INDEX + **COMP** + GO

Exhibit A.6 Bloomberg Typing Code = DEMSO COMP

ETF value; as with the DEMSO example, you are seeing and comparing returns of shares outstanding changes of various ETFs, but typing in DEM + Equity + COMP + Go will get you price return over a certain period of time, typing in DEMIV + INDEX+ COMP will get you price return on the intraday NAV of DEM, and so on. "COMP" is a universal tool to help you compare any sort of change of an instrument and view results in nominal and graphical terms.

ETF Descriptions and Fund Searches

The following are a selection of codes for ETF-relevant functions:

CF—Company filings.
CN—Company news and research.
DES—Description. This screen has five description pages for each fund. Each page has a broad topic: Profile, Performance, Holdings, Allocations, and Organizational. You can type DES1, DES2 . . . DES5 to get directly to each page.
EXTF—ETF home page.
FL—Fund lookup.

FREP—Fund report.
FSRC—Fund screening.
NI ETF—News on ETFs.

Fund and Portfolio Analytics

COMP—Comparative total returns.
DVD—Dividend split summary.
HDS—13F holders by size. This screen gives holder information based on filings data. There are five tabs that break the information down into different categories: Current, Historical, Matrix, Ownership, and Transactions. In Exhibit A.8, you can see the ownership breakdown for DEM, the WisdomTree Emerging Markets Equity Income Fund.

HFA—Historical fund analysis.
HPA—Historical portfolio analysis.
LRSK—Portfolio liquidity risk (IWM example).
MHD—Mutual fund holdings. You can access the creation unit for each fund from this page by typing 97 <GO>.
PRT—Equity portfolio real-time monitor.

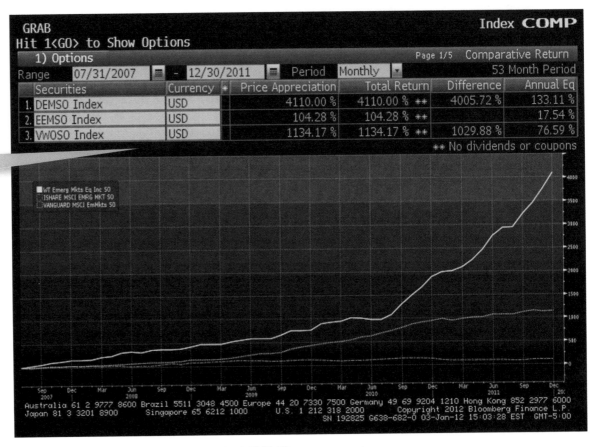

These three funds would have to be added after the initial screen is brought up.

Exhibit A.7 Shares Outstanding Multi-ETF Chart

GRAB				EquityHDS			

DEM US Equit   25) Customize ▼ 99) Feedback CUSIP 97717W31 WisdomTree Emerging Markets Eq

1) Current   2) Historical   3) Matrix   4) Ownership   5) Transactions

Compare Current Stats Against   12/18/2011 ▼

Institutional - Based on Current Filings				▼		Insider - Based on Last 6 Months				▼
Institutional	12/18	12/19	Change		Insider	12/18	12/19	Change	
11) % of Shares Held	36.18	36.25	+0.07 ▣		21) % of Shares Held	0	0	N.A. ▣	
12) % of Float Held	36.18	36.25	+0.07 ▣		22) % Change in Holdings	0	0	N.A. ▣	
13) # of Holders	136	135	-0.74% ▣		23) # of Insiders	0	0	N.A. ▣	
14) # of Buyers	62	63	+1.61% ▣		24) # of Buyers - Opn Mkt	0	0	N.A. ▣	
15) # of Sellers	28	27	-3.57% ▣		25) # of Sellers - Opn Mkt	0	0	N.A. ▣	
16) # of New Buyers	25	25	0.00% ▣		26) # of Shrs Bought - Opn Mk	0	0	N.A. ▣	
17) # of Selloffs	20	20	0.00% ▣		27) # of Shrs Sold - Opn Mkt	0	0	N.A. ▣	
18) % Change in Inst Holdings	+15.49	+15.75	+0.26 ▣		28) Avg Opn Mkt Buy Price	0	0	N.A. ▣	
					29) Avg Opn Mkt Sell Price	0	0	N.A. ▣	

Top Geographic Ownership (%) *				▼		Top Ownership Type (%) *				▼
Geographic Ownership	12/18	12/19	Change		Ownership Type	12/18	12/19	Change	
31) United States	88.61	88.63	+0.02 ▣		41) Investment Advisor	95.32	95.33	+0.01 ▣	
32) Switzerland	8.78	8.77	-0.01 ▣		42) Bank	1.93	1.93	0.00 ▣	
33) Germany	1.53	1.52	-0.01 ▣		43) Hedge Fund Manager	1.79	1.79	0.00 ▣	
34) Canada	0.43	0.43	0.00 ▣		44) Insurance Company	0.78	0.78	0.00 ▣	
35) Mexico	0.25	0.25	0.00 ▣		45) Mutual Fund	0.16	0.16	0.00 ▣	
36) Hong Kong	0.24	0.24	0.00 ▣		46) Government	0.01	0.01	0.00 ▣	
37) Puerto Rico	0.12	0.12	0.00 ▣		47) Unclassified	0.00	0.00	0.00 ▣	
38) Great Britain (UK)	0.03	0.03	0.00 ▣						
39) Israel	0.01	0.01	0.00 ▣						

*Based upon publicly reported holdings (HDS<GO>), not total shares outstanding.

Exhibit A.8 ETF Ownership (DES, 4)

Source: Reprinted with permission from Bloomberg. Copyright 2012 Bloomberg L.P. All rights reserved.

Trading Data

AQR—Top trades contributing to VWAP. Useful for seeing the largest blocks in a particular fund.

CACS—Corporate action calendar.

CORR—Correlation matrix. You can see an example of the correlation matrix for ETFs with Indian underlying stocks, other broader market ETFs, and the underlying Indian index in Exhibit A.9. It is restricted to 10 rows by 10 columns.

G—Graph templates. This is an extensive functionality for developing a wide variety of graphs and saving them for future reference.

GP—Price graph w/ volume. This is one of the main graphs used on the Bloomberg for looking at price performance over time.

HCP—Historical percentage changes.

HP—Price table w/ average daily volume.

HS—Historical spread graph, a longer time frame version of SGIP.

IGPC—Candle graph. This is a very valuable graph for intraday trading showing you candles for short time periods over the day. The chart in Exhibit A.10 shows you a five-day period with 10-minute candles for XLB. You can see also a quick bar for changing the date range to shorter (1D) or longer (5Y).

IOIA—Indications of interest and trade advertisements.

IVAT—Intraday volume at time.

MBTR—Monitoring block trade recap.

MKAC—Market maker activity. Shows you the volumes traded with a variety of variables that you can set.

NAV—Premium-discount graph. This is fund closing prices versus fund NAV. So if you are looking at a fund with international holdings, there will be a lag between when those markets closed and the closing price of the fund at 4 P.M. EST.

OMON—Option monitor. If there are options on a particular ETF, this screen will show the available strikes and other data.

QM—Quote montage. Shows all the various quotes on the different exchanges that the fund is trading on.

QR—Trade recap.

QRM—Trade/quote/recap. This will show you the spread and trades on a rolling basis throughout the day.

RANK—Broker dealer rankings. This is showing you advertised trade volume information.

REQ—Related equities. Will show you if the ETF is cross-listed on foreign exchanges.

SGIP—Spread graph. This is a very valuable tool, enabling you to create a graph of the ETF versus another ETF or versus its indicative value to highlight periods of cheapness or richness. In Exhibit A.11, you can see a graph of DTN versus its indicative value (DTNIV) over one day.

SI—Short interest.

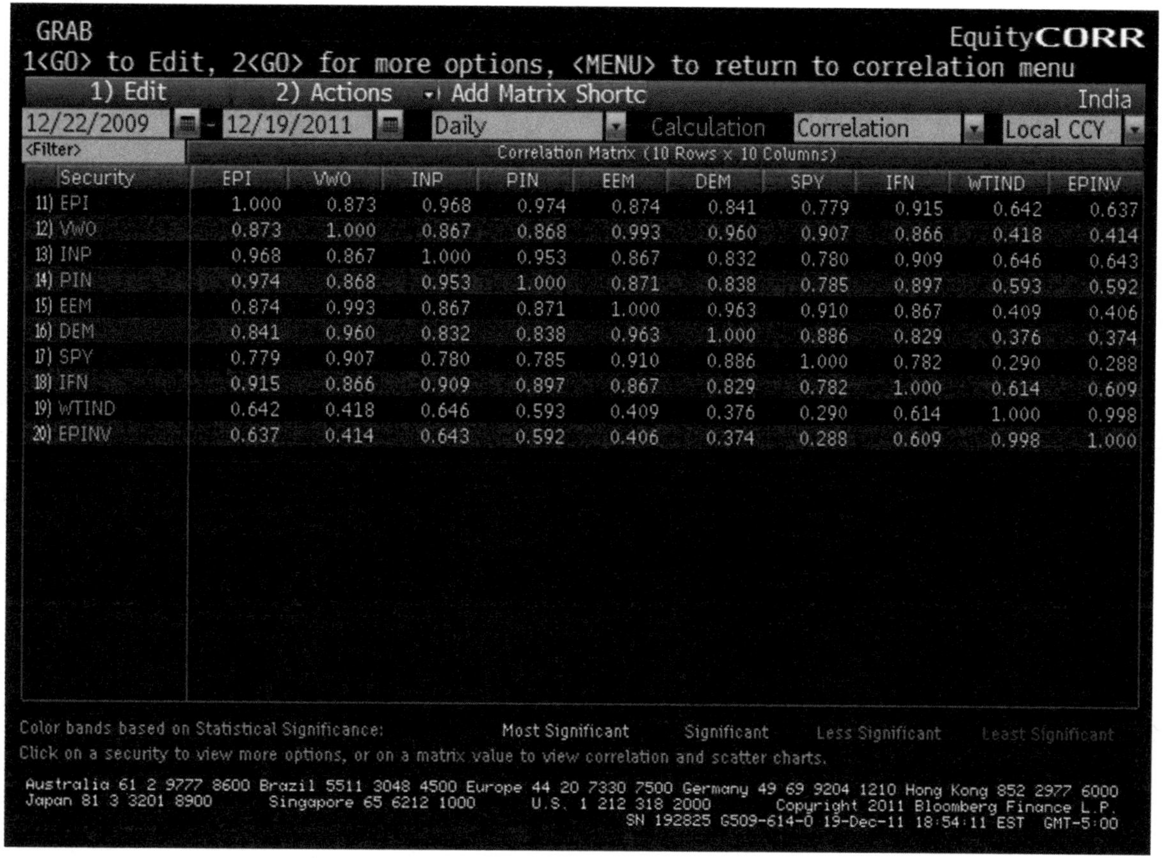

GRAB EquityCORR
1<GO> to Edit, 2<GO> for more options, <MENU> to return to correlation menu
1) Edit 2) Actions Add Matrix Shortc India
12/22/2009 - 12/19/2011 Daily Calculation Correlation Local CCY
<Filter> Correlation Matrix (10 Rows x 10 Columns)

Security	EPI	VWO	INP	PIN	EEM	DEM	SPY	IFN	WTIND	EPINV
11) EPI	1.000	0.873	0.968	0.974	0.874	0.841	0.779	0.915	0.642	0.637
12) VWO	0.873	1.000	0.867	0.868	0.993	0.960	0.907	0.866	0.418	0.414
13) INP	0.968	0.867	1.000	0.953	0.867	0.832	0.780	0.909	0.646	0.643
14) PIN	0.974	0.868	0.953	1.000	0.871	0.838	0.785	0.897	0.593	0.592
15) EEM	0.874	0.993	0.867	0.871	1.000	0.963	0.910	0.867	0.409	0.406
16) DEM	0.841	0.960	0.832	0.838	0.963	1.000	0.886	0.829	0.376	0.374
17) SPY	0.779	0.907	0.780	0.785	0.910	0.886	1.000	0.782	0.290	0.288
18) IFN	0.915	0.866	0.909	0.897	0.867	0.829	0.782	1.000	0.614	0.609
19) WTIND	0.642	0.418	0.646	0.593	0.409	0.376	0.290	0.614	1.000	0.998
20) EPINV	0.637	0.414	0.643	0.592	0.406	0.374	0.288	0.609	0.998	1.000

Color bands based on Statistical Significance: Most Significant Significant Less Significant Least Significant
Click on a security to view more options, or on a matrix value to view correlation and scatter charts.

Australia 61 2 9777 8600 Brazil 5511 3048 4500 Europe 44 20 7330 7500 Germany 49 69 9204 1210 Hong Kong 852 2977 6000
Japan 81 3 3201 8900 Singapore 65 6212 1000 U.S. 1 212 318 2000 Copyright 2011 Bloomberg Finance L.P.
SN 192825 G509-614-0 19-Dec-11 18:54:11 EST GMT-5:00

Exhibit A.9 Correlation Grid (CORR)
Source: Reprinted with permission from Bloomberg. Copyright 2012 Bloomberg L.P. All rights reserved.

Exhibit A.10 Intraday Candle Chart (IGPC)

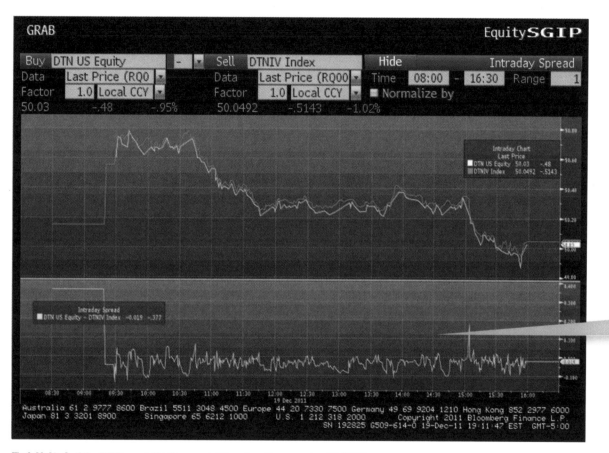

> Notice that since both the fund and its basket are trading at the same time there is almost no spread between them.

Exhibit A.11 ETF and IV Spread Charts–Domestic (SGIP)

DTN consists of U.S.-listed stocks and thus trades tightly around its NAV. However, if the underlying constituents aren't accessible during U.S. hours, such as EEM, which contains global stocks, some of which are closed during U.S. hours, then you will see deviations for the ETF away from its NAV. These premium or discounts can be seen in Exhibit A.12 and are a representation of the price discovery tool inherent in this ETF and not necessarily an arbitrage or faulty pricing.

TSM—Trades summary table of price levels. Used for calculating VWAP.
VAP—Trade summary chart of price levels.
VBAR—Volume at price.

Additional Tools

BTMM—Bloomberg Treasury and money market monitors.
CMDS—Bloomberg monitors for commodities.

FLDS—Field finder. Shows the list of related fields for building queries.
FSTA—Fund style analysis.
IMAP—Intraday market map.
LVI—Largest volume increases.
NDF—Nondeliverable forwards analysis.
PORT—Portfolio analytics.
RVC—Relative value correlation.
SOVR—Global sovereign monitor.
TCA—Transaction cost analysis.
TECH—Technical indicators.
WB—World bond markets.
WCRS—World currency ranker.

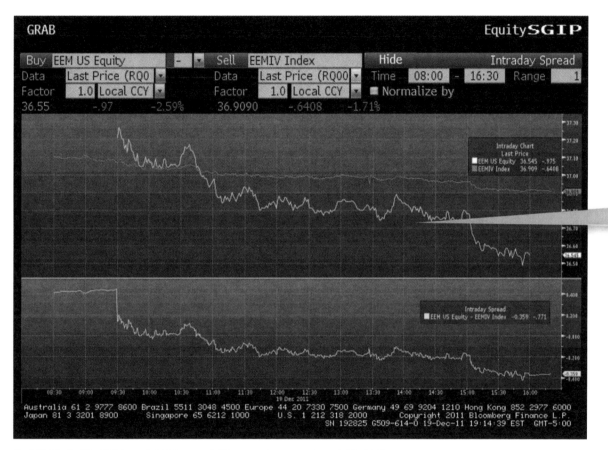

Exhibit A.12 ETF and IV Spread Chart – International (SGIP)

Source: Reprinted with permission from Bloomberg. Copyright 2012 Bloomberg L.P. All rights reserved.

Index